Death of Labour Law?

Comparative Perspectives

Martin Vranken

MELBOURNE
UNIVERSITY
PRESS

MELBOURNE UNIVERSITY PRESS
An imprint of Melbourne University Publishing Limited
187 Grattan Street, Carlton, Victoria 3053, Australia
mup-info@unimelb.edu.au
www.mup.com.au

First published 2009

Text design by Phil Campbell
Cover design by Phil Campbell
Typeset by J & M Typesetting
Printed and bound by CPI Group (UK) Ltd, Croydon, CR0 4YY

National Library of Australia Cataloguing-in-Publication entry:

Death of labour law?: comparative perspectives / Martin Vranken

9780522856293 (pdf)
9780522856309 (pbk.)

Includes index.
Bibliography.

Labour laws and legislation—Western countries.
Labour laws and legislation—Developed countries.

344.172201

In memory of Dr Szakats (1915–2001)

Contents

Abbreviations

AC	Appeal Cases
ACJ	Arbitration Court Judgments
ACTU	Australian Council of Trade Unions
AFL	American Federation of Labor
AILR	Australian Industrial Law Reports
ALR	Australian Law Reports
APEC	Asia-Pacific Economic Cooperation
ATR	Australian Taxation Reports
AWA	Australian Workplace Agreement
Benelux	Belgium, the Netherlands, Luxembourg
BGB	*Bürgerliches Gesetzbuch*
C	Case
CA	Court of Appeal
CAR	Commonwealth Arbitration Reports
CIO	Congress of Industrial Organizations
CLR	Commonwealth Law Reports
CMLR	Common Market Law Reports
Cth	Commonwealth
EC	European Community
ECR	European Court Reports
ECSC	European Coal and Steel Community
EEA	European Economic Area
EEC	European Economic Community
ETUC	European Trade Union Confederation
EU	European Union
Euratom	European Atomic Energy Community
HCA	High Court of Australia
ILO	International Labour Organization
IR	Industrial Reports
ITEA	Individual Transitional Employment Agreement
KB	King's Bench
L	Legislation
MB	Management Board
NAFTA	North American Free Trade Agreement
NATO	North Atlantic Treaty Organization

NES	National Employment Standards
NLRA	National Labor Relations Act
NZLR	New Zealand Law Reports
OECD	Organisation for Economic Co-operation and Development
OEEC	Organisation for European Economic Co-operation
P	President
QB	Queen's Bench
SB	Supervisory Board
SE	*Societas Europaea*
SEA	Single European Act
SH	Shareholders
SME	Small and Medium (-sized) Enterprise
TCR	Termination, Change and Redundancy
TEU	Treaty on European Union
UNICE	Union of Industrial and Employers' Confederations of Europe

Preface

Labour law is no longer the trendy subject to research and teach it once was. In Europe the golden period of labour law lies squarely in the 1960s (at a national level) and in the 1970s (at the supranational level of what was then called the European Economic Community). Today the bright young minds of legal scholars with a social conscience tend to be focused on areas such as environmental law or, even more in vogue, refugee law and international human rights. Labour law, as a major object of study in its own right, risks rapidly becoming a relic of the past.

At one level this book has been written by way of a nostalgic reflex. It retraces the birth and subsequent growth, especially after World War II, of labour law as an autonomous academic discipline. It demonstrates the gradual fall from grace of labour law as a *Sonderdisziplin* ('special discipline')—as the Germans would have it, commencing with the deregulation movement of the 1980s but continuing long after Reaganomics and Thatcherism gave way to the new buzz words of 'globalisation' and 'international competitiveness'. However, the purpose of this book is not to add to the existing literature of tirades against the free market. Publications with such suggestive titles as *Travail flexible, salariés jetables*[1] (*Flexible Work, Throw-Away Employees*), edited by French economist Michel Husson, while undoubtedly thought-provoking, can be overly negative and needlessly cynical.

Instead, *Death of Labour Law?* seeks to invite constructive debate about the relevance of labour law in shaping the social fabric of the Western industrialised world for the twenty-first century. The book has been written in the firm belief that labour law, even when defined narrowly in terms of employee protection law, must continue to have a role that is equal in importance, rather than merely subservient, to the perceived imperatives of a globalised economy. Civilised society, now and into the future, depends on a proper balance between stability and flexibility. In Europe a newly coined term in this regard is 'flexicurity'. This term represents the focal point of an influential Green Paper by the European Commission on modernising labour law in the twenty-seven member states of the European Union. Parallels can be drawn with the legislative reform agenda of the

Rudd-Gillard administration in Australia where a revamped system of collective (workplace) bargaining is meant to operate against the double backdrop of a 'reinforced' floor of statutory employee entitlements and a 'modernised' award system.

For an Australian audience the immediate relevance of the book derives from the 'Forward with Fairness' approach to the labour law reform agenda of the Rudd government. New Zealand readers, for their part, may wish to peruse this text against the backdrop of particularly challenging parliamentary elections faced by the Labour-led coalition of Helen Clark in late 2008.

When writing an initial draft of the manuscript I had occasion to test some of my ideas on some unsuspecting, yet willing participants in a summer course organised by Louisiana State University at the University of Lyon III in France. I am grateful to then Chancellor Costonis for this opportunity. A visiting professorship to teach comparative labour law at the University of Virginia allowed further useful feedback and fine-tuning. I also wish to put on record my sincere appreciation of the warm hospitality received from European colleagues at the University of Leuven over many years.

Melbourne, Solstice Day, 2008

Notes

1 Husson, *Travail flexible, salariés jetables. Fausses questions et vrais enjeux de la lutte contre le chômage.*

CHAPTER 1

Comparative Study of Labour Law: The Proverbial Apples and Oranges?

During twelve years in office from 1996 to 2007 the Howard government substantially rewrote the statutory framework of industrial relations in Australia. The introduction of Australian workplace agreements, in particular, epitomises the radical nature of the change on both a legal and a philosophical plane. Questions arise as to the implications for the field of labour law. Has Australia gone too far in promoting the interests of the individual (whether business or worker) over the collective? How do Australia's workplace relations reforms relate to the debate about labour law flexibility internationally? Do the Australian reforms reduce labour law to a mere tool for the regulation of the labour market? Are these reforms simply a sign of the times, with its increased emphasis on individualism and self-reliance, regardless of which political party happens to be in power? The industrial relations policy of the Rudd-Gillard government does not envisage an unqualified return to the pre–Work Choices era. This suggests a more permanent shift in the labour law landscape of Australia. Is this the end of labour law as we know it?

The purpose of this book is to reflect on the state of contemporary Australian labour law from a comparative perspective. There are clear benefits in adopting a comparative approach to the study of domestic law. This approach allows the researcher to take distance. It in turn helps sharpen the focus. As Otto Kahn-Freund, the *doyen* of comparative labour law once put it:

> One of the virtues of legal comparison is that it allows a scholar to place himself outside the labyrinth of minutiae in which legal thinking so easily loses its way and to see the great contours of the law and its dominant characteristics.[1]

It is by looking at one's own legal system through the eyes of, in effect, an outsider that the otherwise seemingly obvious may become questionable. At the very least comparativism allows one to see where one's own legal system fits in, if at all, internationally. The information and knowledge thus acquired may even lead to law reform, although the intrinsic value of the comparative method does not depend on this actually occurring. From the outset a note of caution seems appropriate, though. To study law from a comparative perspective is never a straightforward proposition. The discussion below shows why the comparative study of labour law tends to be particularly problematic.

Labour Law: The Poor Cousin of Comparative Law

Early precedents as regards the study of foreign laws and the use of the comparative method can be found in the writings of Plato and Aristotle. It has also been suggested that comparative research preceded the drafting of the XII Tables for Rome. Montesquieu's *L'Esprit des Lois* was similarly based on comparison. But the development of comparative law as a legal discipline in its own right is relatively recent. It is only from the nineteenth century onwards that the term 'comparative law' has become established. As a consequence there remains ample scope for trial and error in the design and practical application of various approaches to the comparative method.[2]

Europe led the way.[3] The first meeting of the International Congress for Comparative Law was held at the instigation of Lambert and Saleilles in Paris in 1900. Neither the venue nor the timing proved entirely accidental. That year the World Exhibition was held in France and there existed a quasi-absolute faith in progress generally at the start of the new century. This spirit did not leave the legal community untouched, hence the dream of a new world law: a common law of mankind (*droit commun de l'humanité*). The task of comparative law then was to help create this new legal order.

Contrary to other fields of law—contracts or torts, for example—comparative law has no predefined contents or subject matter. Rather, comparative law essentially represents a particular approach to the study of law. In other words, comparative law is a method rather than a subject. The French and German translations of the label 'comparative law'—*droit comparé* and *Rechtsvergleichung*, respectively—capture the essence of comparative law rather better than their equivalent in the English language.

In principle, the comparative method can be applied to just about any established field of law. In labour law, however, problems tend to surface almost immediately. The concept of legal families has evolved into a major classification device available to comparative scholars when studying legal systems that display certain common features. Unfortunately, this device is of limited assistance when dealing with labour law. The labels of civil law and common law—the two most important legal families in the Western world today—traditionally allow for legal systems to be distinguished in terms of their private law dimension only. The usefulness of these labels in areas beyond private law, including labour law, is marginal at best.

By way of clarification it must be recalled that the classic European legal codes, the French *Code civil* of 1804 and the German *Bürgerliches Gesetzbuch* of 1896 in particular, while claiming to be all-encompassing as to their contents, are effectively restricted to the domain of private law. The primary focus of these civil codes is on relationships among private parties. Thus the core provisions governing contract law and tort law, for example, have been traditional features of civil codes throughout Europe. Public law, on the other hand, because of its emphasis on regulating the relationship between the state and the citizens thereof, largely escapes the reach of the grand nineteenth-century codes. Instead the legal rules of constitutional and administrative law typically are contained in legislation outside the code. Labour law does not really fit in either category of law.

Of course, to the extent that the individual employment relationship is legally founded in contract, labour law might justifiably be viewed as forming part of private law. But, even so, labour law in Europe is essentially a post-codification development. Further, the regulation of large parts of contemporary labour law is more in the nature of public law anyway. The collective dimension of labour law, in particular, ranging from the legal regulation of trade unions, works councils and employment courts to the extended binding effect of collective agreements beyond the immediate bargaining parties, is what gives labour law in that part of the world its specialist flavour. In France, for instance, even a constitutional dimension attaches to the right to strike! Little wonder, then, that not even an in-depth study or understanding of legal families, along civil law and common law lines, is likely to yield much insight when dealing with matters of comparative labour law.

Nationalism need not be an impediment to comparative study, parochialism almost invariably is. It may be trite to observe that legal systems ultimately remain the fundamental expression of their own national identity. Yet, nationalism—even in the patriotic sense of the word—and comparativism are by no means mutually exclusive concepts. In Europe the codification movement and national identity building went hand in hand. But, once in place, the various European codes provided a strong basis and reference point for legal comparative study during much of the twentieth century. The problem of parochialism in labour law is of a different nature.

From time to time it has been suggested, arguably correctly, that labour law, perhaps more than any other area of law, tends to be peculiarly parochial. By this it is meant that labour law is often shaped by features that are uniquely local. Historical, political, economic, cultural and social factors all combine to give labour law its special shape and flavour. In the process it risks turning comparative labour law research into a hazardous enterprise. Specifically, in order to understand fully why any given system of labour law displays certain specific features, intimate familiarity with the broader context can be of paramount importance.[4]

Of course, to some extent the above observation applies to other areas of law as well. But the problem of parochialism easily becomes magnified when dealing with labour law. Take, for example, the comparatively narrow scope for lawful industrial action in Australia and New Zealand, even where strikes or lock-outs occur in the pursuit of legitimate collective bargaining. History, rather than ideology, provides an explanation for this state of affairs. Indeed, widespread public condemnation of the open strife that occurred in the streets of many cities and towns throughout the early part of the 1890s triggered an unequivocal government response on both sides of the Tasman Sea. As a result industrial disputation was compulsorily removed from the streets and handed to a newly established specialist public body—the Arbitration Court—entrusted with wide-ranging conciliation and arbitration powers. Protection of the public interest remained the primary yardstick for the exercise of these powers until the close of the twentieth century. Not even the move away from compulsory arbitration towards a system of 'free' collective bargaining in recent years has quite managed to remove the shackles of the past. A fuller treatment occurs in the context of the discussion on deregulation later in this book.[5]

Comparativism and Australian Labour Law

Some four decades ago Kahn-Freund delivered a brilliant submission to the effect that 'comparative law has long ceased to be a purely academic pursuit'.[6] And it was his firm expectation that 'a moderate familiarity with comparative methods and a measure of comparative "know-how" may in due course become part of the necessary equipment of an English lawyer'.[7] Intriguingly, for most of the twentieth century the Australian—and, for that matter, the New Zealand—system of compulsory conciliation and arbitration represented a landmark for the international legal community and many labour law scholars from abroad expressed fascination with what was then a unique system for the prevention and resolution of industrial disputes.[8] How things have changed. Today stability is no longer the hallmark of Australia's labour laws. But even prior to the enactment of the Workplace Relations Act 1996 (Cth) it could be observed that the desirability and indeed the necessity of undertaking comparative study in Australia increases in line with the ever-increasing 'volatility' of the regulatory system of industrial relations.[9] It must indeed be remembered that the 1996 legislation builds upon reforms introduced under a Keating (Labor) administration in 1993. At the time I suggested that 'history may prove that the Industrial Relations Reform Act 1993 (Cth) constitutes a crucial factor in reconsidering Australia's commitment to the compulsory arbitration model'. In light of the nature and extent of the subsequent reforms under Howard, culminating in the infamous 2005 amendment on Work Choices, it seems appropriate to set out the extract in full:

> The federal reforms of 1993 warrant closer examination. Important changes to the regulatory framework of industrial relations have been identified by commentators to include a move towards a collective bargaining system as well as the insertion of a new 'individual rights' flavour into the legislation. The move away from primary reliance on centralised arbitration for the resolution of industrial disputes arguably brings Australia in line with its trading partners in America and Europe. In particular, the introduction of concepts like the duty to bargain in good faith and the right to take industrial action for purposes of securing a successful outcome to each bargaining round, are eminently suitable for cross-national comparisons so as to assist in determining their meaning and scope. Similarly, the 'individual rights' component of what remains, in essence, a collective piece of labour legislation calls for a re-assessment of the relationship between the individual and the collective components of labour law. Here again, several Western European systems of labour law may offer guidance as to how to use individual employment rights effectively in order to raise the threshold for collective bargaining. At the same time the respective functions of the formal legislature (the Parliament) and the social legislature (the bargaining parties) may need to be re-examined as well. The European experience shows that the gap left by the ever-diminishing emphasis on award protection cannot be adequately filled by collective bargaining alone. Paradoxically, perhaps, it follows that an increased emphasis on collective bargaining goes hand in hand with the need for greater parliamentary vigilance to ensure that overall living and working standards remain acceptable.[10]

The sentiments expressed in the above quote remain as pertinent today as when they were first formulated in 1995.

The Comparative Method: Benefits and Pitfalls

The comparative study of labour law may be difficult, but it is not without its rewards. At a most basic level, comparative law as an academic pursuit never fails to satisfy one's intellectual curiosity and hunger for knowledge—both as regards domestic and foreign legal systems. From this general perspective the comparative study of labour law may therefore justifiably be contemplated for its own sake, that is, as an exercise in its own right. André Tunc, a celebrated French comparative scholar, describes this benefit of comparativism in exuberant terms of an enrichment and an opening-up of the mind (*la culture et l'ouverture d'esprit*).[11]

Less idealistic perhaps, and certainly much more pragmatic, is the pursuit of comparative law for purposes of guiding domestic law reform. Historically, this has been a primary incentive for comparing different legal systems especially, and somewhat intriguingly, in the legal family of the common law.[12] Zweigert and Kötz, two other (German) *gurus* of comparative law on the Continent, refer to 'legislative comparative law'—where foreign laws are examined for purposes of drafting new national laws—as one of two distinct 'roots' of comparative law.[13] Of course, the wider goal of international unification of the law worldwide—much in vogue at the end of the nineteenth century—may seem a rather naïve ambition at present, the current climate of globalisation notwithstanding. Regional harmonisation, on the other hand, may be a less futile aspiration. The establishment of a European Economic Community in 1957 has provided a trigger for the harmonisation and/or co-ordination of national legislation in a whole range of areas beyond the (original) economic domain. Fifty years on, the results of this process of 'communitarisation' directly affect the national legal orders of twenty-seven member states in the European Union (EU).[14]

At this side of the world no such stellar progress can be reported. Certainly, the ambitions of APEC (Asia-Pacific Economic Cooperation) are modest ones and, on a much smaller scale, even the potential of the Closer Economic Relations (CER) initiative between Australia and New Zealand remains largely untapped. Furthermore, Kahn-Freund's classic warning about the problems associated with the so-called transplantability of foreign law must always be heeded.[15] The construct of transplantability operates from the assumption that not all aspects of foreign law are equally suited to exportation. To paraphrase Kahn-Freund, it is easier to transfer a mechanical part of a car (say, the carburettor or a wheel) successfully than to transfer part of a living organism (the cornea of an eye or a kidney, for instance). Even allowing for breathtaking advances in modern medicine, Kahn-Freund's basic point remains valid. A careful consideration as to which aspects of foreign law are most suitable for importation into the domestic legal scene continues to be of the utmost importance if the risk of 'rejection' of the foreign part by the receiving body is to be minimised. In light of the earlier observations about its parochial nature, the problem tends to be particularly acute in the domain of labour law. For example, it may seem a relatively straightforward (albeit financially onerous) proposition to copy the generous annual leave entitlements of German workers into Australian labour law.[16] Much more risky would be, again by way of example, a transplantation of the German model of employee representation on the supervisory boards of companies. So-called institutionalised forms of employee representation in Europe are indeed premised upon a fundamental assumption that at least some commonality of interests exists between workers and management.[17] The labour law systems of common-law based legal systems, including Australia, often assume the opposite.

The distinction between 'organ' transplants and transplants of 'mechanical parts' is easier to state than to apply. The reader is therefore urged to be mindful when perusing the material in this book. A separate but related difficulty concerns the comparative methodology. As comparative law is a relatively young discipline, its methodology continues to evolve. Two principal approaches to comparative study have attained some prominence to date. They can be labelled the institutional and functional approaches to comparative study.[18] The institutional approach is relatively formalistic in that it generally does not look beyond the particular institution, concept or rule that forms the subject of comparative study. In contrast, the functional approach seeks to take into account the substantive, underlying reasons for the existence (or absence!) of any such institution, concept or rule in each of the legal systems being compared.

Conventional wisdom has it that, by and large, the functional approach is to be preferred because of the richer results it yields.

However, it need not follow that the institutional (or formal) approach lacks merit. As has been argued elsewhere, while each method may reflect a different level of comparative inquiry, that does not mean that one method is automatically superior to the other. Take, for instance, the presence of labour courts in Western Europe.[19] These owe their origin to the probiviral court or *conseil de prud'hommes* (literally: court of wise men) set up at Lyon pursuant to a Napoleonic law passed in 1806. Historically, the idea behind this type of court was to have certain labour disputes settled promptly and without great expense by a council composed of representatives of employers and employees.[20] In a more contemporary context, the very existence of labour or employment courts can be viewed as reflecting a political choice to award special treatment to the resolution of (justiciable) labour disputes as opposed to legal disputes in general, whereby the latter continue to be within the jurisdiction of the ordinary courts of law. This observation raises several issues for comparative scholars. Thus, it may be asked whether different degrees of specialisation exist among labour courts internationally. An institutional approach to comparativism allows that question to be addressed most adequately. Application of this first comparative methodology then entails an internal comparison of labour or employment courts in the various legal systems where they exist and yields useful information as regards, *inter alia*, court personnel, jurisdictional powers, appellate structure and representation of parties.[21]

When exploring the above example of labour courts somewhat further, it may be asked why these specialist courts are not omnipresent. They indeed appear absent in several systems of labour law, whether in Europe (the Netherlands and Italy are the two most notable instances) or beyond. By adopting a functional (or substantive) approach the search can be turned towards functional equivalents of labour or employment courts. Here the discussion logically extends to the North American system of personal grievance administration (involving private arbitrators) or, in Australia, the role of the Industrial Relations Commission and Federal Court when asked to adjudicate upon dismissal disputes.

The European model of labour courts is discussed in some detail later in this book. The point that must be made here is that different approaches yield different information. In any event, the functional approach is invariably more difficult: it presupposes that one is able to formulate the correct questions upfront. In the above example, the question is not simply in which legal systems labour courts exist. Instead, under the functional approach the question is which means are available for the peaceful resolution of employment or (more broadly) labour disputes. Similarly, it can be asked, under an institutional approach, in which legal systems works councils and/or employees on supervisory boards are present. Under a functional approach, that question becomes a query into the various means available to employees for influencing the decision-making role of company management. It is a query that logically extends into an examination of the longstanding practice of enterprise bargaining in the United States or, closer to home, the traditional model of compulsory conciliation and arbitration in Australia and New Zealand, including its progressive replacement with Australian workplace agreements.

This book will adopt a combination of the institutional and functional approaches.

Overview of Topics Selected for Discussion

Death of Labour Law? begins with some reflections on the definition of labour law. What does the notion of labour law stand for? What is the function of labour law? It seems appropriate to address these very basic questions at the outset, especially since the traditional answers have proven not entirely uncontroversial. Labour law is a relatively young discipline in academic terms. In Europe labour law was not really recognised as a subject worthy of study in its own right until after World War II. German scholarship, in particular, played a key role in its conceptualisation. Hugo Sinzheimer can be said to be the father of contemporary labour law, with Otto Kahn-Freund as his brilliant pupil. It was Sinzheimer who defined labour law in terms of employee protection law (*Arbeitnehmerschutzrecht*).

The central theme of *Death of Labour Law?* is that labour law in essence is, and continues to be, about employee protection law. Yet, at the start of the twenty-first century this concept of labour law as employee protection law is being questioned in some circles. Alternatively, labour law is being described as (merely?) an instrument for regulating the labour market.[22] In part, this re-formulation of labour law is occurring in recognition of the use—or rather, usefulness—of labour laws as tools to promote domestic employment opportunities and increase international competitiveness. Chapter 2 examines the current state of the debate about the *raison d'être* of labour law. In the process we briefly trace the history of labour law.

The best way to try and make sense of the current volatility in labour law regulation is to go back to basics. Chapter 3 sets the scene through its focus on the core concept of the employee. Employee status represents the cornerstone and the underlying rationale of labour law under the Sinzheimer approach. Various judicial tests for determining employee status have evolved over time. The distinction between employees and contractors, especially, can prove difficult. The problem here is not a purely legal one. At times the debate about employee status acquires a distinctly political dimension and the real question becomes who *ought* to be treated as an employee for purposes of labour law protection.

Chapter 4 looks at various mechanisms for the official representation and protection of employee interests in labour law. While unions constitute a traditional vehicle for the promotion of these interests, differences in the methods for selecting the collective spokesperson of employees exist internationally. A discussion of the American, European and Australasian approaches shows that each union selection device may not be entirely value-neutral. Employees in America, Australia and New Zealand, in particular, have to make do with relatively few statutory employee rights compared with their European counterparts. The collective bargaining 'stakes' for employees in these countries are especially high. Continental European workers, by contrast, benefit additionally from so-called institutionalised forms of employee participation at the place of work.

When looking for alternatives, or rather supplements, to union representation, policy-makers on both sides of the Tasman from time to time examine two forms of institutionalised worker participation in Europe. These are works councils and employee representation on the supervisory boards of companies. A high degree of interdependence typifies and conditions the effective functioning of each. Chapter 4 provides an overview of both institutions that thus far have not been caught up in the deregulation and flexibility debate.

Chapter 5 examines the role of specialist tribunals in the resolution of labour and employment disputes. That role differs depending on the type of dispute at issue. The jurisdiction of European labour courts typically evolves around the legal enforcement of individual (employee) rights. While their Australian and New Zealand counterparts historically operate from a radically different premise, it would seem that the contemporary evolution is towards a convergence of sorts with a European-style labour court.

Chapter 6 addresses the international scope of labour law. The main focus is on the regional dimension within the context of the EU. It is at this supranational level that the current debate about 'flexicurity', explored in greater detail in the final chapter, must be situated. Chapters 6 and 7 help set the scene for that discussion. Chapter 6 demonstrates how the tension between economic and social concerns has shaped European labour law from its very inception. It also sketches the broader backdrop against which the EU's infatuation with fundamental (social) rights must be placed. Parallels can be drawn with the deregulation movement in Australia and New Zealand, discussed in Chapter 7. The Transition to Forward with Fairness Act 2008 (Cth) and, in particular, the drafting of statutory minimum rights for employees—the so-called National Employment Standards in federal Australia—represent the latest phase in a move away from collectivism as the primary pillar upon which labour law is built.

The book concludes by reflecting upon the future of labour law. The focal point of the discussion is the Green Paper released by the Commission of the European Communities on 22 November 2006. Entitled *Modernising Labour Law to Meet the Challenges of the 21st Century*,[23] its key feature is the notion of 'flexicurity'. That term captures the universally applicable objective of balancing the need for flexibility in the labour market with the need for security by the various participants thereof.

Notes

1 Kahn-Freund, 'Comparative Law as an Academic Subject', p. 40.

2 Zweigert and Kötz, *An Introduction to Comparative Law*, pp. 48–62; Hanza, *Comparative Law and Antiquity*; Kamba, 'Comparative Law: A Theoretical Framework', p. 485.

3 Vranken, *Fundamentals of European Civil Law and Impact of the European Community*, p. 2ff.
4 Ziskind, 'Cultural Bias in Labor Law Comparison', p. 275.
5 See Chapter 7.
6 Kahn-Freund, 'Comparative Law as an Academic Subject', p. 59.
7 ibid.
8 One New Zealand commentator aptly put it that 'There is nothing quite like it anywhere else that we know of, although the Australian (state) systems are similar in a number of ways': Woods, *Industrial Conciliation and Arbitration in New Zealand*, p. 9. New Zealand's Industrial Conciliation and Arbitration Act 1894 predates Australia's federal legislation, the Commonwealth Conciliation and Arbitration Act 1904, by some ten years. The book by Woods is the New Zealand counterpart of Macintyre and Mitchell (eds), *Foundations of Arbitration*.
9 Vranken, 'Comparativism and Australian Labour Law', p. 125.
10 ibid.
11 Tunc, 'L'Enseignement du droit comparé: présentation', p. 703.
12 Collins, 'Methods and Aims of Comparative Contract Law', p. 397.
13 Zweigert and Kötz, *An Introduction to Comparative Law*, p. 51. The second 'root' in their view is the 'scientific or theoretical' approach referred to by Tunc, n. 11.
14 Vranken, *Fundamentals of European Civil Law and Impact of the European Community*.
15 Kahn-Freund, 'On Uses and Misuses of Comparative Law', p. 5. See also Schregle, 'Comparative Industrial Relations: Pitfalls and Potential', p. 15.
16 See Chapter 2 for a discussion of statutory employee rights in Europe.
17 See Chapter 4 for a discussion of the institutionalised form of employee participation in Europe.
18 The discussion that follows draws heavily from Vranken, *Fundamentals of European Civil Law and Impact of the European Community*, pp. 8–10.
19 A more detailed discussion of labour or employment courts can be found in Chapter 5.
20 Kassalow, *Trade Unions and Industrial Relations: An International Comparison*, p. 169.
21 For an application, see Vranken, 'Specialisation and Labour Courts: A Comparative Analysis', p. 497.
22 See the various contributors in Arup and Mitchell (eds), *Labour Law and Labour Market Regulation*. See also Arup, 'Labour Market Regulation as a Focus for a Labour Law Discipline', p. 29.
23 Commission of the European Communities, *Modernising Labour Law to Meet the Challenges of the 21st Century*.

CHAPTER 2

Labour Law: Subject or Method?

A major problem facing labour lawyers today is uncertainty about what the subject stands for. Questions are even being asked about whether there is a continuing need for labour law as a legal discipline separate from the general law of, in essence, contract and tort. These questions go to the very core of labour law. Why have separate rules for dealing with the employer-employee relationship? Why not make do with the general law of contract? Why have special rules to deal with unions? Why not deal with them in the same way as other incorporated societies or bodies? Broadly speaking, the debate in the scholarly community is between the purists or traditionalists, on the one hand, and the (self-proclaimed) pragmatists or realists, on the other hand. The purpose of this chapter is to present an overview and evaluation of the main arguments on either side. To provide some context for that discussion, the historical formation of labour law is sketched first.

Building Blocks in History

Conventional wisdom has it that the antecedents of contemporary labour law, and thus also the seeds for the current debate as to whether labour law constitutes a subject (in its own right) or a method (for regulating the labour market), can be found in the Industrial

Revolution and its aftermath. It must be borne in mind, though, that industrialisation reached various parts of the Western world at different times. When compared to the situation in Great Britain, industrialisation arrived relatively late on the Continent. Somewhat paradoxically, the response of the legislature there was more readily forthcoming than in Britain. This leads Hepple to suggest that it would be wrong to assume too close a correlation between the advent of industrialisation in any particular country and the birth of labour law in that country.[1] A more direct trigger for the birth of labour law may have been the economic recession that hit various parts of the world during the 1880s and 1890s. On the Continent industrialisation was in full swing at that time. The severity of the recession and the accompanying social unrest led to a questioning of the absolute freedom ideals promoted by the French Revolution a century earlier. Ultimately, the move towards what today is called labour law then occurred in response to the acknowledged excesses of economic and individual freedoms. In other words, the legal regulation of economic and social conditions has been intertwined from the very beginning of labour law.

France

As indicated above, the French Revolution of 1789 proved to be a momentous occasion on the Continent. It meant the end of the old order (*Ancien Régime*) and the abolition of the social and economic privileges previously bestowed upon certain classes—the nobility, the clergy and the bourgeoisie, in particular. The old corporations, guilds of artisans and merchants really, had to go. Instead, individual freedoms, including those of labour, commerce and industry, became elevated to quasi-absolute rights. In 1791 one of the revolutionaries was immortalised when his name was attached to a piece of legislation, the Act *Le Chapelier*, the essence of which was to suppress all forms of collectivism. Barely a decade later, that same philosophy of individualism became enshrined in the much-celebrated civil code (*Code civil des français*) of 1804. The French *Code civil* continues in force today. When neighbouring Belgium gained its independence in 1830, the *Code civil* was adopted as the civil code for the Belgians. The 1804 code similarly continues to be a dominating force in shaping the legal system of Luxembourg. As well, the former Dutch civil code

(*Burgerlijk Wetboek*) of 1838 was largely, and often literally, based on the 1804 *Code Napoléon*.[2] This focus by the legislature on freedom of the individual, together with a deeply held suspicion of anything collective, remained by no means confined to France alone. It was this (legally enshrined) philosophy of individual freedom that ruled the day when the Industrial Revolution reached the Continent in the latter half of the nineteenth century.

The *Code civil* predates the large-scale industrialisation of France by some fifty years or more. While it contains more than 2000 provisions, only two are devoted to labour law. Neither provision is particularly groundbreaking, which is not surprising in light of the sentiment prevailing at the time of drafting. A general (but direct) reference to labour law can be found in Articles 1780 and 1781. The latter provision was abolished well before the country celebrated the Code's first centenary.[3] Article 1780 holds greater interest in that employees cannot commit themselves to serve the employer forever. Specifically, Article 1780 stipulates that one can engage one's services for a period of time or for a specific task only.[4] In essence, this means that an employment relationship cannot be entered into for life. This follows logically from the (revolutionary) principle of freedom of labour and the associated abolition of personal servitude or 'forced labour'[5] in the wake of the French Revolution.

Interestingly, once industrialisation had gained momentum, growing concern about abuse of the individual freedom ideals by the employer led to follow-up legislation rather swiftly. Pursuant to a French Act dated 27 December 1890, several paragraphs were added to the original text of Article 1780 *Code civil*. Their combined effect was to confirm the legal validity of so-called open-ended employment contracts, that is, contracts that do not specify in advance the length of their duration. This type of individual contract constitutes the backbone of contemporary employment law. An important proviso allowed either party to elect to bring the contract to an end, at any time, unilaterally. Currently, the terminating party is expected to give advance notice. Back then the legislature sought to protect the interests of the non-terminating party (often, but not always, this would have been the employee) by stipulating that the exercise of the option to terminate triggered an entitlement to financial compensation. All in all, though, it is clear that, whereas at first the promotion of individual freedom led to the abolition of lifelong personal serfdom, (admittedly, rudimentary) dismissal protection laws were already in place by the close of the nineteenth century.[6]

Belgium: A Variation on the French (and German) Model

Concern for the protection of individual employees against arbitrary employer behaviour in Belgium similarly led to the enactment of special legislation to deal with individual employment contracts as early as 1900. The focus of the Act of 10 March 1900 concerning the Individual Employment Contract did not remain confined to matters of employee protection against dismissal. But, even then, the drafters of the Belgian Act were at pains to stress their limited ambitions. The Act was not to be a comprehensive employment code. It was not intended to move away from the ideals contained in the civil code, especially not the legal consecration of individual liberty and equality. Rather, the declared objectives of the 1900 legislation were, on the one hand, to fill some of the gaps in the civil code and, on the other hand, to provide greater clarity and promote legal certainty through the removal of certain (unspecified) 'ambiguous customs and habits' that prevailed at the time.[7]

Such false modesty! Yes, it is true that the 1900 Act did not cover all employees in Belgium. Its personal scope of application centred on, in essence, labourers active in the new factories. So-called white-collar workers (as distinct from blue-collar workers), were excluded as well as artisans and domestic servants. These categories of employees had to wait until after the end of World War I before being absorbed by the protective legislation. On the other hand, the Act provided a statutory definition of the employment contract, reiterated the prohibition on lifelong contracts, listed the various rules of evidence permissible in employment matters, stipulated how wages were to be calculated, and stated how claims under the employment contract expired in time. Further, the Act contained a (non-exhaustive) list of rights and obligations bestowed upon each of the parties to an employment contract. As for the employee, the core commitment to work was given expression through such specific obligations as a duty to obey lawful employer orders, keep factory secrets, and return work equipment at the end of the employment relationship. For his part, the employer had a legal obligation to pay wages. In addition, the employer had to commit to behave as a good head of family (the famous *bonus paterfamilias* obligation originating in Roman law) which, among other things, translated into an obligation to ensure the health and safety of the worker, look after any tools owned by the worker, allow time for workers to perform their religious—Belgium was a fiercely Catholic country at the time—and civic duties, and provide a certificate (not quite a reference) upon request at the end of the employment relationship that would allow the worker to seek alternative employment elsewhere.

Given the early timeframe of the legislation, the above list of reciprocal rights and duties is squarely impressive. On top of all that, the 1900 Act contained a dozen provisions on the various ways in which these obligations came to an end. Noteworthy are provisions that stipulated how the length of a temporary employment contract was to be determined and the requirement of advance notice in the absence of just cause justifying instant dismissal of employees engaged on the basis of an open-ended employment contract. This type of statutory provision continues to form the core of Belgian dismissal law to date. The 1900 Act even stressed that certain events—Article 28 is particularly progressive in that it made express reference to employer bankruptcy—need not signal the end of the employment relationship. Finally, incorrect application of the statutory termination provisions resulted in the payment of damages. Initially, the amount of compensation to be paid was fixed at half the wages that corresponded to the length of the (unexpired) notice period.[8] The following extract from an 1896–97 report by the House of Representatives sums up the general sentiment of the legislature rather nicely:

> Under a modern perception of the (employment) contract the labourer is not an object at the free disposal and absolute control of the employer.[9]

Germany

Germany only became a nation-state in 1871 under Bismarck. The drafting of a civil code, a prime instrument in the building of a national identity for the newly founded state, was only accomplished thereafter. Completed in 1896, the *Bürgerliches Gesetzbuch* (hereafter: the BGB) took effect on 1 January 1900—largely for symbolic reasons. Unlike its French counterpart, enacted nearly a century earlier, the BGB tried to capture the past rather more than project the future. In practical terms, it shows that both the French and the German civil codes are very much products of the nineteenth century. It helps explain why the German code also placed its faith in individual freedom and 'the belief that the general good would spontaneously ensue from the interplay of economic forces provided that the state did not interfere'.[10] According to comparative scholars Zweigert and Kötz:

> [T]he draftsmen of the BGB seem to have taken no notice of the great social change which was occurring in Germany in the final decades of the nineteenth century; commerce and industry were becoming much more important economically than farming, and urban populations were expanding rapidly, especially with industrial workers. Yet for the BGB the typical citizen is not the small artisan or the factory worker but rather the moneyed entrepreneur, the landed proprietor, and the official, people who can be expected to have business experience and sound judgment, capable of succeeding in bourgeois society with freedom of contract, freedom of establishment, and freedom of competition, and able to take steps to protect themselves from harm.[11]

Perhaps the picture for the average German (industrial) worker was not quite as negative as the above quote may suggest. Already in the 1870s and 1880s, some movement towards social justice had seen the adoption of early labour and welfare legislation. Best known are legislation on health insurance (1883), accident insurance (1884), and old age pension and disability insurance (1889). In part, the reasons for this legislative intervention were undoubtedly altruistic. In part, they may also have reflected an attempt at keeping the socialist (political) cause at bay. In any event, the BGB did not repeal these reforms from the Bismarck era. Thus the scene was set for the development of Germany's vast array of social and employee protection laws in place to date. Interestingly, as happened in France and Belgium, this development typically occurred outside the civil code.

Thilo Ramm, writing as a professor of both civil and labour law at the University of Hagen in Germany, observes that protective labour laws across Europe remained largely piecemeal in their focus throughout the nineteenth century.[12] Before protection could be extended to employees generally, the focus was often narrowly on especially vulnerable groups—children, in the first instance. Things only changed with the introduction of universal (male) suffrage as 'there was the hope for politicians of winning ... votes by promising protective legislation'.[13] During this formative period of labour law, the initiative often depended on the advocacy efforts of 'philanthropic' individuals, especially where they were backed by a strong conservative or Christian political party. Ramm points out the special position occupied by German university professors in this regard. The good reputation of academics is said to have helped form public opinion in favour of interventionist labour laws and this, in turn, influenced the situation in neighbouring France and Italy.[14] The relatively high status traditionally enjoyed by scholarship (*la doctrine*) in the family of the civil law can be linked to the hands-on role of law professors when advising on, and even participating in, the drafting of the grand nineteenth-century codes in both France and Germany. To this day the status of scholarship in the civil law resembles that of the judiciary in the common law.[15]

Great Britain and, by Extension, its Former Colonies

Historically, the legislature cannot be said to have acted as the prime mover in promoting the idea of employee protection in England. Instead it has been a longstanding British tradition to accord legal regulation a secondary role in favour of an emphasis on voluntary regulation by the industrial relations parties themselves. This voluntary regulation typically took the form of 'free' (from state interference) or 'autonomous' collective bargaining. In fact, the first unambiguous sign of a shift towards legal regulation did not really occur until the 1960s.[16] Prior to that, labour law was all about staying out or, at best, about according legal immunity from the constraints of civil or criminal liability. The pervasive nature of this climate of legal abstention helps explain the peculiar (from a continental

European perspective) opening sentence in Lord Wedderburn's classic text on *The Worker and the Law* to the effect that:

> Most workers want nothing more of the law than that it should leave them alone.[17]

Where did this lack of expectation that the law can positively and proactively assist employees originate? The short answer is: hostility breeds contempt. Wedderburn recounts how any worker who 'failed' in his duties to the 'master' has been subject to criminal penalties as far back as the Statute of Labourers of 1351.[18] Similarly legislation to outlaw 'combinations' of workers can be traced to the fourteenth century.[19] Building on a long legislative history of this type, but also in a direct reaction to the French Revolution on the Continent and associated concerns about where this might lead, additional punitive statutes—the Combination Acts of 1799 and 1800, in particular—were adopted that generalised the prohibition on collective organisations for workers.

A hostile judiciary added to a climate of fear and distrust among workers long after the statutory abolition of criminal liability in the latter half of the nineteenth century. Here it must be borne in mind that English law resorts under the legal family of the common law. It follows that, contrary to the situation in the civil law, judge-made law qualifies as an official source of law. As a practical matter, this means that the legal binding effect of individual court decisions does not remain confined to the immediate parties in dispute. Of particular interest is the display of judicial creativity as regards civil liability in tort. Today, conspiracy, intimidation, and interference with contractual relations are collectively known as economic or industrial torts. They are torts that have been developed in and by the common law courts for the very purpose of curtailing social unrest on the factory floor.

The Industrial Revolution reached England well ahead of the Continent. By the time pressure on the legislature to enact minimum protective standards for workers generally came to the fore in Europe, the British labour movement had not only managed to survive the prolonged (statutory and judicial) onslaught on unions and their members, but organised labour had also started to acquire considerable strength. In the circumstances, collective self-reliance seemed the best way forward. In a way, the social legislature 'missed the boat' in Britain.

The common law approach to legal reasoning was exported to the colonies. Goldman records how it affected the United States of America at the time of its independence in 1787.[20] Less obvious was the continued, pervasive influence of the common law for another hundred years or so following independence. Throughout the nineteenth century the American approach to employment also came with a peculiar twist. Slaves formed an integral part of the American workforce until well after the Civil War (1861–65) had ended. In their case, the employment relationship was deemed to be based upon notions of property law. Even 'free' workers faced a hostile legislature and judiciary. Tellingly, it was not until the Great Depression of the mid-1930s that the US Supreme Court withdrew the 'constitutional barriers'—freedom of contract and property rights, in particular—to social legislation.[21] In practical terms, the only alternative to state help seemed, once again, (collective) self-help. Not unlike the situation in Britain, this proved moderately successful, especially in areas where skilled trades were present. In the early 1880s a federation of unions was formed; it subsequently became known as the American Federation of Labor (hereafter: the AFL). Goldman records that during the formative years of the AFL its leadership firmly believed that American workers could best promote their interests through collective bargaining with their employer. The influence of one person in particular, Samuel Gompers, is said to have been so powerful that collective bargaining continues to be 'the principal tool through which the American labour movement pursues its goals' today.[22] This statement may come as somewhat of a surprise, given the consistently low union density rate of the American workforce compared to some of its European counterparts.

In the former colonies of Australia and New Zealand, the legislature deliberately sought to avoid following in the footsteps of mother England. Legislative abstention, or collective *laissez faire*, was not considered a real option. The period of social unrest during the early 1890s, characterised by a series of, at times, violent strikes and lockouts in the pastoral (sheep shearers!), mining and maritime sectors, is the conventional and also the most direct explanation for the willingness, extent and nature of government intervention on both sides of the Tasman. Politically, it must have been difficult for the government of the day to ignore the plight of the workers. In New Zealand the right to vote for all adult European men had been in place since 1879. In 1889 plural voting was abolished and replaced with the 'one man, one vote' principle.[23] Linked to this was the persuasive influence of strong personalities. Charles Cameron Kingston in South Australia and William Pember Reeves in New Zealand are two names that readily come to mind.[24] Both men sought to remove industrial warfare from the streets in the wider public interest. Macintyre and Mitchell add that the desire to build a national identity further 'fostered a willingness to fashion new institutions' and, thus, to experiment with new forms of industrial relations regulation.[25] Reference must also be made to the physical conditions of both countries. First, there was the sheer size and harshness of the local terrain, together with the tyranny of distance from the outside world. Any need for individual resilience this undoubtedly required aside, the citizens in these young nations of necessity came to rely on government assistance in a variety of domains other than industrial relations. The building of essential infrastructure (roads, the telegraph system, hospitals, schools) provides a case in point. And then, as always, of course, there was the economic factor to consider. Macintyre and Mitchell describe the situation in the late nineteenth century as follows:

> [T]he limits of growth based on existing methods of production had been reached. The principal gold discoveries had been depleted. Over-stocking, exhaustion of pasture and a downturn in world prices struck the pastoral industry heavily. Speculative investment in land and urban development resulted in a financial collapse ... After their recent and chastening misfortunes in the world trading economy, the two countries began to restructure their export sectors. Using the new opportunities presented by refrigeration, New Zealand developed dairy products, while Australia restructured its pastoral industry, diversified agriculture and developed new mineral exports. But the domestic sectors, which provided a livelihood for the majority,

> remained highly sensitive to fluctuations in the volume and price of these export staples. The desire to stabilise the domestic economy and protect it from sudden shocks had political as well as economic impulses. For in the absence of correctives, there was the prospect of recurrent contractions, continued conflict between employers and wage-earners, and endemic social instability.[26]

Two vehicles for cushioning the domestic economy were immigration controls and customs tariffs. They allowed indirect regulation of the labour market, both in terms of access and cost. The first national, industrial-relations specific legislation was New Zealand's Industrial Conciliation and Arbitration Act 1894. Similar legislation for the Commonwealth of Australia followed a decade thereafter.[27] Each time the focus of the legislature was not—unlike the situation in Europe—individual employees directly but the collective representative of these workers. Further, these statutes did not set individual employment standards as such. Rather the emphasis was on collective bargaining, if that is what it can be called as state control affected both the formulation and the resolution of industrial disputes, including even the selection of parties permitted to engage in such disputes.

Twentieth-Century Developments

The International Labour Organization

In Europe World Wars I and II—or rather their aftermath—were events that helped shape the outlook of contemporary labour law. The Peace Treaty of Versailles (1919) provided for the establishment of the International Labour Organization (ILO), a specialist tripartite body currently within the organisational structure of the United Nations. The Preamble to the ILO's Constitution stresses the close nexus between social justice and world peace.[28] Significantly, it also emphasises the interdependence that exists among the member states when developing 'humane' conditions of employment nationally:

> Whereas also the failure of any nation to adopt humane conditions of labour is an obstacle in the way of other nations which desire to improve the conditions in their own countries.[29]

Indirectly, at least, herein lies a call for countries to resist settling for a minimalist or lowest common denominator approach to the regulation of employment standards. Australia has been a member of the ILO since its inception.

The actual achievements of the ILO must not be exaggerated. The two most important ILO Conventions to date were only adopted after World War II. The first deals with the right of workers to join a union; the second addresses the right of unions to engage in collective bargaining.[30] Both conventions were ratified by Australia, rather belatedly, in 1973 under a Whitlam (Labor) government. Neither convention seeks to create direct, substantive employment rights for individual employees. Probably the most famous contrast in this regard can be found in an ILO Recommendation of 1963, concerning 'termination of employment at the initiative of the employer'[31] and a Convention of 1982 on that same topic.[32] Pursuant to the latter Convention the employment of an employee shall not be terminated unless there is a valid reason for such termination. Valid reasons for dismissal can be either personal or structural. The former relate to the employee's capacity to perform the work as well as employee misconduct. The latter are based on 'the operational requirements of the undertaking, establishment or service'.[33] The 1982 Convention inspired and guided the (short-lived) dismissal reforms introduced under Keating in the early 1990s.[34]

The ILO provides an international (if, initially, somewhat Eurocentric) forum for representatives of government, unions and employer organisations to meet and confer. Considerable symbolic significance attaches to this elevation of labour and social issues to the world stage.[35]

National Developments: Europe

International labour law does not operate in a vacuum. It draws its inspiration from the input and national experience of the countries that together make up the membership of the international legal community. This inevitably forces a return to the study of developments at the level of the nation-states. The case of France stands out. That country introduced a Labour Code (*Code du travail*) in 1910. Admittedly, this Code has nothing of the hallmarks of the grand—private law—*Code civil* of 1804. Certainly the Labour Code is not intended to be revolutionary: it does not seek to break with the past. It is therefore best understood as a formal compilation of existing laws.[36] Limited in number at first, the laws contained in the Code, as adopted, would have been unable to provide much decisive momentum for any move towards the establishment of an autonomous labour law, free from the constraints of the general civil law and worthy of study as an academic discipline in its own right. By the same token, though, the Labour Code is also very much an open-ended document. Once in place, new laws and regulations can be added all the time.[37] The net result to date is formidable, both as regards the (largely prescriptive) regulation of the individual employment relationship and the (more facilitative) regulatory framework for the orderly conduct of collective labour relations. The latter type of legal regulation includes provisions for the establishment, at the level of the shop floor or individual company, of personnel representatives and union delegates, works councils, and health and safety committees. All amount to opportunities for employees and management to interact and, in the process, get to know one another—a prerequisite for developing mutual trust and confidence.

It would be time-consuming, and not particularly fruitful, to attempt an exhaustive overview of twentieth-century labour legislation in Europe. What needs to be stressed is that the Continental legislature did not restrict itself to producing a mere catalogue of individual labour laws. Javillier's account of the French situation is a good illustration. Thus an Act of 25 March 1919 introduced the legal construct of collective bargaining agreement. Javillier comments that, in doing so, French labour law was allowed to commence its drift away from the general law of obligations.[38] In 1936 further legislation provided for the appointment of an official spokesperson for the workers on the factory floor.[39] Purely altruistic it probably was not, as the direct backdrop for the 1936 Act was the economic recession of the 1930s. Even so, gradually an infrastructure was put in place that allowed for the orderly interaction between employees and management. Post–World War II, a national social security system was created and the subject matter of the Labour Code expanded more rapidly. The 1946 Constitution formally proclaimed the existence of social rights (*droits sociaux*). Works councils, a new form of institutionalised employee participation at the level of the company, were introduced[40] and the pre-war use of the employee spokesperson was broadened.[41] Collective bargaining came under stricter state control pursuant to an Act of 23 December 1946. Other achievements of the Fourth Republic saw the right to strike enshrined in legislation,[42] the period of paid annual leave extended to three weeks,[43] and a minimum period of one month's notice guaranteed for all employees facing dismissal.[44] In turn, the (current) Fifth Republic introduced a semi-presidential system of government under Charles de Gaulle. Politically conservative, the president nonetheless put his own stamp on social policy developments. Of note is employee participation in the financial results of the company—aimed at strengthening the link between business and labour.[45]

A formal labour code does not exist in all legal systems elsewhere in Europe. Even so, the story of labour law development in neighbouring Belgium and Germany is a very similar one, the absence of a formal code notwithstanding. Blanpain describes how the role of the state in regulating labour matters has been an integral and largely undisputed feature of labour law in Belgium since the 1886 strikes that occurred against the backdrop of a deepening economic recession.[46] In some respects this role has tended to be a proactive and interventionist one. In other areas the state has been content to act merely as a facilitator. The former is most evident in the extensive coverage of just about every aspect of the individual employment relationship. To this effect, the 1900 Act on the Individual Employment Contract, referred to earlier in this chapter, has been amended and added to on numerous occasions. Consolidating legislation is currently contained in the Act of 3 July 1978. The 1978 Act constitutes the core instrument for the regulation of the individual employment relationship in contemporary Belgium. It must be read in conjunction with two further pieces of legislation of major significance in this area. They are the Act of 12 April 1965 on the protection of employee wages and the Labour Act of 16 March 1971 on the regulation of working time. Illustrative of more facilitative legislation is the Act of 5 December 1968 regulating collective bargaining agreements and the functioning of so-called joint committees. Joint committees are committees established by government regulation, either upon request of the parties or *ex officio* by the relevant minister, at the level of a particular sector of industry (such as metal manufacturing and banking). Their composition consists of equal numbers of representatives from the relevant organisations of employers and employees. Meetings are chaired by a government-appointed president or vice-president. These joint committees are directed at providing a non-adversarial forum for the discussion and, ideally, resolution of industrial disputes—typically, but not exclusively, disputes arising out of collective bargaining rounds.

While the establishment and composition of joint committees may be controlled by the state, their operation is not. Thus, unlike the former Arbitration Court in Australia and New Zealand, there is no scope for the exercise of compulsory arbitration powers should the resolution of a particular dispute drag on. On the other hand, the joint committees stand for a tripartite approach to industrial relations. Even more symptomatic of the presence (and role) of the state in this regard is the presence in several European countries of an umbrella (tripartite) advisory council, covering social or economic matters that affect all industries throughout the private sector of the national economy (rather than simply a particular industry). For Belgium the relevant body is the National Labour Council, established by Act of 29 May 1952. Its functional equivalent in the Netherlands and France is the Social and Economic Council (*Sociaal Economische Raad, Conseil économique et social*, respectively). In both countries its creation once again took place in the immediate aftermath of World War II.

In Germany no labour code operates. But Germany has no equivalent of Belgium's 1978 Act on the Individual Employment Contract either. Weiss laments that German attempts at consolidating at least the principal rules on the individual employment relationship have failed thus far.[47] Fortunately, contrary to the situation that prevailed throughout most of the twentieth century in Australia, federalism has not proved an additional impediment to clarity and legal certainty in Germany. Specifically, under the Constitution (*Grundgesetz*) the competence to deal with matters of labour law lies with the federal legislature rather than with the states. It follows that German labour law is uniform across the various states (*Länder*), with staff representation in the public sector the only exception of significance.[48] A further feature of German labour law is the role played by the specialist Labour Courts. These, like their counterparts in France or Belgium, interpret the legislative provisions of both the general law and labour law. However, they also 'fill in the gaps left open by the legislature'.[49] Weiss suggests that, in the field of German labour law, the specialist judiciary may have acquired a standing comparable to, and possibly greater than, the legislature. A good illustration is the development and regulation, by the courts, of the right to strike in pursuit of a collective bargaining agreement. A fuller discussion of labour courts occurs in Chapter 5.

The legal basis for collective bargaining in contemporary Germany is the 1949 Act, as amended in 1969, on collective agreements (*Tarifverträge*). Collective bargaining typically occurs at a level that surmounts the employee's place of work, as is the case elsewhere on the Continent. The primary focus of the legislation on various forms of institutionalised worker participation, on the other hand, is the workplace. In this fashion both vehicles for the protection of employee interests complement each other rather well. Pursuant to the Works Constitution Act (*Betriebsverfassungsgesetz*), works councils must be created in every 'establishment' (*Betrieb*) with more than five employees over the age of eighteen.[50] In addition, the legislature introduced three different models of employee representation on the supervisory board of (large) companies. Two of these were adopted in the aftermath of World War II, the third and most recent model dates from the mid-1970s. Again, an in-depth analysis can be found in Chapter 4.

National Developments: Britain and Beyond

While the above account is by no means comprehensive, it contains sufficient detail to provide an interesting contrast with the situation in Britain and elsewhere in the English-speaking world. On the Continent, the proactive role of the state gained both momentum and acceptance as the twentieth century unfolded. State involvement there was typified by a steady expansion of statutory employee protection rights in the domain of what is commonly referred to as individual labour law. Equally important was the role of the state in putting in place the infrastructure for the orderly exchange between the collective representatives of employees and employers. This part of labour law is known as collective labour law. It accommodates the role of the union, especially its central place in the collective bargaining process. Clearly, not all employee representation devices as set up on the Continent were meant to be dependent on union involvement. Works councils, for instance, have been specifically designed to represent all employees at the place of work rather than just the unionised segment of the workforce. Equally, employee representation on the supervisory board of companies stands for more than union representation. In the same vein, access to the labour or employment court is neither restricted to union members nor dependent on union assistance.

In the various English-based legal systems referred to earlier in this chapter, the labour law scene throughout the larger part of the twentieth century was one of relative calm. Certainly, no frenzy of legislative activity comparable to the Continent can be detected there. As indicated already, in Great Britain no real change in government policy as regards collective *laissez faire* occurred until the 1960s. Once the government did start displaying an interest in regulating the conduct of industrial relations, any associated increase in the role of the law did not reflect a change of heart as regards the primary role of collective bargaining in protecting the interests of employees. Rather, the purpose of the so-called Donovan reforms[51] was to tie bargaining to the state's incomes policy, aimed at controlling inflation and curbing wage drift.[52] Similarly, any growth in individual employee protection legislation during the 1970s was largely 'a quid pro quo for wage restraint'.[53]

In the United States, the Great Depression of the 1930s resulted in the adoption of the National Labor Relations Act of 1935. No substantial change in the statutory framework has proven politically feasible since,[54] although allowance must be made for the impact of the civil rights movement from the 1960s on employee protection against discriminatory treatment by the employer. Closer to home, the Australian/New Zealand model of compulsory conciliation and arbitration, with its associated philosophy as regards the pivotal role of the state in industrial relations, only started to be challenged seriously in the final decades of the twentieth century.[55]

Turning of the Tide?

And then something changed. In a first (and somewhat predictable in light of the preceding history of labour law) reaction to the economic recession of the 1970s, a series of protective measures was adopted by various national governments including, in Europe, measures at the supranational level of what was then the European Economic Community (EEC). The purpose of these measures was to maintain the *status quo* and shield employees from the harshest effects of change in the economic environment.[56] Typical were the adoption of several European Community Directives for the protection of 'acquired rights' of employees in instances of collective redundancy,[57] whenever the employer's business changed hands,[58] or when the business became insolvent.[59] Only this time it was followed by a period—from the 1980s onwards—of questioning the appropriateness of this type of intervention. Ever louder calls were heard that an employee protectionist approach only added rigidity to the labour market, that precisely the opposite was required: that is, greater flexibility, including social flexibility so as to be able to better ride the wave of internationalisation of the national economies and the associated challenges presented by a more globalised competition.

The immediate trigger for this querying of the purpose of labour law—the recession and successive oil crises in 1973 and the early 1980s—might have been temporary. But questions about the role of labour law remained. As a result, Australia and New Zealand opted for drastic change in the pre-existing approach to labour law regulation. Witness the complete dismantling of the centralised system of compulsory conciliation and arbitration in these countries over the past few decades. Thus far, the reaction in Europe has been more muted and, arguably, more cautious, although there as well a growing consensus appears to have emerged as to the need for change. In late 2006 the Commission of the European Communities released a discussion document—a Green Paper—entitled *Modernising Labour Law to Meet the Challenges of the 21st Century*.[60] A key aspect of the Green Paper is embodied in the term 'flexicurity'. By seeking to combine the need for economic flexibility with the desire for social stability and (social) security, it would seem that the core concern in Europe remains how to avoid throwing out the proverbial baby with the bath water.[61]

A First Attempt at Appraisal: Purists or Traditionalists

The above timeline, while sketchy, provides an appropriate backdrop for the current scholarly debate about the nature and purpose of labour law. One point to note is that there exists a traditional perception of labour law. It is a perception that has been held widely across much of the Western industrialised world for most of the twentieth century. It is a perception that views labour law as necessarily going beyond the mere application of the rules of general law to the employment relationship. Rather, labour law is treated as an area of law with a mission: it is about employee protection law. For these 'traditionalists' or 'purists' the employer-employee relationship is fundamentally and inherently unequal. The relationship is fundamentally unequal because the inequality goes to the very core of that relationship. The relationship is inherently unequal because it is an inequality based on the consideration that one party is dependent on the other party for his or her very livelihood. It follows that to apply, for instance, general contract law to the employment relationship is most inappropriate as to do so would be tantamount to legally consolidating this economic inequality. To overcome economic inequality, special legal rules are needed. The proper focus of labour law thus also displays a justified bias in favour of the employee.

Traditionalists acknowledge the existence of differences between legal systems, but these merely concern the various methods available for tackling inequality in the employment relationship. For ease of reference, a distinction then can be made between the direct interventionist approach of the legislature on the European Continent and the more indirect, procedural approach preferred by English-based legal systems. When adhering to the primary classification device of legal families as used by comparative scholars, the distinction roughly corresponds to the divide between the worlds of civil law and common law.

Continental Europe: Specialisation of Labour Law

As the historical overview at the start of this chapter showed, continental legal systems by and large opt for direct statutory intervention. Under this approach individual employees are awarded statutory rights that boost their position *vis-à-vis* the employer. Union assistance for the enforcement of these rights is available but not compulsory. To be clear, employees have direct access to law courts specifically created for the enforcement of their rights. Incremental legislative growth over time has resulted in an extensive body of individual employment rights across continental Europe.

The current extent of protective employee legislation in Europe can be usefully illustrated through an examination of the labour laws in Belgium. Belgian law displays features from both main representatives of the civil law, that is, France and Germany. A series of statutes there has had as their primary objective to boost the legal protection of Belgian employees. The 1978 Act on Individual Employment Contracts takes pride of place. It is the successor of the 1900 Act by the same name.[62] This legislation consolidates statutory entitlements as regards not only the contents of the individual employment relationship, including its termination, but also its creation and format. Specifically, the 1978 Act contains an express requirement for individual employment contracts, other than those that provide full-time employment and are entered into for an indefinite period, to be in writing. A statutory limit on the number of successive fixed-term contracts and restrictions on the use of probationary periods applies. In addition, numerous 'events' are stipulated to merely 'suspend' the individual employment relationship rather than formally terminate the contract or provide grounds for its termination by the employer. In this manner the 1978 Act catalogues employee entitlements to various forms of leave for reasons of personal health, family commitments or the performance of civic duties (such as military service, jury service). Further, detailed provisions aim at avoiding arbitrary dismissals. These extend to procedural safeguards applicable in situations where substantive grounds for terminating the employment relationship may exist.

Apart from the 1978 Act, separate statutes in Belgium regulate working time, annual leave, public holidays, paid educational leave, remuneration, equal pay, and—not without significance in a multilingual country—the use of language in the workplace. As a rule, any statutory employee entitlements are minima only: they provide the threshold for any subsequent individual and/or, more likely in practice, collective bargaining. In this fashion they also act as a shield for employees against the vagaries of fluctuations in economic conditions and the impact of these on the outcome of collective bargaining.

Legal commentators have sought to capture the European approach to employee protection by describing it in terms of 'specialisation' or 'specificity' of labour law.[63] French scholars use the expression of *particularisme du droit du travail* in this regard.[64] The functional equivalent in Germany is *Eigenständigkeit des Arbeitsrechts*.[65] Each expression in its own language stresses a need for special concepts, rules, institutions and procedures to cater for the legal relationship between employer and employee.

Two qualifications to the above labelling of labour law are in order. First, the argument in favour of specialisation can never amount to a complete break with the general law. If labour law is to remain part of the overall legal order, it cannot be wholly 'free' as complete independence would place labour law in a 'juridical void'.[66] Thus the question of specialisation in labour law must always be phrased in relative, not absolute, terms. To maintain a proper balance between general law and specialist labour law may prove problematic at times. Certainly, the issue here defies any separation of legal systems along family lines. A recent illustration concerns the tension between the Labour Court and the supervisory role performed by the more generalist Court of Appeal in New Zealand.[67] Second, it would be wrong to assume that specialisation is a feature only of individual labour law. It applies equally to collective labour law in continental Europe. Certainly, the role of the collective representative (of employees as well as, most commonly, employers) in the formation of contemporary labour law can hardly be ignored. Hueck and Nipperdey, in their assessment of labour law as a discipline in its own right (*selbstandige Sonderdisziplin*), specifically commend the unique dimension of collective labour law.[68] However, these authors also caution against a temptation to over-emphasise its significance. Specifically, they argue against the precedence of the collective over the individual in all circumstances. This makes perfect sense. Unions, collective bargaining and collective bargaining agreements are never goals in themselves. Instead, they are a means towards an end: the promotion of the interests of the employee. Individual and collective labour law complement one another. But the ultimate question in labour law must always be how well or how badly off the individual employee is.

Anglo-American Approach: Autonomy of Labour Law

The Anglo-American approach to labour law also acknowledges the unequal relationship between the individual employment parties. However, in contrast to the European approach, it shifts the focus away from the individual towards the collective employment relationship rather more swiftly and more fully. Any inequality that exists between the parties at an individual level is addressed by preference indirectly, that is, by having a collective representative of the employee deal with the employer.

Typically, the type of legal rule enacted to accommodate the Anglo-American approach to collective representation tends to be procedural rather than substantive in nature. Herein lies a first meaning of the label 'autonomy' in a labour law setting. Labour law is autonomous in that the terms and conditions of employment are set by the (collective) parties themselves. In Britain this notion of autonomy has long gone accompanied with a struggle for freedom from (interference by) the common law.[69]

Complete state abstention proved a futile dream, even in Britain. Certainly, any social consensus there might once have been that the role of the state in industrial relations should be kept to a minimum, has since been obliged to accommodate—arguably as early as the 1960s and therefore several decades prior to Tony Blair's 'Third Way'[70] approach—an expansion in legislation creating individual employee rights enforced by newly established industrial tribunals for that very purpose. Unlike the experience in continental Europe, though, the British evolution towards individualisation and 'juridification'[71] of labour law has come in for severe criticism almost from the very beginning. That criticism seems to have been two-fold. On the one hand, while the development of a statutory framework for employee protection might have been intended to leave the essential autonomy of the collective parties undisturbed,[72] in reality there are said to have been 'profound implications for voluntary regulation'.[73] On the other hand, individual employees were not unqualified winners either. As regards protection against unfair dismissal, for instance, Lewis refers to research carried out during the 1980s indicating 'a poor success rate in the tribunals, low levels of compensation, a marked reluctance to order reinstatement, and a judicial attitude geared towards the needs of managerial efficiency'.[74] Somewhat ironically, the 1980s is precisely the period during which Australia and New Zealand began a move in the opposite direction, away from centralised state control in industrial relations and with a greater emphasis on (collective, at first) self-regulation.

In the United States, 'proceduralism' has been the hallmark of American labour law ever since the National Labor Relations Act of 1935. Still the core statute on federal labour law today, various provisions of the 1935 Act deal with the establishment of bargaining units, union certification, duty to bargain in good faith, and the prohibition of so-called unfair labour practices. These statutory provisions in turn must be read in conjunction with the vast case law emanating from the Act's principal administrative agency, the National Labor Relations Board. Overall, though, the substantive contents of American labour law remains the domain of the bargaining parties themselves. Relatively comprehensive statutory schemes that govern the (legal) relationship between management and organised labour are also a feature of labour law in neighbouring Canada.

Whenever collective bargaining is conceived as the main vehicle towards avoiding unilateral decision-making by the employer, individual labour law is easily, if bluntly, dismissed as nothing but 'the sum of archaic common law of master and servant along with a (limited) number of statutes of more or less modern vintage'.[75] Even a cursory inspection of individual labour law courses on offer in North American law schools today reveals a paucity of contents by European standards: in essence, the focus tends to be on employment discrimination and/or occupational health and safety in the workplace. The dismantling 'down under' of the compulsory conciliation and arbitration model has not of itself triggered a shift in focus away from the collective and towards the individual. Not even the introduction of a so-called personal grievance procedure in New Zealand made much difference at first, with access confined to union members only.[76]

All in all, under the traditional Anglo-American approach, the legislature seeks to be merely a facilitator and does not see it as its primary function to spell out the actual terms and conditions of employment for workers. The hands-off label of labour law 'autonomy' then captures the difference with the continental European approach rather well.[77]

An adequate explanation for the difference in approach between the continental Europeans and the Anglo-Americans is not easily found. In part, no doubt, any differences are a matter of historical accident. Whereas the British Labour Party was the creation of the union movement, on the Continent developments have tended to be in the reverse order. In part, different perceptions about the role of the state undoubtedly and, perhaps, different perceptions about the role and concept of law itself play a role as well. In the civil law systems on the Continent the legislature constitutes the supreme law-maker, hence the emphasis on positive rights. By contrast, the English common law has a long tradition of judge-made law, and this helps explain the focus on practical remedies and self-help. On the Continent the role of the state in organising human relationships is questioned less. Elsewhere, relatively more faith is placed in the judiciary and its independence. Finally, on the Continent democracy tends to operate along principles of proportional representation, including the presence of multiple parties on the political scene. Unlike the first-past-the-post system found elsewhere, this last feature both enhances the chances of employee-friendly laws being introduced and reduces the likelihood of abrupt, radical reverses in social policy legislation over time.[78]

Pragmatists or Realists: A Challenge from Within?

Towards the end of the twentieth century some legal commentators started to question the underlying rationale of labour law as employee protection law. Intriguingly, these commentators have tended not to come from Europe, where one might have expected concerns to be raised about the tension between the seemingly endless scope for improvement in substantive employment rights and the competing need for flexibility in a more globalised economy. Rather, the calls for change have been loudest in the Anglo-American world, its traditional, more limited focus on creating a level playing field procedurally notwithstanding.[79] These 'new generation' labour lawyers stress the role of labour law as a tool for regulating the labour market, including its actors (employers, unions, and so on). Employee protection is said to constitute too narrow (and, possibly, inappropriate) an objective of labour law. Instead its goals are stated to include things like maximising productivity, boosting (international) competitiveness, or even reducing unemployment. When viewed in this light, the legitimate but broader goal of job creation becomes as important or, arguably, even more important than the promotion of job security. It also follows that the creation of, in European parlance, 'McDonald jobs'—that is, jobs deemed inferior because they provide employment under precarious conditions—is to be preferred over the alternative of no jobs.

The contrast with the continental European approach is a sharp one. In March 2006 mass demonstrations throughout France successfully blocked government proposals for a new type of 'first job contract' (*contrat première embauche*). Under these ill-fated proposals some of the existing labour laws would have been amended to allow young (under the age of twenty-six) persons without previous job experience to be offered employment with, in effect, a two-year probationary period. During that period dismissal without reason would have been legally permissible.

It may be tempting for outside observers to dismiss this and other instances of European resistance to expanding forms of precarious employment as exceedingly reactionary, elitist even, especially since the unemployment rate of the target group—young people, often from the outer suburbs (*banlieues*)—has been in the double digits for some time now. Equally perplexing, though, again from a European perspective, is the implementation in that same year of Australian legislation facilitating dismissals across the board with the stated objective of stimulating employment growth. In effect, the Workplace Relations Amendment (Work Choices) Act[80] introduced into Australia the equivalent of the American employment-at-will doctrine.[81] Pursuant to the Act, employees in companies with a workforce of 100 or less could no longer query the fairness of their dismissal. In larger companies as well, protection against dismissals 'for operational reasons' was removed. Especially intriguing is that the adoption of the federal legislation occurred against an economic backdrop of acute labour shortages. In May 2007 Australia's overall unemployment rate had reached a historically low level of 4.2 per cent.

Labour Law: Employee Protection Law or Labour Market Regulation?

When trying to make sense of these seemingly opposing views of labour law, a number of considerations must be borne in mind. First, the traditionalist (European) perception of labour law arguably carries more weight, if only because it is the more conventional as well as the oldest perception of labour law. Additionally it has the advantage of providing a positive normative perspective that facilitates the evaluation and critique of any labour laws adopted over time. The pragmatist view of labour law is more recent and has not, as yet, stood the test of time. It also is itself the product of a particular timeframe. Specifically, the doctrine of labour law as labour market regulation must be seen against the economic backdrop of the recession of the 1970s and the political backdrop of deregulation that followed in the 1980s. Both the recession and the deregulation movement were profoundly unsettling events. They led to a questioning of accepted practices. It was a period typified by Margaret Thatcher in the United Kingdom and Ronald Reagan in the United States. Both political leaders reflected a 'small business' outlook on life. They stood for less, rather than more government regulation, in exchange for greater recourse to self-reliance and individualism. When applied to labour law, deregulation does not remain confined to a reduction in government intervention as a matter of mere practicalities. Rather, the shift towards self-regulation and individualism in industrial relations has been profoundly ideological in nature.[82] As self-regulation and individualism represent longstanding, traditional aspects of the American psyche and culture, the question that arises then is whether the world—and, in particular, Australia—is 'simply' catching up with the United States.

Labour law as employee protection law and labour law as labour market regulation need not be mutually exclusive. Creighton and Stewart argue that both views of labour law can co-exist in Australia.[83] To the extent that this is indeed the case, the net effect may very well be to enrich the experience of all those who study labour law, if only by broadening the scope of this study. The perception of labour law as labour market regulation stands for the proposition that the government pursuit of employee protection cannot and does not occur in splendid isolation from other, at times competing, public interest objectives—such as competitiveness, productivity or employment opportunities. To use a somewhat tired slogan, no (lasting) social paradise was ever built on top of an economic graveyard. A practical compromise therefore may be to design a genuine (instead of a mere token) minimum floor of employee rights. Here the continental European experience may be of assistance. This proposition is revisited in chapters 7 and 8 of this book.

It does not follow from the above that no differences exist between both perceptions of labour law whatsoever. In particular, to view labour law as a tool for regulating the labour market carries the risk of treating social wellbeing as an afterthought, as something that will fall into place of itself once economic priorities are taken care of first. The fallacy of such an assumption is by no means confined to labour law.[84] It has been demonstrated rather vividly by the attitude to social policy making at EU level in the early years, when the EU was still known as the EEC.[85] Blanpain has used the image of European social policy as a trailer rather than a locomotive when describing the European integration movement during the 1960s.[86] The social policy of the EU is discussed more fully in Chapter 6.

Death of Labour Law? adopts a normative stance. It is written from the premise that employee protection continues to be, not just a worthwhile objective of labour law, but rather its very *raison d'être*. Economic and fiscal government policies aimed at boosting productivity, containing inflation and promoting employment, while unquestionably worthwhile, risk detracting from the main game. From a purely pragmatic perspective, the risk of diluting the contents of labour law can and must be avoided. Conceptually, government economic and fiscal policies clearly fall outside the proper scope of labour law as an academic discipline in its own right.

Notes

1 Hepple, 'Introduction', p. 4.

2 Most of the 1838 Code remained in force until 1992. Since then a new Dutch civil code (*Nieuw Burgerlijk Wetboek*) draws from a wide variety of sources besides France.

3 Act of 2 August 1868.

4 *On ne peut engager ses services qu'à temps, ou pour une enterprise déterminée.*

5 Blanpain uses the expression 'forced labour' in regards to an identical

provision in the Belgian civil code: Blanpain, 'Belgium', 2006 update, [422].
6 Initially, the French Labour Code of 1910 reproduced the text of Article 1780 *verbatim*: see Articles 20 and 23. Since 1928 this is no longer the case. The relevant provisions in the new Labour Code are Articles L 121 and L 122.
7 Senate Commission Report 1977, p. 39ff.
8 Article 22 of the 1900 Act.
9 *In de moderne opvatting van de overeenkomst is de werkman geen zaak waarover de werkgever vrij kan beschikken en waarover hij een absolute macht heeft:* Belgian House of Representatives (Gedr. Stuk Kamer), Session 1896–97, Number 26.
10 Zweigert and Kötz, *An Introduction to Comparative Law*, p. 144.
11 ibid.
12 Ramm, '*Laissez-faire* and State Protection of Workers', p. 111.
13 ibid.
14 ibid., p. 112.
15 Vranken, *Fundamentals of European Civil Law and Impact of the European Community*, pp. 66–7; Merryman, *The Civil Law Tradition*, pp. 56–60.
16 Lewis, 'The Role of the Law in Employment Relations', p. 1.
17 Lord Wedderburn, *The Worker and the Law*, p. 1.
18 ibid., p. 141.
19 ibid., p. 514.
20 Goldman and White, 'United States of America', 2002 update, [62].
21 ibid., [68] and [72].
22 ibid., [64].
23 Woods makes a direct link between the voting rights of workers, the return of a sympathetic government following the 1890 elections and the 1894 Industrial Conciliation and Arbitration Act. See Woods, *Industrial Conciliation and Arbitration in New Zealand*, p. 37. New Zealand was also the first 'major' nation to grant universal suffrage (including women) as early as 1893. South Australia followed in 1894.
24 ibid., pp. 42–3; Macintyre and Mitchell, 'Introduction', p. 11.
25 Macintyre and Mitchell, 'Introduction', p. 10.
26 ibid., pp. 9–10.
27 Conciliation and Arbitration Act 1904 (Cth).
28 Landau, *The Influence of ILO Standards on Australian Labour Law and Practices*, p. 1.
29 ibid.
30 Convention No. 87, 1948, concerning Freedom of Association and Protection of the Right to Organise; Convention No. 98, 1949, concerning the Right to Organise and Collective Bargaining.
31 Recommendation No. 119.
32 Convention No. 158.
33 ibid., Article 4.
34 Industrial Relations Reform Act 1993 (Cth).
35 See also Chapter 6.

36 In the terminology of Bergel, the French Labour Code qualifies as an instance of formal rather than substantive codification. See Bergel, 'Principal Features and Methods of Codification', p. 1073.
37 A side-effect is increased complexity. The recent adoption of a 'new' Labour Code, on 12 March 2007, appears to have been a missed opportunity to simplify the legislative provisions on French labour law: Regulation (*Ordonnance*) No. 2007–329.
38 Javillier, *Droit du travail*, p. 14.
39 Act of 24 June 1936.
40 Regulation (*Ordonnance*), 22 February 1945.
41 Act of 16 April 1946.
42 Act of 11 February 1950.
43 Act of 27 March 1956.
44 Act of 19 February 1958.
45 Regulations (*Ordonnances*), 7 January 1959 and 17 August 1969.
46 Blanpain, *Schets van het Belgisch arbeidsrecht*, p. 26.
47 Weiss, 'Labour Law', p. 301.
48 ibid.
49 ibid.
50 The original legislation goes back to the *Betriebsrätegesetz* of 1920. Amendments were introduced in 1952, 1972 and, more recently, in 2001. See Ramm, 'Workers' Participation, the Representation of Labour and Special Labour Courts', p. 252.
51 Lord Donovan chaired a Royal Commission on Trade Unions and Employers' Associations. The Commission published its report in 1968: Cmnd 3623.
52 Lewis, 'The Role of the Law in Employment Relations', pp. 32–6.
53 ibid., p. 34.
54 Finkin, 'Law Reform American Style: Thoughts on a Restatement of the Law of Employment', p. 139.
55 A detailed discussion can be found in Chapter 7.
56 See also Chapter 6.
57 Directive 75/129/EEC, *Official Journal of the European Communities*, 1975, L 48.
58 Directive 77/187/EEC *Official Journal*, 1977, L 61.
59 Directive 80/987/EEC *Official Journal*, 1980, L 283.
60 Commission of the European Communities, *Modernising Labour Law to Meet the Challenges of the 21st Century.*
61 For an in-depth discussion, see Chapter 8.
62 See the discussion at the beginning of this chapter.
63 See the overview in Vranken, 'Autonomy and Individual Labour Law. A Comparative Analysis', p. 100.
64 Durand, 'Le particularisme du droit du travail', p. 298.
65 Hueck and Nipperdey, *Lehrbuch des Arbeitsrechts*, p. 26.
66 Lord Wedderburn, 'Labour Law: From Here to Autonomy?', p. 2.
67 Vranken, 'The Role of Specialist Labour Courts in an Environment of Substantive Labour Law Deregulation', p. 303.

68 Hueck and Nipperdey, *Lehrbuch des Arbeitsrechts*, p. 29.
69 Lord Wedderburn, 'Labour Law: From Here to Autonomy?'.
70 Hardy, 'Great Britain', 2007 update, [70] and [71].
71 Hepple, 'Individual Labour Law', pp. 393–4.
72 Lewis, 'The Role of the Law in Employment Relations', p. 19.
73 ibid., p. 21.
74 ibid. Lewis draws on the major study by Dickens, Jones, Weekes and Hart, *Dismissed.*
75 See Vranken, 'Autonomy and Individual Labour Law', p. 104 and the references there.
76 The personal grievance procedure was introduced in 1970. It was modelled on the US system of grievance handling. Its application extends beyond dismissal disputes, and includes any type of employer action allegedly to the disadvantage of the employee's employment. An overview of the procedure's early history can be found in Department of Labour, *Industrial Relations. A Framework for Review*, vol. 2, pp. 146–8, 156–71.
77 Vranken, 'Autonomy and individual Labour Law', p. 108.
78 In recent times New Zealand has moved away from the traditional Anglo-American preference for a first-past-the-post system. The first national election under a system of (mixed member) proportional representation took place in 1996. Thus far, however, this change appears to have had little if any effect on the formulation of labour or employment policy.
79 The argument is put most forcefully by Gahan and Mitchell, 'The Limits of Labour Law and the Necessity of Interdisciplinary Analysis', pp. 67–70. That same book provides a more comprehensive overview of the debate about labour law as a tool for regulation of the labour market in a chapter by Arup, 'Labour Market Regulation as a Focus for a Labour Law Discipline', pp. 29-61. Since 2006 an even more comprehensive text on 'new' labour law is Arup et al. (eds), *Labour Law and Labour Market Regulation*, xvi + 752 pp.
80 Act no. 153 of 2005.
81 For a recent critique of the American approach to employment security from within, see Dannin, 'Why At-Will Employment is Bad for Employers and Just Cause is Good for Them', p. 5.
82 Vranken, 'Common Law versus Specialist Jurisdiction in Labour Law', pp. 21–8.
83 Creighton and Stewart, *Labour Law*, pp. 5–10.
84 Here a parallel can be drawn with the treatment of the environmental—climate change—policy as being subordinate to economic policy under the Howard government.
85 The second 'E' in EEC stands for 'Economic'. It stresses the political emphasis placed by the founders of the European Economic Community on achieving economic integration first and foremost.
86 Blanpain, *European Labour Law*, pp. 232–3.

CHAPTER 3

Employee Status

> *An attempt to define the subordinate worker is as hard to make as it is to define an honest man. Everybody recognises an honest man, without being able to give a good definition of him.*[1]

The Cornerstone of Labour Law

The late Sir Otto Kahn-Freund referred to the individual employment contract as 'the corner-stone of the edifice' of labour law.[2] Freedland agrees and elaborates in the following terms:

> The law of the contract of employment, although obsolete in some respects and misconceived in others, has a critical role not only in individual employment law but in collective labour law also. As a conceptual starting point, the contract of employment still preserves a central position in a rapidly developing part of the law.[3]

The above observations were originally made several decades ago, in the context of English labour law. However, they remain valid today, and their scope of application extends to the legal systems from both the common law and—perhaps even more—the civil law.[4] In both families of law the individual employment relationship between employer and employee provides the basis upon which labour law is built. In legal terms this basis is typically described by reference to the (individual) employment contract or contract of service.

Contracts of service constitute a special type of contract. Unlike other types of contract such as, for example, contracts of sale, they are not one-off events. Rather, contracts of service establish an on-going relationship between the parties. More importantly, unlike contracts in general including, in particular, contracts for services, the parties to a contract of service are not (legally) treated as equals. Rather, it is assumed that the party providing the service, that is, the employee, is the subordinate of the party for whose benefit the service is provided, that is, the employer. It is this presumption of legal subordination that triggers the (employee) protective rules of labour law.

How does one determine whether a particular type of contractual relationship qualifies as a contract of service? The answer may require a detailed examination, one that delves deep into the contents of the factual relationship between the parties. Not everyone who works in exchange for payment legally qualifies as an employee. Thus the pivotal question becomes which workers, in a general sense, can be said to be employees.

Since access to the protective rules of labour law depends on it, one would expect a clear, unambiguous understanding of what the concept of employee stands for. However, and intriguingly, an unequivocal definition is lacking in labour law systems throughout the world. Effectively, the legislature has left it to the courts to decide, on a case by case basis, whether someone qualifies as an employee. In principle, this allows the flexibility to cater for evolving work patterns over time. But it can also come at a serious cost, as legal certainty risks being compromised in the process.

The debate about employee status is arguably as old as labour law itself. However, in a contemporary setting, the problem has acquired special significance.[5] As the protective rules of labour law expand, pressure mounts to avoid situations where non-employees become caught up in its web. This presents the classic dilemma between legal (social) paternalism and contractual (economic) freedom. From a labour law perspective, though, the focus is squarely on countering abuse, in that certain employment situations risk being labelled relationships between equals whereas, in reality, they are not. The crucial question to be addressed in this chapter therefore is how to ensure that economic dependence and legal subordination match one another.

Role of the Legislature

Legislative assistance in determining employee status has not proven particularly helpful. The limits of statutory intervention are apparent in both the civil and the common law.[6] Typical of one approach is the federal labour legislation in the United States. The National Labor Relations Act of 1935 defines 'employee' in a circular and otherwise negative fashion only. Using an ambit claim of sorts, the Act stipulates that 'the term employee shall include any employee'.[7] Next are listed the categories of workers who do not qualify as employees. Expressly excluded are, *inter alia*, supervisors and independent contractors.[8] This exclusionary type of definition raises questions as to why supervisory staff are rather unceremoniously lumped with the employer side for purposes of American labour law, especially since the term 'supervisor' can be open to a broad interpretation. Furthermore, the American legislation begs the question as to how (non-supervisory) employees can be distinguished from, in particular, independent contractors. Technically, the latter are deemed to be engaged pursuant to a contract for services instead of a contract of service.

This circular approach to the American definition of employees closely resembles the description of employee used in the Australian Workplace Relations Act 1996.[9] Similarly in Great Britain the legislature uses the type of contract as the basis for determining employee status. An employee is said to be someone who works under a 'contract of employment'.[10] Alas, a contract of employment, in turn, is defined as 'a contract of service'![11]

The civil law approach provides equal cause for despair. As in Britain, no statutory definition of employment contract exists under French law. The French legislature assumes—correctly, no doubt—that the distinction between employees and contractors poses no great practical problems in most instances. Where uncertainty may arise, so-called deeming provisions in the *Code du travail* seek to infuse clarity by expressly categorising certain groups of workers as employees. The use of this type of legislative device is not restricted to France. Even so, the list of deemed employees pursuant to the *Code du travail* is peculiarly diverse. It includes outworkers (*travailleurs à domicile*),[12] a form of employment that has come in for renewed attention in many labour law systems of late. But the list extends further to sales representatives and commercial travellers,[13] journalists, performing artists and fashion models,[14] as well as building supervisors (*concierges*) and certain child minders (*assistants maternelles*).[15]

For the greater part of the twentieth century the Belgian legislature defined 'employee' as someone who, in exchange for remuneration, commits himself to work under the authority, command and supervision (*onder gezag, leiding en toezicht*) of an employer. Since 1985 that definition has been simplified, yet without the intent to change its meaning, by substituting 'authority' (*gezag*) for the more elaborate (but not necessarily less obscure) expression of 'authority, command and supervision'.[16] Largely for historical reasons, as discussed in Chapter 2, Belgian labour law is one of several legal systems on the European Continent where the distinction between blue-collar and white-collar employees continues to linger. Traditionally, the former type of employee is hired to perform predominantly manual labour, whereas the latter are meant to use, again predominantly, their brain. Archaic though the distinction may seem today, it does serve as an indication that, unlike the situation prevailing in the United States, supervisory personnel need not be excluded from the employee concept *per se*.

This last point warrants closer examination. The Belgian approach has always been to acknowledge the special position occupied by managerial staff. Here a parallel can be drawn with the situation in Germany where the distinction between blue-collar and white-collar employees goes back to the nineteenth century. The recognition that not all white-collar employees are alike, however, is a more recent development. While the labels may differ somewhat between both legal systems, supervisory personnel in Germany are assumed to have professional 'problems and interests' that are incompatible with the needs and aspirations of other (white-collar) employees in several respects.[17] In particular, because of the very nature of their function, supervisory staff can at times find themselves in a position of being the 'opponents' of the employee.[18]

The basic premise in Belgium as well as Germany is that all managerial personnel, including top managers, qualify as employees.[19] This means that, in principle, the full range of protective labour laws are applicable to these employees. In practice, however, the legislature tends to differentiate, by taking into account the type of labour legislation at issue in any particular instance. Thus, statutory protection against unfair dismissal is typically available to high-income and low-income earners alike. In fact, earning a high income even triggers extra generous length of notice requirements under the Belgian Act of 3 July 1978. On the other hand, the statutory rules on working time, especially those restricting overtime, may very well not apply across the board.[20] A further factor of differentiation in this regard is the recognition that not all supervisory personnel are alike. Thus, Belgian law draws a sharp distinction between the—narrowly construed—notion of 'leading personnel' (*leidinggevend personeel*) and the broader category of 'executive staff' (*cadres*). The latter encompass all high-ranking white-collar employees who may perform managerial functions but do not qualify as 'leading personnel'.[21] Leading personnel in turn comprise those charged with the daily management of the company; they are entitled to represent the employer and to commit the employer legally.[22] Leading personnel are not eligible for election as an employee representative on the works council, nor do they have voting rights in works council elections. By contrast, the *cadres* were recognised in 1985 as a separate category of white-collar employees for purposes of the legislation on works councils.[23]

The functional equivalent of *leidinggevend personeel* in Germany are the *leitende Angestellte*. Only, in Germany the special position of this type of executive staff creates further problems for the various forms of employee representation on the supervisory board of companies. A fuller discussion of institutionalised forms of employee representation can be found in Chapter 4. Of note, at this stage, is that separate organisations for the collective representation of executive staff exist in Europe. In Germany they are amalgamated in the Union of Executive Staff (*Union leitender Angestellter*).

The above excursion into different types of employee cannot disguise ongoing difficulties in defining the employee concept itself. Reference can be made to the quote from the Belgian Minister for

Labour at the start of this chapter. For Germany, Weiss and Schmidt suggest that the absence of a statutory definition of 'employee', especially for purposes of determining the personal scope of application of labour law, may not necessarily be for want of trying. Rather, obtaining a political majority in the federal parliament (*Bundestag*) is said to have proved elusive to date.[24] In other areas of law more success was had. Thus, a statutory definition of 'employee' was adopted in 1998 (although substantially amended in 1999) for purposes of social security law.[25] A statutory definition of 'self-employed' persons also appears in the German Commercial Code. By applying an argument *a contrario*, some inferences can be drawn that, indirectly at least, may assist in fine-tuning the employee concept. Section 84 *Handelsgesetzbuch* reads as follows:

> He who essentially is free in organising his work and in determining his working time is presumed to be self-employed.[26]

Enter the Judiciary

The various statutory definitions of 'employee' make clear that two main types of workers exist: those who work for themselves and those who work for someone else. Only the latter qualify as employees proper. The former are not considered employees as they are self-employed, that is, they are their own boss. The label most commonly used for these workers is that of 'contractors'. Borderline cases remain to be decided by the judiciary in both the civil and the common law. In reaching their decisions, courts tend to examine closely the specific circumstances of each individual case. Interestingly, in making case-specific determinations, the judiciary looks for signs of actual or *de facto* (and not merely formal) equality in the relationship between the parties. Where the relationship is found to be, on balance, a subordinate rather than a co-ordinate one, employee status ensues.

In recent years particular problems have emerged regarding so-called 'dependent contractors'. These are contractors in name only as they are economically dependent on one employer (the 'principal') to provide them with work. As the use of contractors to perform certain tasks increases in popularity, so does the risk of abuse. Somewhat ironically, perhaps, at one stage this even led to Australian industry proposals for a (voluntary) labour code specifically for contractors!

How does one distinguish genuine contractors from the not-so-genuine ones? A method needs to be found that allows dependent contractors to be offered at least some of the protections available under labour law. Economically, dependent contractors are as vulnerable as employees proper. The three case studies below illustrate the judicial search for legal recognition of the distinction between dependent and independent contractors.

Case Study 1: Performing Right Society v Mitchell and Booker (Palais de Dance)

Palais de Dance[27] is an early 1920s English case decided by the (then) King's Bench. The defendants ran a dance hall by the name of Palais de Dance in Hammersmith. They hired a jazz band to perform live music at the hall. The written terms of the band's contract with the dance hall stipulated that no music should be played that infringed copyright. In addition, a notice posted in the hall read that only such music as might be played without fee or licence was allowed to be played. The plaintiff owned copyright over certain music performed by the band in breach of the terms of the contract. A successful claim was brought in damages together with an injunction, that is, a court order preventing the performance of unlicensed copyright material in the future.

Vicarious Liability

Prima facie this case has no bearing on labour law. However, in litigating the breach-of-copyright matter, a question was raised as to whether the defendants could hide behind the terms of their contract with the band. In other words, was the breach of copyright really the band's problem, as claimed by the defendants? Or could it also be the defendants' problem, because the band members legally qualified as employees of the defendants? If the band members were to be treated as contractors, they would be self-employed in the eyes of the law and, thus, they would not be able to trigger the vicarious liability of the employer. Known in the United States as the *respondeat superior* doctrine, employers are legally liable to third parties for the tortious conduct of their employees, always provided that such conduct falls within the scope of employment. Scope of employment tends to be defined broadly by the courts. The question then becomes whether what the employee does amounts to 'an improper mode of performing an authorised act'.[28] Not even employee conduct contrary to the employer's express instructions—including, in certain circumstances, malicious conduct—necessarily produces an exonerating effect for the employer. In legal parlance, vicarious liability attaches to employee conduct that is sufficiently 'incidental' to authorised conduct. A classic case in point is the High Court of Australia decision in *Bugge v Brown*.[29]

Bugge v Brown involved a dispute between neighbouring property owners. The defendant was a farmer who instructed a labourer to cut thistles on a remote part of his land. The terms of employment included the provision of food. The farmer gave specific instructions about the location at which to prepare the food. The labourer ignored these instructions. His negligence caused a fire which spread to the plaintiff's property. The leading judgment was written by Isaacs J who observed that vicarious liability is not simply a question of checking whether the employee's conduct was authorised, either expressly or implicitly. On the other hand, his Honour acknowledged that it would be unjust to make employers legally responsible for every act of their employees. Isaacs J continued as follows:

> The limit of the rule expressed in the widest form by the phrase 'the course of the employment' or 'the sphere of the employment' is when the servant so acts as to be in effect a stranger in relation to his employer with respect to the act he has committed *so that the act is in law the unauthorised act of a stranger*.[30]

Whether the employee's act is legally that of a stranger is a question of fact and, thus, it is entirely dependent upon the specific circumstances of each individual case. In *Performing Right* the court acknowledged that the band had not breached copyright knowingly or wilfully.[31] Put differently, *Performing Right* did not involve a situation where the band could be said to have acted 'on a frolic of its own'.[32]

A wide interpretation of the doctrine of vicarious liability is undoubtedly beneficial to the victim. It allows injured parties to take advantage of the 'deep pockets' of the business that employs the person inflicting the harm. But it may seem unfair for the employer. Specifically, what could the defendants in *Performing Right* possibly have done to avoid incurring liability, apart from incorporating an express prohibition clause in the contract with the band? Further, how does the legal system avoid the risk of sending the wrong signal in terms of expected behaviour by the various band members if they end up enjoying, in effect, a form of immunity because of their status as employees? The proverbial soup is never eaten as hot as it has been served. In plain English, employees do not enjoy absolute immunity. They certainly do not do so automatically. In the absence of specific (labour) legislation to the contrary, employees can always be sued in their own right. Alternatively, the employer can ask to be indemnified. Vicarious liability indeed does not create a new cause of action by allowing for someone other than the actual tort-feasor to be sued. At common law the employer and employee are both liable, concurrently and jointly.[33] And, as for the availability of practical avoidance action on the part of the employer, all that was required was for the operators of the dance hall to have applied (and paid!) for a licence to perform copyright music.

Employee status

In *Performing Right* the court applied the so-called control test to determine whether the band members were the 'servants' of the dance hall operators. It seemed reasonably clear to McCardie J that:

> The final test, if there be a final test, and certainly the test to be generally applied lies in the nature and degree of detailed control over the person alleged to be a servant.[34]

In addressing the question whether a formal, legal right to control rather than actual control is determinative, the court suggested that in the present case both types of control might have been present. The court observed that the 'right' of 'continuous, dominant and detailed control' existed.[35] Factual control was clearly present in that the band could not freely choose the place, time or hours of its performances. Also pointing towards the existence of an employment relationship were the method of payment (a fixed amount irrespective of attendance figures) and the obligation of exclusive service throughout the period of engagement (one year in length, with a provision for seven hours' daily service). On the other hand, more in the nature of the relationship being between contractor and principal rather than between employee and employer were the band's ownership of the 'tools of the trade' (their musical instruments), the band's control over the selection of music to be played (apart from a general reference in the contract that the band should play 'the latest music'), as well as the presence of termination modalities in the contract. Regarding the latter, the court assumed that there would have been less need for this type of contract clause in employment settings as termination of employment is typically controlled by statute in any event.

Somewhat intriguing are the *obiter* observations by the King's Bench to the effect that, even if the band members had been treated as contractors, this would not *per se* have exonerated the operators of the dance hall. Presumably, this is a reference, in passing, to the possibility of some independent negligence on the part of the defendants.[36]

Case Study 2: Stevens v Brodribb Sawmilling

The second case study concerns a decision by the High Court of Australia dating from the mid-1980s.[37] In this case Australia's top court decided against granting employee status. It reached this conclusion upon application of a revamped control test. The test it applied is best described in terms of a multiple indicia or totality test.

Brodribb was a company that carried out logging operations. These operations involved the engagement of three different types of personnel. First, there were 'fellers' in charge of cutting down the trees. Next a group of 'sniggers' would pull the logs to a central collection point in the forest. Finally, 'truckers' transported the trees to the mill for processing. On this particular occasion, a snigger by the name of Gray negligently injured one of the truckers called Stevens. Stevens commenced compensation proceedings in the Supreme Court of Victoria. The trial judge at first instance held that Gray and Stevens were both employees. On appeal, a 2–1 majority of the Full Court disagreed. A further appeal to the High Court of Australia was dismissed.

Of particular interest is the part of the reasoning by the High Court of Australia that focuses on the argument by Stevens that

Brodribb was vicariously liable for the negligent act by Gray. In addressing this issue the central question quickly became whether Gray could be regarded as an employee of Brodribb. Here the High Court observed that, over the years, various employee tests had been developed by the judiciary. The High Court acknowledged the traditional importance of the control test, including the shift from factual control to the right of control as first articulated in *Zuijs v Wirth Brothers.*[38]

The case of *Zuijs* involved the engagement of two acrobatic artists in a circus. Both men had been hired because of their special skills on the trapeze. They were obliged to rehearse and be present prior to the start of each circus performance, march in the grand parade and execute their act. They were not required to do any other work. One of artists accidentally injured the other while performing on the trapeze. Access to compensation depended on proof that the injured party, Zuijs, was a circus employee rather than an independent contractor. In holding in favour of Mr Zuijs, the High Court of Australia dismissed the suggestion that the circus management could not possibly exercise actual control over the manner in which the various acts on the trapeze were to be performed. The Court said:

> The duties to be performed may depend so much on special skill or knowledge or they may be so clearly identified or the necessity of the employee acting on his own responsibility may be so evident, that little room for direction or command in detail may exist. But that is not the point. What matters is lawful authority to command so far as there is scope for it.[39]

Needless to say, what goes for circus artists has implications for a whole range of business activities that involve the contemporary employment of often highly skilled workers, university teachers included.

In *Brodribb* the High Court of Australia also acknowledged the existence, under English law, of the so-called organisation test and its bearing, in some instances, on the issue of control. But the High Court stressed that, ultimately, control needs to be viewed as just one of a range of factors in assessing the overall relationship in place between the parties. In the factual circumstances of this particular case, the parties' own labelling of their relationship as one of independent contract weighed against Stevens. The absence of classic *indicia* of an employment relationship, in particular the obligation of personal and exclusive service, also pointed away from employee status. Thus, Gray had his son replace him from time to time on the job and Brodribb had condoned this practice in the past. Brodribb also left sniggers and truckers free to undertake work elsewhere in the local community whenever its operations were temporarily disrupted because of bad weather. Further, the Court found that the men 'provided and maintained their own equipment, set their own hours of work and received payments, not in the form of fixed salary or wages, but in amounts determined by reference to the volume of timber which they had been involved in delivering, through the use of their equipment, to the sawmill'.[40] Overall, the totality of the situation on the ground was held to point towards the relationship being one of independent contractors supplying their services to the Brodribb sawmilling corporation.

Brodribb stands for the acceptance in Australia of the multiple indicia test for determining employee status. The test is sometimes referred to as the common sense test in that the totality of the situation before the court is examined. However, a note of warning is appropriate. It would be misleading to view the test as simply replacing the control test. Many of the indicia that make up the totality test are themselves emanations of control. The label of revamped control test thus seems most apt. A recent application of this multiple indicia test, incorporating the role of the control factor, can be found in the next case of *Hollis v Vabu.*

Case Study 3: Hollis v Vabu (trading as Crisis Couriers)

Vabu is a company in the business of delivering parcels and documents in the Sydney area. The company engages the services of some twenty-five to thirty people as bicycle couriers and a number of others as motorcycle or motor vehicle couriers. A pedestrian was injured when struck on the footpath by a cyclist. While the identity of the latter remained unknown, it was established that the cyclist had been wearing a jacket with the words 'Crisis Couriers' on it. The victim brought proceedings in negligence against Vabu, arguing that the company was vicariously liable for the wrongful conduct of its couriers.[41] Somewhat ironically, the victim himself was a courier working for a different business organisation.

Split (Legal) Personalities?

The trial judge found that the cyclist was a courier employed by Vabu.[42] However, his Honour considered that he was constrained by an earlier decision in *Vabu v Federal Commissioner of Taxation*.[43] In that decision the New South Wales Court of Appeal had ruled that Vabu's couriers were independent contractors for taxation purposes. This then raises a preliminary point: how fragmented is the concept of employee? Can someone be an employee in some respects, for purposes of the protective rules of labour law for instance, but not in other respects, say for purposes of tax liability? The majority decision of the High Court of Australia effectively confirms this to be the case. Admittedly, in *Vabu* the High Court preferred to examine the matter of any ensuing split in legal personality narrowly. Specifically, the question of employee status was confined by the Court to the issue of vicarious liability at common law, not coverage of bicycle couriers by the rules of labour law in general.

Terms of the Contract

Couriers starting work at Vabu were handed a three-page document. The first page carried the title 'Contract for Service', and contained spaces for the recording of each courier's personal details. The second page, referred to by the Court as an inventory sheet,[44] was headed 'Radio Equipment & Uniforms'. It came with boxes or columns for checking whether the equipment was 'in' or 'out'. The third page listed a series of matters 'to be adhered to and understood' by each courier. Some of these terms of engagement read as follows:

1. Drivers terminating contracts of carriage will have their last week's pay held against any overcharges or unpaid cash jobs ...
2. This company does not pay hospital bills ...
3. A uniform with the company's logos attached must be worn at all times ...
4. Drivers must be neat and tidy at all times ...
5. Loss or damage to goods in transit is the responsibility of the sub-contractor.

6. Marine and public liability insurance is $7.65 per week. Please note that any claim is subject to $1000 excess.
7. All equipment and uniforms issued by the company shall remain its property.[45]

Clearly, the above list is incomplete and not all work rules were stated in writing. In determining the legal status of Vabu's bicycle couriers, the High Court stressed the need to examine 'the totality of the relationship between the parties'.[46] It expressly rejected the suggestion, articulated in the dissenting opinion by Callinan J, that considerations about economic independence and freedom of contract pointed to a legal status of independent contractor. The majority also ruled that the lower court had erred 'in making too much'[47] of the fact that the couriers were expected to provide their own bicycle and keep it in a proper state of repair. The bicycle couriers were held not to run their own business. They had no independence in the conduct of their operations. The Court acknowledged, however, by way of an *obiter* observation, that things might have been judged differently if a more significant capital layout had been required, together with greater skill and training to operate it.[48] One wonders whether the members of the High Court are fully aware of the vast array of quite sophisticated bicycles currently on the Australian market and, thus, the substantial variations in purchase price of this mode of transport.

Having dismissed any suggestion that the couriers 'somehow' could be running their own business as 'intuitively unsound',[49] the majority of the Court held that the bicycle couriers were employees for three principal reasons. First, on the evidence the couriers had little control over the manner in which the work was to be carried out. They were required to present themselves for work by 9 a.m. Upon arrival they were assigned a work roster. Vabu thus controlled the allocation and direction of the various deliveries. They were not able to refuse work. Any leave (including annual leave) had to be applied for. While it was unclear whether work could be delegated to others, the Court thought it unlikely in the circumstances.[50]

Second, the couriers were presented to the general public as 'emanations' of Vabu.[51] In this regard the Court attached particular importance to the consideration that the couriers were made to wear tops that prominently displayed the company logo. They were issued with company radios and bags with the Vabu logo. By contrast, the couriers did not wear a number or other sign that would allow the public to distinguish between couriers individually. This the Court said encouraged the public to identify the couriers as being an integral part of Vabu's business.[52]

The third stated reason for labelling Vabu's couriers as employees is closely linked to the second. But, in addition, it has a distinct public policy dimension to it. Vabu knew that the conduct of some of its couriers had created a danger to pedestrians in the past. Yet it had failed to encourage bicycle couriers to operate in a more responsible manner. It had also neglected to adopt effective means for the personal identification of its couriers by the public. By holding Vabu vicariously liable for the wrongful conduct by one of its couriers, the Court then sought to deter unsafe conduct in the future.[53] Social standard setting is an appropriate role for the law. Behaviour modification forms an essential, if not always successful,[54] aspect of that role.

Search for Consistency

When applying the multiple indicia test, there will inevitably be factors that point in opposite directions. In *Vabu*, the couriers owned their own bikes and carried the cost of maintaining them. They were paid per delivery and not by the time period engaged. The company did not pay medical or hospital costs. It took out insurance for the couriers but deducted the amounts from their pay package and passed on any excess. In the end, though, courts must form a total picture for themselves by weighing the various factors that together typify the legal nature of the relationship between the parties. While this reflects a common sense approach, it does not always promote legal certainty and predictability.

All up, the High Court of Australia was swayed in favour of employee status, the previous treatment of Vabu's bicycle couriers as independent contractors for taxation purposes notwithstanding.[55] The Court acknowledged that it might have decided the case differently had the couriers been expected to commit to a greater capital lay-out, including, in particular, if the tools of the trade had involved motor vehicles rather than bicycles. As noted by the High Court itself,[56] the New Zealand Court of Appeal decision in *TNT Worldwide Express (NZ) Ltd v Cunningham*[57] provides an interesting contrast in this regard.

Cunningham was a case decided under New Zealand's Employment Contracts Act 1991.[58] The case deals with an issue that goes to the very heart of labour law, that is, its scope of application. The question before the New Zealand courts was whether an owner-driver employed as a courier can be treated as an employee for purposes of the statutory provisions on unjustifiable dismissal. Specifically, Cunningham had been engaged by TNT to conduct a courier service for the company. The parties had entered into a written standard form contract used by TNT for all its couriers. Less than two years into the contract, the company sought to terminate the relationship by giving four weeks notice as stipulated under the contract. In response Mr Cunningham invoked the personal grievance provisions of the 1991 legislation, claiming he had been dismissed unjustifiably. In its defence TNT submitted that Cunningham was an independent contractor. Since the relevant statutory provisions were restricted to employees, a judicial determination as to the legal status of Cunningham became imperative.

To fully appreciate the legal proceedings that followed, it must be borne in mind that New Zealand only has a specialist court structure at the first instance and intermediate appeal stages of any litigation concerning employment matters. Any final appeals go to a court of general jurisdiction. At the time[59] this was the Court of Appeal, the functional equivalent of the High Court of Australia. Both specialist judicial bodies at the trial stage, the Employment Tribunal and the Employment Court respectively, found in favour of Cunningham. In reaching their decision considerable emphasis was placed on the extensive control exercised by TNT over Cunningham in the performance of his contractual obligations. This control included the requirement for Mr Cunningham to exclusively conduct the courier service over such routes and service such customers as directed by TNT. Mr Cunningham provided (and maintained) his own vehicle, but the type and colour had to be approved by TNT. Cunningham had to affix to his vehicle any advertising signs as required (and paid for) by the company. Cunningham had to take out TNT-approved insurance in respect of his vehicle. He was expected to wear a uniform while on the job, with both the type and colour subject to company approval. Any money received on behalf of the company had to be accounted for. Cunningham's own income was paid directly by the company. That payment, while performance-based, was subject to a guaranteed monthly minimum.

The New Zealand Court of Appeal overturned the decision of the lower courts. It expressly acknowledged that the contract gave the company 'very extensive control' over the activities of the owner-driver so as to 'tie' him to the company.[60] However, it ruled that too much emphasis had been placed on the control factor by the trial judge. Approaching the case as essentially one of contractual interpretation, the President of the Court of Appeal held that there could be 'little doubt' that the parties 'intended' the owner-driver to be an independent contractor.[61] Cooke P referred approvingly to the English decision in *Ready Mixed Concrete (South East) Ltd v Minister of Pensions and National Insurance*[62] and called it 'the closest case of authority' in the matter.[63] Great significance was attached to the comprehensive nature of the (written) contract. The terms of the contract stated unequivocally that the relationship between the parties was one of principal and contractor. The Court considered that the contract was not a sham to avoid the application of New Zealand's employee protection legislation. Thus it saw no reason not to uphold the parties' intention as reflected in the terms of their contract.

Ultimately, not unlike the judicial reasoning in *Hollis v Vabu*, the decision in *Cunningham* has a strong undercurrent of public policy—only this time they were considerations of legislative policy and these were said to point away from the courier having employee status. Specifically, the New Zealand Court of Appeal expressed its reluctance to disrupt what it called 'established practice in the industry'. It felt strengthened in its conviction by what it regarded as 'legislative policy to preserve existing principles'.[64] In this regard Cooke P noted that the definition of 'employee' was essentially the same in both the 1991 Act and that Act's predecessor, the Labour Relations Act 1987. Casey J went one step further. His Honour observed that, pursuant to both statutes, the common law concept of employee had only been extended to include homeworkers. No other category of contractor was expressly deemed to be an employee for purposes of the labour legislation. Reasoning *a contrario*, Casey J inferred that owner-drivers therefore were precluded from similarly being treated as employees. In further support of this type of reasoning, his Honour noted that a 1988 government report on the matter[65] had not been implemented.[66]

Back to the Legislature?

The above case studies show that the judicial tests for determining employee status produce unpredictable outcomes. An extreme solution would be to reduce, or eliminate altogether, the special treatment that attaches to contracts of service *vis-á-vis* contracts in general. This approach must be resisted as it is overly drastic and, in the end, it represents an intellectually dishonest 'solution' to the problem of distinguishing between employees and contractors proper. More useful, and certainly more benign, might be an expansion of the legislative assistance offered to courts through the use of so-called employee deeming provisions in selective labour statutes. While this undoubtedly allows policy-makers to go beyond the constraints of the traditional common law tests, a major drawback of this approach is its statute-specific nature. It therefore tends to consolidate an already fragmented notion of employee status. Given that the issue here touches upon the very core of labour law, a more unitary and principled approach seems appropriate. Besides, in practice, deeming provisions tend to be adopted *post factum*, whereas a more proactive stance by the legislature is generally to be preferred.

A variation on the same theme has been the adoption of legislation, in various Australian states, aimed at protecting contractors operating in certain industries against the excesses of contractual freedom. Although the purpose of this state legislation typically is not to treat these contractors as fully fledged employees, the sheer detail of the regulation at times can suggest otherwise. Chapter 6 of the Industrial Relations Act 1996 in New South Wales and the Owner Drivers and Forestry Contractors Act 2005 in Victoria are two cases in point. As the difference in their titles suggests, only the former statute seeks to place the protection of contractors squarely within the legislative framework of (state) labour law.

Chapter 6 of the Industrial Relations Act 1996 (NSW)

Chapter 6 of the NSW Act targets contracts for the transport of people (bailment) or goods (contracts of carriage). It provides for the collective representation of the contractors in question, principally taxi drivers, hire car drivers and owner-drivers, via the registration of associations of contractors. The Act also provides for the active involvement of the Industrial Relations Commission in contract negotiations, including the approval of the outcome of these negotiations. To this effect the Act distinguishes between the hands-on involvement of the Commission in the actual contents of contract 'determinations'[67] and the relatively hands-off role of the Commission in approving contract 'agreements'[68] entered into by the parties themselves. Even as regards the latter type of contract the Commission is expected to check whether the parties 'understand' the agreement, whether they might have entered into the agreement 'under duress' and, most intriguingly, whether the agreement does not 'on balance' provide a 'net detriment' to the drivers or carriers who are to be covered by it.[69]

Owner Drivers and Forestry Contractors Act 2005 (Vic)

Victoria's Owner Drivers and Forestry Contractors Act 2005 obliges contractors to be provided with an information booklet. The form and contents of the booklet are determined by the state legislature.[70] The Act makes further provision for the adoption of compulsory codes of practice by state regulation.[71] Contrary to the situation in New South Wales, the Victorian legislature opted for the resolution of disputes by a newly established Small Business Commissioner and, ultimately, the Victorian Civil and Administrative Tribunal.[72] Tellingly, the Act expressly prohibits so-called unconscionable conduct. Unconscionable conduct is identified as potentially emanating from either party. As regards hirers, the Act stipulates in surprisingly detailed and at times verbose terms as follows:

(1) A hirer must not engage in unconscionable conduct with respect to a contractor.

(2) Without in any way limiting the matters to which the Tribunal may have regard for the purpose of determining whether a hirer has contravened subsection (1), the Tribunal may have regard to any one or more of the following –

  (a) the relative strengths of the bargaining positions of the hirer and the contractor;

(b) whether, as a result of conduct engaged in by the hirer, the contractor was required to comply with conditions that were not reasonably necessary for the protection of the legitimate interests of the hirer;
(c) whether the contractor was able to understand any documents relating to the acquisition or possible acquisition by the hirer of services from the contractor;
(d) whether any undue influence or pressure was exerted on, or any unfair tactics were used against, the contractor or a person acting on behalf of the contractor by the hirer or a person acting on behalf of the hirer in relation to the acquisition or possible acquisition of the services from the contractor;
(e) the amount for which, and the circumstances which, the contractor could have supplied identical or equivalent services to a person other than the hirer, including as an employee;
(f) the extent to which the hirer's conduct towards the contractor was consistent with the hirer's conduct in similar transactions between the hirer and other like contractors;
(g) the requirements of any applicable code of practice;
(h) the extent to which the hirer unreasonably failed to disclose to the contractor –
    (i) any intended conduct of the hirer that might affect the interests of the contractor;
    (ii) any risks to the contractor arising from the hirer's intended conduct being risks that the hirer should have foreseen would not be apparent to the contractor;
(i) the extent to which the hirer was willing to negotiate the terms and conditions of any contract for the acquisition or possible acquisition of services from the contractor;
(j) the extent to which the hirer and the contractor acted in good faith;
(k) whether or not the regulated contract allows for the payment of any increases in fixed and variable overhead costs on a regular and systematic basis.[73]

The same provisions apply, *mutatis mutandis,* to contractors.[74]

International Approaches to Employee Status

The International Labour Organization

In June 2006, at the occasion of the ninety-fifth session of its International Labour Conference, the International Labour Organization (ILO) adopted Recommendation No. 198 on the Employment Relationship. The Recommendation directly addresses the legal uncertainty that currently exists regarding the distinction between employees and contractors. The Recommendation has been formulated against a broader backdrop of the overall mandate of the ILO, that is, the protection of workers internationally. Related, more general considerations at the basis of the Recommendation are the desirability of national laws and practices aimed at the provision of 'decent work' and addressing 'what can be an unequal bargaining position between the parties to an employment relationship'.[75]

Recommendation No. 198 is timely in that it places the uncertainty about employee status in the broader context of a more globalised economy and the associated increase in mobility on the part of workers as well as businesses. As regards the former, the Preamble to the Recommendation draws attention to new risks of abuse through 'circumvention of national protection by choice of law'. As regards the latter, the Preamble stresses that 'in the framework of transnational provision of services, it is important to establish who is considered an employee in an employment relationship, what rights these employees have' but also—and this can be just as problematic—who the employer is.

Part I of Recommendation No. 198 postulates that protection of workers is the responsibility of the member states in the first instance.[76] To this effect each country is urged to formulate a national policy for reviewing the personal scope of application of its labour laws and regulations on a regular basis.[77] Any such national policy review should take into account international labour standards including, presumably, Recommendation No. 198 itself.[78] Here special emphasis is placed on the need for guidance to be offered to employers and employees alike, together with the need to 'combat disguised employment relationships'.[79] Both the formulation and implementation of national policy measures should occur in consultation with the collective representatives of employers and employees.[80]

Part II of Recommendation No. 198 provides guidelines for the member states when determining the existence, or otherwise, of an employment relationship.[81] In doing so, Recommendation No. 198 confirms existing national practice not to rely solely on the characterisation of the relationship by the parties themselves, especially where this would contradict the facts as these relate to the performance of the work and the remuneration for that work.[82] To promote greater clarity, two principal legal tools are said to be available. A first device is the deeming technique identified earlier in this chapter, only this time the option is expressly left open for workers to be deemed either employed or self-employed.[83] Second, the burden of proving that an employment relationship exists can be alleviated considerably by the introduction of a legal presumption in favour of employee status.[84] The technique of legal presumption is used across different areas of law, and it is not unique to labour law. Provided that at least some indicators of an employment relationship are present, this can offer a simple yet effective means of testing employee status. Provided also that there remains scope for rebuttal during litigation, it need not be an inflexible tool either. Flexibility is important if commercial realities are not to be judicially undermined unnecessarily. Article 8 of the Recommendation is most explicit on this point:

> National policy for protection of workers in an employment relationship should not interfere with true civil and commercial relationships ...

Strictly speaking, Recommendation No. 198 is not legally binding. It follows that its listing of indicators for the existence of an employment relationship can only be suggestions. The list itself is not exhaustive, and holds no real surprises, but does provide a good summary of typical signals pointing towards employee status. Article 13 distinguishes in this regard between indicators that relate to the conditions for performance of the work and those addressing modalities for the payment of the work. They are, respectively:

(a) the fact that the work is carried out according to the instructions and under the control of another party; involves the integration of the worker in the organisation of the enterprise; is performed solely or mainly for the benefit of another person; must be carried out personally by the worker; is carried out within specific working hours or at a workplace specified or agreed by the party requesting the work; is of a particular duration and has a certain continuity; requires the worker's availability; or involves the provision of tools, materials and machinery by the party requesting the work;

(b) periodic payment of remuneration to the worker; the fact that such remuneration constitutes the worker's sole or principal source of income; provision of payment in kind, such as food, lodging or transport; recognition of entitlements such as weekly rest and annual holidays; payment by the party requesting the work for travel undertaken by the worker in order to carry out the work; or absence of financial risk for the worker.

The European Union

The European Commission formally welcomed ILO Recommendation No. 198 in its 2006 Green Paper on *Modernising Labour Law to Meet the Challenges of the 21st Century.*[85] As the broad title suggests, employee status in the EU is seen as part of a wider problem facing contemporary labour law. At the basis of the Green Paper lie fears about the development of a two-tier labour market, with privileged 'insiders' enjoying full access to the protective rules of labour law—including job security, while 'outsiders' comprise the unemployed and anyone working under precarious employment conditions.[86] The latter group includes the nominally self-employed.

It would seem that the authors of the Green Paper faced a serious dilemma. The European Commission acknowledges, and implicitly supports, the reliance by business on self-employment as one of several means to cope with change. Self-employment is said to allow for a reduction in labour costs as well as greater flexibility when managing resources in response to fluctuating economic circumstances.[87] Here, of course, the risk of abuse is real. Recourse to self-employment might benefit one party to the employment relationship but not necessarily the other. The Green Paper plays down somewhat the significance of that risk. It does so by (correctly) presenting self-employment as the reflection of an increasingly popular business model in its own right, especially in the service industry. The Green Paper observes that:

> In many cases it [self-employment] reflects a free choice to work independently despite lower levels of social protection in exchange for more direct control over employment conditions and terms of remuneration.[88]

Because of this, the introduction of minimum requirements in all contracts involving dependent contractors, let alone contracts covering dependent and independent ones alike, is not particularly favoured by the Commission even if such a 'floor of rights' would increase certainty and transparency.[89] In adopting this stance the Commission is not entirely neutral. To be clear, the distinction between employees and contractors is not of purely academic interest for the legal order of the EU itself. Not only is the EU acutely aware of the need for national laws in its member states that are truly effective, but in recent years it has become a directly affected party. In the aftermath of a recent enlargement of the Union's membership base, transitional restrictions on access by employees from the new member states to national labour markets elsewhere within the Union can and, reportedly, have been circumvented by means of 'bogus self-employed work, fictitious service provision and extended subcontracting'.[90]

Accurate figures can be hard to come by. The Green Paper relies on data from the Community's own 2006 *Employment in Europe* report. An indication of the scale of the problem facing Europe can be gleaned from the numbers for 2005. More than 31 million people, an estimated 15 per cent of the total workforce, were self-employed in the EU that year. Of that number, two-thirds are said to be single-person businesses that employed no (other) employees. Inevitably, because the data relates to the enlarged EU of twenty-five, agriculture (together with retail businesses) features rather heavily in these figures. Self-employment is particularly significant in Poland, Hungary, Lithuania, Latvia and Estonia. Since 2007 Bulgaria and Romania can be added to that list. Among the older member states, four countries—the United Kingdom, Ireland, Portugal and the

Netherlands—stand out as well. Self-employment is said to be 'a growing feature' of the construction and service industries.[91] It is in these sectors of the economy, in particular, that use is made of practices such as outsourcing, subcontracting and project-based work. All are practices that present real challenges for contemporary labour law. The European Commission does not claim to have the definitive answer. For jurisdictional reasons it sees the problem as primarily one for the member states to deal with.[92]

A sense of *déjà vu* is inevitable. Not unlike the approach adopted by the ILO, the EU claims to be able to offer limited assistance only. Not without some irony, perhaps, the Commission applauds the adoption of Recommendation No. 198 on the Employment Relationship for its 'strategic approach'.[93] The ILO Recommendation is specifically commended for encouraging the member states, in consultation with the representatives of employees and employers, to formulate national policies and periodically review the scope of existing national laws in terms of their overall effectiveness.

A rare instance of direct EU involvement in the regulation of working conditions for the self-employed is Directive 86/653/EEC.[94] Adopted in 1986, the Directive seeks to co-ordinate the laws of the member states relating to commercial agents. The Directive defines a commercial agent as a self-employed intermediary with continuing authority to negotiate the sale or purchase of goods on behalf of a principal.[95] While the meaning of self-employed is not elaborated upon, the Directive bestows certain rights upon commercial agents. Generally, principals must act 'dutifully and in good faith' in their relationship with agents.[96] More specifically, agents are entitled to receive—upon request—a written document setting out the terms of the agency contract.[97] Further, they must be provided with the information 'necessary' for the performance of the contract;[98] they are entitled to 'reasonable' remuneration;[99] and they may qualify for an indemnity upon termination of the contract.[100] All of the above safeguards for commercial agents remain vague, presumably to allow for maximum flexibility. More reminiscent of provisions enjoyed by those with protective employee status are Articles 14 and 15 of the Directive. Article 14 stipulates that, where an agency contract for a fixed period continues to be performed by both parties after that period has expired, the contract is deemed to have converted into an agency contract for an indefinite period. While agency contracts for an indefinite period can be terminated by either party by giving notice, the period of any such notice is set at a minimum one month for every year of the contract, albeit with a maximum of three months. Pursuant to Article 15, the member states are given the option to double the maximum period of notice.

The Green Paper is discussed more fully in Chapter 8.

Back to the Future? The Independent Contractors Act 2006 (Cth)

The above European legislation on commercial agents reflects a broader concern not to go overboard in the assimilation of the legal position of employees and contractors. A desire to safeguard the freedom of genuine independent contractors, rather than protect economically dependent contractors against abuse, features even more prominently in Australia's Independent Contractors Act of 2006.[101] Adoption of the federal statute was preceded by a parliamentary inquiry into the legal status of independent contractors.[102] The inquiry triggered a government response that has been severely criticised by scholars for going against international efforts to avoid abuse of independent contractor arrangements.[103] To be clear, the stated objectives of the Independent Contractors Act 2006 (Cth) amount to an unequivocal act of faith in the principle of contractual freedom. These objectives are listed in Section 3(1) of the Act in the following terms:

(a) to protect the freedom of independent contractors to enter into services contracts; and
(b) to recognise independent contracting as a legitimate form of work arrangement that is primarily commercial; and
(c) to prevent interference with the terms of genuine independent contracting arrangements.

To achieve these objectives the primary source of legal regulation of contracts for services is meant to be the contract itself. The Act expressly excludes any state or territory laws 'more commonly associated with employment relationships'.[104] Specifically excluded in this manner are, *inter alia*, the employee deeming provisions in state laws.[105]

Personal Scope of Application

If the legislation is to avoid overreaching its intended objectives, it is imperative that the Act's personal scope of application be unambiguous. Not surprisingly, the 2006 legislature faced problems similar to those encountered when drafting employee protective rules. The statute defines a services contract as encompassing a contract for services to which an independent contractor is a party and that relates to the performance of work by that contractor.[106] Yet, the term 'independent contractor' itself, while stated not to be limited to natural persons, is not statutorily defined.[107]

Intriguingly, although the application of state laws extending employee protection to contractors is precluded, an exception is made for so-called 'outworkers'.[108] Once again, outworkers are not defined by the 2006 Act. Rawling traces the origins of the term back to the employment of, in essence, migrant women from non–English speaking backgrounds in the textile, clothing and footwear industries during the post–World War II period.[109] These outworkers were the original 'home' workers in that they typically worked from home rather than on the factory floor. Historically, the application of protective labour laws was avoided by treating these workers as independent contractors. However, in response to public concerns about exploitation, as well as a concerted effort by the union movement, a number of state governments enacted legislation regulating outwork from the late 1990s onwards. The Independent Contractors Act 2006 allows for the continued application of these state laws.[110] Also 'saved' from the scope of application of the federal legislation are Chapter 6 of the Industrial Relations Act 1996 (NSW) and the Owner Drivers and Forestry Contractors Act 2005 (Vic).[111]

Intervention Powers of the Federal Court of Australia

Contemporary contract law makes provision for unconscionable conduct. In this vein, each party to a services contract may ask the Federal Court to review the contents of the contract on the grounds that the contract is either unfair and/or harsh.[112] In its determination the Court may, among other things, take into account the relative bargaining strength of the parties in negotiating the contract.[113] The remedial powers of the Court are of a substantive nature. They are therefore not restricted to striking out one or more terms of the contract including, where appropriate, an order setting aside the whole contract. The Court effectively can rewrite the contents of the contract.[114] The ramifications of judicial intervention can thus be far-reaching, especially since inadequacy of the negotiated remuneration package is expressly listed as one aspect of the judicial fairness test. Of special note in this regard is that the Court has been authorised to make comparisons with the remuneration 'an employee performing similar work' is likely to receive.[115] Apart from the issue of remuneration, comparisons with the employment conditions of employees are also allowed, so it would appear, regarding leave entitlements, hours of work, and even the modalities for terminating the contract.[116]

Notes

1 Reply by the Belgian Minister for Labour when asked to define an 'employee' in the early 1920s. See Engels, 'Belgium', p. 30.

2 Kahn-Freund, 'Legal Framework', p. 45.

3 Freedland, *The Contract of Employment*, p. 1.

4 See the various country studies, covering both civil and common law systems, in Brooks and Engels, *Employed or Self-Employed.*

5 A conceptual framework and contemporary critique can be found in Fudge, 'Fragmenting Work and Fragmenting Organisations: The Contract of Employment and the Scope of Labour Regulation', p. 609.

6 Brooks and Engels, 'General Overview', p. 2.

7 Section 2(3) of the Act.

8 ibid.: 'The term employee ... shall not include ... any individual having the status of an independent contractor, or any individual employed as a supervisor ...'

9 Section 4(1) of the Workplace Relations Act 1996 (Cth) stipulates that the notion of employee 'includes any person whose usual occupation is that of employee'.

10 Section 230(1) of the Employment Rights Act 1996.

11 Section 230(2) of the Employment Rights Act 1996.

12 Article L 721.

13 Article L 751.

14 Article L 761.

15 Article L 771.

16 Articles 2 (blue-collar employees) and 3 (white-collar employees) of the 1978 Act on the Individual Employment Contracts, as amended by the Act of 17 July 1985.

17 Weiss and Schmidt, 'Germany', 2000 update, [92].

18 ibid.

19 Blanpain, 'Belgium', 2006 update, [37]; Weiss and Schmidt, 'Germany', 2000 update, [92] and [93].

20 The Belgian Act of 16 March 1971 on Working Time excludes 'leading personnel' from its scope of application.

21 These *cadres* are said to be employees who perform a function in the company which is generally reserved for holders of a higher degree or persons with equivalent on-the-job experience: Blanpain, 'Belgium', 2006 update, [37].

22 Article 1 of Royal Decree 15 May 2003 concerning Works Councils and Committees for the Prevention and Protection of Employees at the Workplace.

23 Act of 1948 on the Organisation of Life at the Workplace as amended by the Social Recovery Act of 1985.

24 Weiss and Schmidt, 'Germany', 2000 update, [82].

25 ibid.

26 Translation by Weiss and Schmidt: ibid., [80].

27 [1924] 1 KB 762.

28 Stallybrass, *Salmond's Law of Torts*, pp. 94–5. Sir John Salmond has been described as New Zealand's most famous judge and author. See Frame, *Salmond. Southern Jurist.*

29 (1919) 26 CLR 110.

30 ibid., at 118 (emphasis added).

31 [1924] 1 KB 762 at 772.

32 For an instance of an employee deemed to be acting on a frolic of her own, see *Deatons v Flew* (1949) 79 CLR 370.

33 Sappideen, Vines, Grant and Watson, *Torts. Commentary and Materials*, p. 809.

34 [1924] 1 KB 762 at 767.

35 ibid., at 771 (per McCardie J).

36 ibid., at 773.

37 (1986) 160 CLR 16.

38 (1955) 93 CLR 561.

39 ibid., at 571.

40 (1986) 160 CLR 16 at 25 (per Mason J).

41 (2001) 207 CLR 21.

42 ibid., [3].

43 (1996) 33 ATR 537.

44 (2001) 207 CLR 21, [23].

45 ibid.

46 ibid., [24].

47 ibid., [46].

48 ibid., [47].

49 ibid., [48].

50 ibid., [49].

51 ibid., [50].

52 ibid., [52].

53 ibid., [53].

54 Compare and contrast, in this regard, the largely successful effect of contemporary 'pooper scooper' laws applicable to pet owners and the

more mixed public response to the prohibition of using a hand-held telephone device while driving a motor vehicle.

55 *Vabu v Federal Commissioner of Taxation* (1996) 33 ATR 537.

56 (2001) 207 CLR 21 [58].

57 [1993] 3 NZLR 681.

58 That statute has since been replaced by the Employment Relations Act 2000.

59 A new court of final appeal, the Supreme Court, has since been established in New Zealand pursuant to the Supreme Court Act 2003.

60 [1993] 3 NZLR 681 at 684 (per Cooke P).

61 ibid.

62 [1968] 2 QB 497.

63 [1993] 3 NZLR 681 at 684.

64 ibid., at 689 (per Cooke P).

65 Department of Labour, *Report of the Committee Enquiring into Dependent Contracting*.

66 [1993] 3 NZLR 681 at 694 (per Casey J).

67 Part 2 of Chapter 6.

68 Part 3 of Chapter 6.

69 Section 325 of the Industrial Relations Act 1996 (NSW).

70 Sections 10 and 13 of the Owner Drivers and Forestry Contractors Act 2005 (Vic).

71 Section 27 of the 2005 Act.

72 Section 40 of the 2005 Act.

73 Section 31 of the 2005 Act.

74 Section 32 of the 2005 Act.

75 Recommendation No. 198, Preamble, Considerations 2 and 3.

76 Part I of Recommendation No. 198 is entitled: National Policy of Protection for Workers in an Employment Relationship.

77 Article 1 of Recommendation No. 198.

78 Article 2 of Recommendation No. 198.

79 Article 4(b) of Recommendation No. 198.

80 Article 3 of Recommendation No. 198.

81 Part II of Recommendation No. 198 is entitled: Determination of the Existence of an Employment Relationship.

82 Article 9 of Recommendation No. 198.

83 Article 11(c) of Recommendation No. 198.

84 Article 11(b) of Recommendation No. 198.

85 Commission of the European Communities, *Modernising Labour Law to Meet the Challenges of the 21st Century*.

86 The labels 'insiders' and 'outsiders' were first used in a 2003 report for the European Council, prepared by a European Employment Task Force chaired by former Dutch prime minister, Wim Kok. See *Jobs, Jobs, Jobs: Creating More Employment in Europe*, cited in the Commission of the European Communities' Green Paper, *Modernising Labour Law to Meet the Challenges of the 21st Century*, p. 3.

87 Commission of the European Communities, *Modernising Labour Law to Meet the Challenges of the 21st Century*, p. 8.
88 ibid.
89 ibid., p. 12.
90 Here the Green Paper cites a Report on the Functioning of the Transitional Arrangements set out in the 2003 Accession Treaty.
91 Commission of the European Communities, *Modernising Labour Law to Meet the Challenges of the 21st Century*, p. 8.
92 The jurisdiction of the EU in labour law matters is discussed in Chapter 6.
93 Commission of the European Communities, *Modernising Labour Law to Meet the Challenges of the 21st Century*, p. 11.
94 *Official Journal of the European Communities*, L 382/17, 31 December 1986.
95 Article 1(2) of the Directive.
96 Article 4(1) of the Directive.
97 Article 13(1) of the Directive.
98 Article 4(2)(b) of the Directive.
99 'Taking into account all aspects of the transaction': Article 6(1) of the Directive.
100 Article 17 of the Directive.
101 Act No. 162, 2006. An Act relating to Independent Contractors, and for related Purposes.
102 House of Representatives, Standing Committee on Employment, Workplace Relations and Workforce Participation, *Making it Work: Inquiry into Independent Contracting and Labour Hire Arrangements*.
103 The *Making it Work* report is discussed in Underhill, 'Labour Hire and Independent Contracting in Australia: Two Inquiries, How Much Change?', p. 306. For an analysis of the legislation itself, see Rawling, 'The Regulation of Outwork and the Federal Takeover of Labour Law', p. 189. See also Riley, 'A Fair Deal for the Entrepreneurial Worker? Self-Employment and Independent Contracting Post Work Choices', p. 246.
104 Section 3(2)(c) of the 2006 Act.
105 Section 7(1)(a) of the 2006 Act.
106 Section 5(1) of the 2006 Act. For constitutional reasons the other party needs to be a corporation.
107 See the definitions' provision in Section 4 of the 2006 Act.
108 Section 7(2) of the 2006 Act.
109 Rawling, 'The Regulation of Outwork', p. 103.
110 Section 7(2)(a) of the 2006 Act.
111 Section 7(2)(b) of the 2006 Act.
112 Section 12(1) of the 2006 Act.
113 Section 15 of the 2006 Act.
114 Section 16(1)(b) of the 2006 Act.
115 Section 15(1)(c) of the 2006 Act.
116 Arguably this is the combined effect of Sections 8(1) and 9(1)(e) of the 2006 Act.

Chapter 4.
Employee Representation

The Story So Far

Employees—unlike genuinely independent contractors—are considered vulnerable and thus in need of special protection. Legally, they are deemed to be in a subordinate relationship with the other contracting party.

One way of tackling inequality at the level of the individual employment relationship is to create additional rights for employees by statute. Specifically, the legislature can give individual employees entitlements that are enforceable by them (with or without union assistance) in a court of law specifically created for that purpose. As we saw in Chapter 3, this has been a major part of the continental European approach to labour law regulation throughout the twentieth century. Special labour or employment courts ensure that any such employee rights are applied in the 'correct spirit'.[1] These courts will be discussed more fully in Chapter 5. Importantly, the European approach has tended to go beyond merely creating a statutory minimum floor of rights. Over the years many continental European legal systems have built an extensive scheme of statutory entitlements that cover just about every aspect of the individual employment relationship.[2]

By and large English-based legal systems prefer a different approach. Rather than boosting employee rights outright, that is, at the individual employment level, these systems have tended to shift the focus to a higher, collective level. They seek to address and remedy the inequality that exists at the individual employment relationship level through the legal recognition of a collective spokesperson of the individual employee. The underlying assumption here is that at the collective level, that is, at the level of the relationship between the collective representatives of employee and management, the chances of achieving a level playing field are greater. Of course, this is not to suggest that legal recognition of a collective spokesperson for employees is not also a feature of continental European systems. Even so, because the stakes are relatively higher in systems that make collective representation a primary device for employee protection, one would expect to find a rather more sophisticated approach to the regulation of unions and the like in non-continental systems of labour law.

This raises two major questions. First, how do various legal systems across the advanced Western world regulate the selection and official designation of a collective representative for individual employees? The discussion below contrasts the North American, Australasian, and continental European approaches to union recognition. Second, which legal rights or privileges attach to the status of officially designated employee representative? This question is important in trying to evaluate how much of a level playing field really exists at the collective level. At the end of the day, the focus on collective representation will always promote procedural rather than substantive equality in the first instance, in that it does not of itself produce any employee entitlements to minimum wages, maximum hours of work, meal breaks, annual leave and the like.

Unions: Official Designation Mechanisms

Certification in the United States

Under federal labour law the collective spokesperson for US workers is selected through a process known as certification. From a comparative perspective, it is interesting to note that collective representation is not considered to be an issue in need of regulation on the management side. Unlike the situation in Europe, no provision is made for the collective representation of individual businesses in labour law. Any lifting of the discussion about employee protection, away from the individual employment relationship to a higher, collective level thus remains partial at best.

Certification, US style, proceeds from the basic premise that employers can recognise a particular union as the spokesperson for the workforce either voluntarily or because they are compelled to do so. Each time the legislature has built in safeguards to ensure genuine employee representation is achieved. The relevant statutory framework is contained in the National Labor Relations Act 1935.

Voluntary Recognition

Voluntary union recognition can be a risky affair for employees as an employer may prefer dealing with a union that is sympathetic to the interests of the business. To avoid the voluntary recognition of employer-dominated unions, the Wagner Act stipulates that employers can only resort to voluntary recognition if they can show good reason for assuming that the particular union effectively represents a majority of the workforce. The statutory technique to help determine whether majority support exists consists of the signing of so-called (union) authorisation cards by the employees. By signing these cards, individual employees give expression to their wish to be represented for collective bargaining purposes.

Authorisation cards have proved to be a simple yet effective device for selecting a collective spokesperson of workers. They also play a role in the forced recognition procedure, as discussed later.[3] The pool of employees from which majority support must come is known as the bargaining unit. The notion of the bargaining unit is crucially important, not least because it has repercussions for both the level and the (personal) scope of any ensuing collective bargaining. The National Labor Relations Act is surprisingly unspecific in its definition of the bargaining unit, though. The Act only prescribes the maximum size of a bargaining unit. Section 9(b), in particular, limits the size of bargaining units to the employer-wide unit. This notion is sufficiently broad to allow for multi-plant bargaining, whenever the employer's business happens to be spread over two or more geographically separated plants. The bargaining unit can also be smaller than the plant or workplace, for instance where employees have traditionally been (and continue to be) organised along craft or occupational lines. However, truly industry-wide bargaining, let alone inter-industry bargaining along continental European lines, is something the concept of the bargaining unit does not allow for. In practice, multi-employer bargaining is dependent on one union obtaining certification in multiple bargaining units simultaneously. Furthermore, it is dependent on the relevant businesses agreeing to the negotiation of a multi-employer contract. Crucially, any union pressure on employers to enter into a multi-employer deal amounts to a prohibited ('unfair') labour practice under the Act. A rare, recent instance of one union successfully organising employees across different companies for bargaining purposes involved the Service Employees International Union and some 5000 janitors (cleaners and caretakers) in the Houston area.[4]

Multi-union bargaining, between one employer and several unions, while not prohibited *per se*, is equally rare. It requires inter-union co-operation between organisations that may very well be direct competitors in the recruitment of employee members.

The rationale behind the concept of the bargaining unit is a desire to ensure that employees share a sufficient commonality of interests. When viewed from this angle, it follows that more than one bargaining unit can qualify as an 'appropriate' unit. The Wagner Act acknowledges this by not requiring that a particular bargaining unit be the 'most' appropriate unit. Of course, opinions of employer and union as to what constitutes an appropriate bargaining unit may readily differ. The ultimate decision rests with the National Labor Relations Board, the federal government agency charged with administering the Act.[5] In making its determinations, the Board invariably views the wishes of the employees themselves as one of several factors to be considered. In effect, the Board tends to stress the need to balance the interests of all parties, including those of the employer.[6]

Forced Recognition

In the absence of voluntary union recognition, the device used to determine whether a majority of employees in a particular bargaining unit favours collective representation of their interests is the ballot box. The statute provides for union certification elections to be administered by the National Labor Relations Board.[7]

Certification elections determine whether employees favour one union over another. Significantly, given the tradition of individualism in American society at large, they can also determine whether employees in a particular workplace favour representation at all. To this effect an election petition can be filed by a union, a group of employees, and even by an employer. Petitions filed by an employer present certain risks for organised labour. The employer may try to boycott the organisational aspirations of a particular union by filing for an election prematurely. Specifically, employers wishing to keep the union out of their plant may wish to file for an election before the organisational drive of the union is completed.[8] To overcome this problem the National Labor Relations Act stipulates that an employer can only file for an election after one or more unions has made a claim for collective representation.[9] The legislature seeks to ensure that there is a genuine basis to every application for an election. Thus, even where the filing party is a union or a group of workers, minimal employee support must be shown first. In practice, this means that union authorisation cards must be submitted indicating a minimum 30 per cent membership support in the bargaining unit.

The outcome of certification elections represents an all-or-nothing approach under the Act.[10] Either the—or a—union wins the election or no union gets a majority vote. In the former scenario, that union becomes the exclusive representative of all members of the bargaining unit, including non-members and members of other unions. The employer may not avoid dealing with the majority union, say by directly negotiating with the employees, whether as a group or individually. If no union obtains a majority vote, there is no union to officially represent the employees. In that case the losing union cannot even represent its own members.

Frequency of Certification Elections

The finality of union certification elections is affected by both the election-bar rule[11] and the contract-bar rule.[12] Under the election-bar rule, once (valid) elections have been held in a particular bargaining unit, no new elections can occur for a period of twelve months. The practical result is that, if the employer 'wins' the election, that is, no majority of employees favours collective representation, the employer need not worry about another election being filed for a year. Thus stability in the workplace is assured. Conversely, if a—or the—union wins the election, that union will be free from rival challenges for at least twelve months as well.

The election-bar rule can be extended by the contract-bar rule. The employer is under a statutory obligation to bargain with the official bargaining agent of the employees. If the certified union succeeds in negotiating a collective agreement with the employer, no new elections can be held during the currency of that agreement. The maximum effect of the contract-bar rule is three years.

Once a collective agreement is in place, the earliest a rival union—or, for that matter, the employees themselves—can file for a new election is ninety days prior to the expiry of the agreement. To ameliorate the risk that the filing for an election hampers the chances of the certified union in persuading the employer to agree to a new collective agreement, the period of sixty days prior to the expiry of the old agreement is treated as a grace period. Thus, any window of opportunity that may have opened up lasts only a month.[13]

The combined effect of the election-bar and contract-bar rules can be illustrated with the following example. Assume union A is the certified bargaining agent for employees AA in a particular bargaining unit. In application of the election-bar rule, union A has one year during which to negotiate a collective agreement with the employer. Assume union A succeeds in negotiating an agreement by the end of that year. Assume also that the stipulated currency of the agreement itself is one year. If the employees AA are unhappy with union A, or if another union B persuades employees AA that it can do better than union A, the earliest employees AA or union B can file for an election is twenty-one months after the first election, that is, after twelve months (because of the election-bar rule) plus nine months (because of the contract-bar rule). Employees AA and union B have exactly one month in which to file. If no election is filed for during this period, employees AA and union B are prevented from filing during the following two months (that is, the final sixty days before the stipulated expiry of the agreement). If union A succeeds in negotiating a new agreement during those two months, the contract-bar rule once again prevents filing during the currency of this new agreement. If union A is unsuccessful in its attempts to renew the first agreement, however, nothing can stop employees AA or union B from filing for an election once that agreement has expired.

The National Labor Relations Board conducts several thousands of union certification elections each year.[14] Election-bar and contract-bar rules notwithstanding, the mere provision for certification elections provides a statutory basis for employer resistance to union representation of the workforce to be brought to the fore on a regular basis. Employer hostility to collective representation can manifest itself in various ways. Targeting individual employees who actively participate in union organisational drives through (often unlawful) termination of their employment continues to occur more than seventy years after the enactment of the National Labor Relations Act.[15]

Registration in Australia and New Zealand

In New Zealand and Australia the traditional procedure for selecting a collective spokesperson of individual employees is registration. Whereas certification in the United States is an openly democratic exercise involving, typically, elections to ascertain employee preferences, its Australasian counterpart of registration has always been in the nature of a largely bureaucratic, administrative process.

Minimum Membership Numbers

In some respects registration is similar to certification. Thus, the Australian equivalent of the American National Labor Relations Board is the Industrial Relations Commission.[16] The functional equivalent in New Zealand is the Registrar of Unions.[17] However, there are also some important differences. The most pertinent one is that the focus of the Australian and New Zealand legislatures throughout most of the twentieth century has not really been on employee representation at the level of the enterprise. Instead the legislative requirements regarding minimum membership numbers have tended to reflect a strength-in-numbers philosophy on both sides of the Tasman. Australia's earliest federal conciliation and arbitration legislation of 1904 put the minimum number at 100. The Industrial Relations Act 1988 (Cth) raised that number to 1000. A 1990 amendment further increased the minimum number to 10 000—ostensibly in an attempt to force rationalisation and facilitate efficiency gains through economies of scale. Intriguingly, it immediately led to an official employer complaint to the ILO where it was argued, successfully, that the Australian legislature, by raising the bar for the registration of unions in this fashion, breached Convention No. 87 on freedom of association. Because of the shift towards an enterprise focus, and the associated move away from national awards as the primary instrument for negotiating terms and conditions of employment, the current trigger for the registration of a federal union in Australia is a low fifty employees. The current minimum in New Zealand stands at an even lower number of fifteen employees. Unlike the situation across the Tasman, the Australian Workplace Relations Act 1996 additionally makes special provision for so-called 'enterprise associations'. This type of decentralised union organisation requires a mere twenty members to qualify for registration.[18]

Traditionally the statutory minimum membership number requirements sought to ensure efficiency, that is, the ability of the organisation to represent and defend its members' interests effectively. The trade-off for this focus on efficiency may have been reduced internal democracy, in terms of opportunities for individual member input into the functioning of the organisation. Some commentators suggest that the Howard reforms sought to encourage competition between unions.[19] Whether the small-is-beautiful approach adopted by the 1996 legislature has also resulted in a union movement that is more in tune with the wishes of its membership is questionable. In any event, the existence of enterprise unions is not a prerequisite for the success of enterprise bargaining. Similarly, democracy is not necessarily a full substitute for efficiency. Some of the continental European union-designation models, discussed more fully below, have sought to tackle this dilemma by combining a requirement for employee representative organisations to be large—minimum 50 000 members in Belgium, a country with a population half that of Australia's—with the notion of union pluralism. Specifically, by allowing for the co-existence of multiple unions as so-called 'most representative' organisations, employees in countries like Belgium, France and the Netherlands have a real choice to join the union they feel most ideologically aligned with.

Apart from, but closely related to, the minimum membership number requirement, Australian and New Zealand unions must be able to demonstrate that they are genuine as well as independent organisations, that is, that they are willing and able to protect the interests of members free from improper employer influence.[20] Thus the legislature seeks to avoid the registration of 'tame cat' staff associations.[21] While these requirements themselves are not new, they address an issue of renewed concern in the context of the current provisions expressly allowing for the registration of enterprise-based organisations in Australia.

In March 2008 the Rudd government introduced transitional measures to phase out certain aspects of the existing workplace relations legislation. The Workplace Relations Amendment (Transition to Forward with Fairness) Act 2008 paves the way for more comprehensive legislation to take effect from 1 January 2010 onwards. While a new workplace relations Bill is yet to be introduced into Parliament, it has been foreshadowed that the emphasis will be on enterprise-level collective bargaining.[22] The implications, if any, for the registration of unions remain unclear.

Democratic Union Rules

The rules of the organisation to be registered must reflect a minimum level of internal democracy. This requirement goes directly to the relationship between the organisation and its members. The union rules on access to membership, expulsion from membership and, generally, member input into the running or operation of the union are subject to official scrutiny. A parallel can be drawn here with the duty of fair representation imposed on American unions. In effect, a wider parallel with the United States can be drawn in that external scrutiny of the union's internal affairs constitutes a traditional *quid pro quo* for the bestowing of exclusive representation rights relating to membership coverage, bargaining rights, and (personal) grievance handling upon registration. In New Zealand at least one of the union objectives is expected to be the promotion of the 'collective employment interests' of its members.[23] Less clear is which, if any, other objectives a union might legitimately seek to pursue. Further, under New Zealand law, union rules may not be 'unreasonable' and must be 'democratic'.[24] Similar constraints attach to the internal rules of applicant unions in Australia. To this effect, a separate Schedule to the Workplace Relations Act 1996—entitled Registration and Accountability of Organisations—spells out the intentions of Parliament regarding federal unions.[25] These include a general requirement for registered organisations to be accountable to the membership while at the same time being able to operate effectively.[26] Further, the active participation of members in the affairs of the organisation is encouraged.[27] Seemingly less relevant is Parliament's declared desire 'to reduce the adverse effects of industrial disputation'.[28] This may entail a reference to the possibility of cancelling the registration of unions that are overly militant or otherwise behave in a fashion that is considered just plain difficult. Tellingly, Section 28 of Schedule 1 stipulates that preventing or even hindering the achievement of Parliament's intention provides grounds for cancellation of the union's registration. Further, the Act prescribes various forms of 'prohibited conduct' in relation to the formation and registration of employee associations.[29] Prohibited conduct includes industrial action, or the threat thereof, in the context of union registration.

Fair Union Competition

Finally, to be registered, there must not be another organisation to which the members of the applicant union can 'more conveniently' belong, that would be able to 'more effectively' represent the interests of these members.[30] On one level, this requirement is acknowledgment of the age-old issue of rival unionism, with the legislature seeking to address scenarios where one union unduly tries to poach members of another union. Interestingly, though, that requirement was not made into an obstacle to the formation and registration of enterprise unions under the Howard government.[31] According to the Rudd government, key elements of the proposed new workplace relations system will be freedom of association and the right of employees to 'genuine' workplace representation.[32]

Most Representative Organisation in Continental Europe

When comparing the United States with the situation in Australia and New Zealand, one major difference to note is the level at which union representation occurs. In the United States, because of its link with the concept of the bargaining unit, certification caters primarily (although, in principle, not necessarily exclusively) for enterprise bargaining. In Australia and New Zealand, the recent focus on the workplace notwithstanding, registration is a procedure that is more readily able to accommodate multi-employer or industry-wide bargaining. High-level bargaining is also a typical feature on the European Continent. This in turn is linked to a particular manner of union organisation on the Continent.

Fifty years of political and economic integration notwithstanding, Europe does not present a uniform picture, and over-generalisations must be avoided so as not to mislead. Even so, with Germany and Scandinavia as major exceptions, a European model of sorts is the union designation technique of most representative organisation.

The term 'most representative' first featured in the 1919 Treaty of Versailles concluded between the Allied forces (including the United States) and Germany following the end of World War I.[33] From there the expression made its way into the parlance of the ILO. In 1922 the Permanent Court of International Justice—the predecessor of the current International Court of Justice and a permanent organisation within the (then) League of Nations—issued an advisory opinion regarding the Dutch government's selection of a union representative to attend the International Labour Conference.[34] The Court based its ruling on Article 389, Paragraph 3, of the Treaty.[35] The Court observed that the drafters of the Peace Treaty, as the Treaty of Versailles is also known, had refrained from providing a definition. While it acknowledged the importance of membership numbers, the Court considered that figures are not the only test of the representative character of an organisation. Rather the International Court held that:

> What these organisations are, is a question to be decided in the particular case, having regard to the circumstances in each particular country at the time when the choice falls to be made.[36]

This reference to local circumstances allows for the recognition of broader, ideological divisions that may exist in European society at large. In some instances it has allowed divisions along religious, secular and even linguistic lines to be accommodated. The presence of union pluralism then is not at all precluded by the requirement for unions to be most representative!

Union Pluralism: Belgium

The simultaneous recognition of several organisations as most representative unions is an integral feature of labour law in the Benelux countries as well as in France, Italy and Spain. Belgium provides an interesting case study to illustrate the ramifications of this pluralism. In that country a largely political decision was made to recognise three umbrella organisations for the representation of employees: a Christian-democratic union, a social-democratic union, and a liberal-conservative union. All three confederations meet the statutory requirements of being national organisations with an inter-industry focus. All three are represented in the core national (government) advisory bodies on economic (the Central Economic Council) and social (the National Labour Council) matters. A final requirement for recognition as a most representative organisation is a minimum membership number of 50 000 employees.[37] There have been repeated employer complaints to the ILO about the lack of transparency of these requirements.[38]

In 1985 the Belgian legislature paved the way for the recognition of unions organising high-level white-collar employees who do not qualify as leading personnel (the so-called *cadres*) as a new type of representative union.[39] A reduced membership threshold of 10 000 applies here. Previously, only the Christian and socialist confederations of unions devoted a separate division to the organisation of any white-collar employees wishing to join.

The existence of linguistic divisions in the country did not leave the structure of the Belgian labour movement untouched. Each of the three main confederations is split into separate Flemish and French arms: the ACV-CSC,[40] the ABVV-FGTB[41] and the ACLVB-CGSLB,[42] respectively. All of the most representative unions can operate in the same industry or company via their member organisations (of which there are dozens for each of the umbrella organisations). On the one hand, this system allows employees freedom of individual choice. In effect, as more than one union has most representative status simultaneously, employees can choose which, if any, organisation they join. On the other hand, collective agreements can be signed, on behalf of the workforce employed in a particular industry, by each and every one of the most representative organisations. Whether just one, several or indeed all of the most representative unions sign the agreement has no repercussions for its legally binding effect or its personal scope of application. This particular feature of the Belgian 'model' acts as a powerful incentive for constructive inter-union co-operation. It certainly represents a more positive and proactive approach to avoiding union rivalry than is found in the United States, Australia and New Zealand.

Unlike the American umbrella union of the American Federation of Labor–Congress of Industrial Organizations (AFL–CIO), the ability to negotiate collective agreements in Belgium extends to the umbrella unions themselves. National (inter-industry or, as they are known locally, inter-professional) agreements, covering the whole private sector of the economy, have become a traditional feature of the Belgian social scene post–World War II. Typically, these are negotiated with the active participation of the government of the day. The net result is a multi-layered approach to collective bargaining, allowing for both uniformity and flexibility in social regulation. Specifically, big-picture issues are negotiated centrally, at the national level, and apply uniformly across the whole private sector of the economy. Decentralised industry and company bargaining then builds upon these national accords by using them as a platform for the negotiation of more detailed, industry- and/or company-specific, agreements.

Union Pluralism: France

The complexity of the Europe's 'most representative' model of union designation inevitably increases with the number of unions officially recognised in this manner. It would be wrong to assume, though, that a direct correlation exists between the number of unions that thus operate in any particular system of labour law and union membership levels. Union density in Belgium, estimated at 69 per cent at the start of the twenty-first century, has always been high.[43] In France, by contrast, not three but five unions qualify for the label of most representative organisation. Yet union density in that country has traditionally been much lower. Most attractive, when judged purely in terms of relative membership numbers, is the communist CGT (*Conféderation Génerale du Travail*), estimated to cover one in three union members. Its main rival, organising one in four members, is the socialist CFDT (*Conféderation Française Démocratique du Travail*).

Each of these two unions triggered its own breakaway union at one stage. The CGT-FO (*Confèderation Génerale du Travail-Force Ouvrière*) is anti-communist (and anti-religious); it claims to be reformist and covers one in seven union members. As its name suggests, the CFTC (*Confèderation Française des Travailleurs Chrétiens*) is a Christian union, organising one in twenty union members. This last figure compares unfavourably with the much stronger position occupied by Christian unions in Belgium and the Netherlands.

Of special note is the existence of a separate union for managerial personnel in France. The CGC (*Confèderation Génerale des Cadres*) organises senior white-collar employees, including supervisors and even executive personnel.[44] As a most representative organisation the CGC covers one in every eight union members in France. It provides a sharp contrast with the situation in the United States where supervisors are formally excluded from the definition of 'employee' pursuant to the National Labor Relations Act.

Elsewhere in Europe

In Germany union pluralism along ideological lines disappeared at the end of the Weimar Republic in the early 1930s. Instead, any previously existing political and ideological wings of the organised labour movement currently are 'amalgamated' in a single confederation, the DGB (*Deutscher Gewerkschaftsbund*). Unlike the umbrella organisations of unions in Belgium, the DGB does not itself enter into collective bargaining agreements with employers. Instead, its main role consists of acting as spokesperson for the labour movement in Germany. The DGB also co-ordinates the activities of its member unions.[45] The Christian unions, however, opted against affiliation with the DGB. Their role—even following political unification of East and West Germany—has tended to be marginal.[46]

In Scandinavia union pluralism never really existed, especially not along religious lines.

Impact on Representation Rights

Differences in Union Organisation

The above differences in union selection mechanisms between the United States, Australasia and continental Europe must be linked to differences in the organisational structure of unions themselves. The precise nature of this link is not entirely clear. There may not be a perfect correlation between union selection and union structure. However, it is clear that a decentralised selection mechanism as it exists in the United States, for instance, tends to promote a workplace focus in the organisational set-up of the collective spokesperson for the employees. Conversely, a broad-based national emphasis in union selection, as can be found in continental Europe, induces a more centralised approach to the structure and operation of the organised labour movement. To appreciate why this is the case, and also to see where the Australasian method of union selection fits in, it is important to look at differences in the historical formation of unions internationally.

There are various ways in which unions can be classified. In terms of organisational structure, two main types of unions exist: craft or occupationally based unions, on the one hand, and industrial unions, on the other hand. Craft unions developed first. Their main representative is Britain, where the Industrial Revolution also happened to come first. From there the craft or occupational model of union organisation was exported to the various colonies—including the United States, Australia and New Zealand. Industrial unionism, by contrast, is a more recent phenomenon. That type of union organisation is typical for continental Europe and coincides with the late arrival of the Industrial Revolution on the Continent.

Craft or occupational unionism forms the backbone of the oldest trade union movements in the world. A feature of craft or occupationally based unions is that any recruited members typically belong to the same craft or occupational category. Traditionally, the emphasis was on organising skilled workers only. Only these workers were deemed to have something in common and worthy of protection, that is, a trade or marketable skill. A most famous illustration in this regard is the central union organisation in the United States. It started life as the AFL (American Federation of Labor), with the CIO (Congress of Industrial Organizations) component of the American organised labour movement having been added in more recent times only.[47]

Industrial unions present a quite different story. Typically, the emphasis of industrial unions is on a broadly understood notion of (working-) class solidarity rather than, more narrowly, job training, apprenticeship, or the marketable skills of the members. The common factor of workers organised by industrial unions is that, irrespective of their actual occupation, all are employed in a particular industry. The notion of industry itself is defined in terms of the product or service provided by the employer. Obvious examples include traditional industries such as construction or manufacturing, but also 'newer' industries such as the banking or insurance sectors. Industrial unions are typical for the whole of the Western European Continent with Denmark as the major exception. In Denmark a strong element of craft unionism continues today.

Representation Rights

The differences in union designation mechanism between the United States, Australia/New Zealand and Europe inevitably have an impact on the employee representation rights of the official union. In essence, any exclusivity that attaches to the representation rights of unions in the United States, Australia or New Zealand, is necessarily absent from the continental European scene once union pluralism comes into play. Further, while the grant of exclusive representation rights constitutes a traditional incentive for submitting to registration (and, hence, submitting to state control) in Australia and New Zealand, the focus in the American system of certification tends to be much more openly on mitigating the side-effects of any such exclusivity rights. Apart from restricting the membership coverage rights of the certified union to the bargaining unit, two core union obligations in this respect are a duty to act in good faith during the bargaining round and a duty to represent all members of the bargaining unit fairly when dealing with any grievances (such as dismissal disputes) that may arise between employee and employer from time to time. The former duty also attaches to the employer party in the collective bargaining process. An express statutory duty to bargain in good faith has made its way into the principal labour legislation in New Zealand since 2000.[48] Interestingly, that duty in New Zealand is part of a broader obligation for parties in an employment relationship—individual as well as collective ones—to deal with each other in good faith.[49] Whether a similar requirement can be read into Australia's Workplace Relations Act has been a matter of some considerable debate.[50] In any event, the Rudd Labor government wishes to formally introduce a duty to bargain in good faith against the backdrop of a focus on greater 'respect (for) democracy in the workplace'[51] from 1 July 2009 onwards.[52]

Figure 4.1 below outlines the traditional representation rights of the official union(s) in three major areas: membership coverage, collective bargaining and personal grievance handling.

<table>
<tr><th>Union</th><th>Aust/NZ</th><th>United States</th><th>EU</th></tr>
<tr><td>Selection Mechanism</td><td>Registration</td><td>Certification</td><td>Representation</td></tr>
<tr><td>Membership Coverage</td><td rowspan="3">E X C L U S I V I T Y</td><td>Bargaining Unit</td><td rowspan="3">P L U R A L I S M</td></tr>
<tr><td>Collective Bargaining</td><td>Duty to Bargain in Good Faith</td></tr>
<tr><td>Personal Grievance Handling</td><td>Duty of Fair Representation</td></tr>
</table>

Figure 4.1: The traditional representation rights of the official unions

Institutionalised Forms of Employee Representation

The Contemporary Relevance of Unions

The relevance of unions has come in for serious questioning,[53] in line with declining membership numbers since the late 1970s.[54] This phenomenon is by no means restricted to the United States. Traditional strongholds, such as Australia and New Zealand, have been similarly affected.[55] To date the decline has been less pronounced in Europe. A partial explanation for this may be that unions on the Continent have managed to become an integral part of society at large. While seemingly more peripheral than their counterparts in English-based legal systems (because European employees rely less exclusively on collective bargaining as relatively more extensive employee rights are enshrined in legislation directly), the role of the organised labour movement on the European Continent includes the performance of certain quasi-delegated government functions. In Belgium, for instance, unions facilitate, and effectively are in charge of, the payment of unemployment and health benefits. For this service the three most representative unions receive a substantial 'administrative fee' (in the order 162 Euros per person in 2005) from the government for the payment of unemployment benefits alone. This may seem odd to an outsider. To be clear, technically, there is no need for union involvement in the payment of these social benefits. Even so, this payment system provides some continuity in the historical link between the union movement and the creation of these social benefits.[56] Continental unions have also been able to maintain relatively close links with the government of the day through their involvement in the periodic, tripartite, inter-industry bargaining exercises referred to earlier in this chapter and encompassing the whole private sector of the economy.

Thus far, any decline in membership numbers has not affected the unions' ability to represent workers on the Continent. The story is different elsewhere. In New Zealand, legislation adopted under a conservative government during the 1990s initiated a trend towards individual bargaining, with employees being encouraged to look for assistance beyond the union. While actual figures of take-up numbers are not available, even law firms have stepped in by offering their services in the negotiation of individual employment contracts. A change of government and the adoption of less (union-) hostile legislation in 2000 may have lessened the need for non-union representation of employees in New Zealand somewhat. In Australia, a similar trend towards individual bargaining led to the appointment of a public official, the Employment Advocate, whose services could be called upon by employees (and employers alike).[57] Any meaningful assistance to individual employees by the Employment Advocate disappeared in the aftermath of the 2005 amendments to the Workplace Relations Act and the abolition of the so-called 'no disadvantage test' relating to the negotiation of Australian Workplace Agreements (AWAs).[58] A negative public reaction, together with a looming federal election, saw the partial reintroduction of the no disadvantage test by means of a newly created 'fairness test' and the replacement of the Employment Advocate by a Workplace Authority Director in 2007.[59]

The function of government-appointed officials such as the Employment Advocate and the Workplace Authority Director partially resembles that of the union and its traditional role as employee spokesperson in the negotiation of terms and conditions of employment. In Europe various institutionalised forms of employee participation exist that provide opportunities for employees to have a voice at their place of work. They have their basis in legislation that predates the recent labour law reforms in Australia. Significantly, they seek to supplement unions rather than replace or even compete with them. All up, the role of unions in European society is not fundamentally questioned by these forms of employee representation in the workplace.

The Concept of Institutionalised Employee Representation

The discussion that follows is not concerned with employee participation in the financial aspects of the employer's business through employee shareholdings, profit-sharing and the like. Rather, the focus is on participation in the management of the company that employs the employee. This form of employee participation may seem radical, in that it encroaches more directly upon traditional employer prerogatives. Arguably, it also constitutes a much more meaningful device for giving employees a voice as well as some control over their own (working) lives.

Institutionalised forms of employee participation are the antithesis of mere *ad hoc* arrangements. Typically the latter are established in response to a specific need, for instance, a special consultative committee set up to deal with lay-offs following a decision to restructure a particular business operation. Institutionalised forms of employee participation, by contrast, are standing bodies: they are in place on an ongoing basis, regardless of whether or not a particular crisis situation has arisen. In continental Europe two main forms of this type of employee participation are works councils and (employee representation on) supervisory boards. Both are compulsory bodies. Their establishment thus does not depend upon employer discretion. In this manner any lingering employee or union distrust about the creation of employer-controlled, in-house consultative committees by legislative fiat is successfully avoided.

It is sometimes suggested that collective bargaining, especially where this occurs in a decentralised fashion, acts as the functional equivalent of the various forms of institutionalised employee participation that exist in Europe. Such a comparison is far from perfect.

Admittedly, enterprise bargaining can be less alienating to employees than centralised bargaining in that it occurs at a level close to the actual place of work. Even so, collective bargaining, including enterprise bargaining, tends to occur *ex post facto*, that is, after a dispute between the employer and employee has arisen. In Australia and New Zealand the existence (and thus, in practical terms, the creation) of an industrial dispute has been a longstanding prerequisite and trigger for the exercise of the conciliation and arbitration powers by the state umpire. Further, collective bargaining represents an adversarial form of conflict resolution. It turns employers and employees (the latter acting via their collective representative, the union) into adversaries. By contrast, institutionalised forms of employee participation are premised upon the assumption that there exists a minimum commonality of interest—that is, the wellbeing of the company—between employer and employee parties. In essence, the European approach to employee participation reflects a co-operative or consensus-based approach to industrial relations.

Works Councils

Composition

Works councils constitute the most widespread form of institutionalised employee participation in Western Europe. Their presence traditionally extends from the Benelux countries (Belgium, the Netherlands and Luxembourg) to France, Germany, Austria, Spain, Portugal and Greece. There now even exists legislation at the level of the European Union on the matter.[60]

Works councils are bodies established at the actual place of work. They are venues where employer and employee meet on a regular basis (once a month or so) and on an equal footing. The official trigger for setting up a works council has always differed from country to country. A minimum workforce of five employees theoretically suffices in Germany, although in reality few if any works councils operate in companies that small. A few years ago the German legislature simplified the process for electing employee representatives in an attempt to make their presence in small and medium-sized companies more attractive, or at least less cumbersome.[61] The minimum number of employees in the Netherlands has been set at thirty-five. That figure rises to a more realistic fifty in France and even to, effectively, 100 in Belgium. In 2007 the European Court of Justice considered the latter threshold too high and Belgium was held in breach of its obligations under community law, specifically its duty to comply with a 2002 Directive for the creation of a general regulatory framework for informing and consulting employees.[62]

The composition of the works council tends to reflect that of the company's workforce generally. The provision for employees and employers to meet on an equal footing does not necessarily mean that the works council comprises an even number of representatives from either side. In some countries (for example, Belgium) the legislature only prescribes the actual number of employee representatives, with the proviso that the number of employer representatives may not exceed the number of employee representatives. Elsewhere (for example, Germany and the Netherlands) the works council is composed exclusively of employee representatives.

The employee representatives on the works council are elected by the workforce at large. All employees, not just union members, have a right to vote. This is significant because the employee representatives on the council are there to represent all workplace employees. In a similar vein, nominations for election as an employee representative are not restricted to union members. Thus the legislature has sought to avoid the formation of company factions and, more significantly, to avoid the appearance of bringing in the proverbial Trojan horse (that is, the union) via the back door. This goal has met with mixed success, especially in legal systems such as Belgium, where the submission of nomination lists remains the prerogative of the most representative unions.

Powers

Equality in the works council means that the employee's voice in principle carries as much weight as that of the employer. The actual degree of influence a works council has in the management of the company depends on the type of issue at stake. Generally, the powers of a works council come in three shades or degrees that build upon one another. They are information-sharing, consultation, and co-determination.

The lowest level of employee participation in the management of companies involves the right to be kept informed. Information-sharing means the communication of knowledge. It is a first, but necessary, step towards meaningful employee participation. The information rights of the works council tend to focus on economic and financial matters. This seemingly modest form of employee involvement can nevertheless be far-reaching. Works councils in Belgium, for example, have information rights that extend into commercially sensitive areas such as the financial structure of the company; the competitive position of the company in the market; production and productivity; budget and calculation of costs; personnel costs as well as budgets for research and development.[63]

Consultation rights build upon information rights. Knowledge, derived from the information made available to the works council, allows informed discussions between employer and employee. Consultation means that the employer has to ask for the advice of the employee. Consultation rights typically extend to social matters, especially the social implications of economic and financial decisions. To use the Belgian scenario once again, the employer must give the works council the opportunity to formulate an opinion about such matters as structural changes in the company; personnel training and retraining; the reorganisation of job classification systems as well as the formulation of general principles on hiring and firing, including lay-offs on economic or structural grounds.[64]

A statutory obligation to ask for the opinion of the works council does not imply a duty for employers to adopt the advice received. Strictly speaking, employers thus are free to ignore the opinion of the works council. Occasionally, however, the legislature has seen fit to boost the advisory powers of works councils.[65] In France, for instance, if the advice of the works council is required but not sought, the company decision on the matter is not legally enforceable. Similarly, in the Netherlands veto powers attach to certain consultation rights. Where applicable, the negative advice of a Dutch works council has the practical effect of delaying the company decision by at least a month and, ultimately, this may lead to an amendment or even the formal withdrawal of the company plans.[66]

Co-determination stands for joint decision-making. This is most developed in Germany. But, even there, the co-determination powers of the works council are limited to thirteen, narrowly defined and specifically enumerated, 'social' matters. Expressly excluded are 'personnel' and, not surprisingly perhaps, 'economic' or 'financial' matters. Of course, the distinction between social and personnel matters is not always entirely clear. Typical instances of social matters are said to include working time, annual holidays and social aspects of redundancy decisions (in particular, the development of a so-called social plan). A legislative amendment introduced in 2001 has added the organisation of teamwork (performance methods only, not the decision to use teamwork itself) to the list of social matters.[67]

The scope of influence exercised by the German works council can be illustrated by reference to its co-determination rights regarding hiring and firing decisions. Technically, these qualify as personnel matters and, thus, the German works council has no formal co-determination rights in this domain. However, its input and influence can still be considerable. First, as regards recruitment German management in principle is free to choose its preferred person to fill a vacancy. However, the works council has input into the hiring procedure in a variety of ways. For example, if the company were to use questionnaires, the works council has co-determination rights as to the contents thereof. Also, once management has selected someone to fill the vacancy, the works council must be informed. The employer's duty to transfer knowledge to the works council in this instance extends to an obligation to allow access to the files of all applicants. If it were to transpire that management failed to comply with its own selection process or appointment criteria, the works council is entitled to block the hiring decision. A veto can only be overruled by the labour court. Similarly, with regard to any decisions to dismiss personnel, the managerial prerogative is tempered by the obligation to inform and consult the works council. Without consultation, the dismissal decision is invalid. In practice, any works council objections are communicated to the employee concerned. This in turn allows the employee to build a stronger case for fighting the dismissal decision in the labour court.[68]

Evaluation and Critique

No institution can ever expect to be entirely free of criticism and the works council is no exception to this general proposition. Any financial costs associated with the operation of the works council are expected to be met by the employer. This adds to the cost of doing business in Europe. Second, employee members of the works council enjoy legal privileges not available to other employees. These risk creating tensions among workers. Thus council members have access to company information that, when commercially sensitive, may not be readily available to the general workforce. Special training leave for members is meant to allow this information to be interpreted in a meaningful fashion. Significantly, to avoid the risk of employer reprisals directed at 'difficult' members of the works council, special dismissal protection rights attach to the position of employee representatives on works councils. In an attempt to tackle any appearance of elitism, the German legislature since 2001 allows the works council to delegate certain tasks to so-called work teams. According to Weiss, the purpose is to reduce the (psychological) gap that exists between employees on the works council and the rest of the company's workforce.[69]

On the positive side, works councils undeniably serve an important symbolic function: they stand for the proposition that companies may not be just about promoting the interests of shareholders after all. Furthermore, because the *modus operandi* of the works council is co-operation instead of conflict, works councils in Europe arguably contribute to a positive change in climate at the company level. Of interest in this regard is that German works councils are expressly prohibited from resorting to strike action. This prohibition in turn ensures that the activities of the works council do not encroach upon the more adversarial role reserved for the union, especially in the context of collective bargaining. Finally, the ultimate value of the works council surpasses the institution itself. Specifically, works councils provide an important link with the representation of employees on the supervisory board of companies.

Supervisory Board Representation

Lack of Uniformity

Not all European legal systems traditionally provide for employee representation on company boards.[70] Two principal models are the German and the Dutch approaches to employee representation on the supervisory boards of (large) companies. Together they have been a primary source of inspiration for the adoption, in 2001, of legislation on this subject matter at the level of the EU.[71]

Impact of a Dual Company Structure

A proper understanding of the European approach, as qualified above, to employee representation on company boards requires a basic familiarity with the rules of company law. European companies tend to be organised along a two-tier structure. A first body is known as the management board or directorate. It deals with the day-to-day running of the business. A second body within the same company is charged with the supervision of the management board. A convenient label for this second body is the supervisory board.[72]

The supervisory board appoints and discharges the management board. On average, it meets between two and four times a year. Typically, it does not deal with issues of daily management itself. Rather, the supervisory board decides upon general policy matters, whether and where to invest, for instance, or whether and how to diversify the company product lines. Employee representation, under both the German and Dutch models, occurs at the level of the supervisory board rather than the management board. It follows that this type of employee involvement in companies does not entail co-management, but rather it is restricted to co-supervision of the management in any particular enterprise.

The German Model(s)

Not one but three different models operate in the German legal system. The oldest model dates from 1951. While it is confined to the coal, iron and steel industries, it remains the sole model to provide for truly equal representation of employees on the supervisory board to date.[73] A second model, introduced in 1952, provides for minority representation only: one-third of seats on the supervisory board are reserved for representatives of the employees. This second model applies to companies with a workforce between 500 and 2000 employees in industries other than the heavy industries listed above.[74] A third model was adopted in 1976. It applies specifically to large companies, that is, companies with a workforce in excess of 2000. This latest model provides for quasi-equal employee representation on the board as the chairperson—the person with the casting vote in instances of deadlock—is always a representative of the shareholders.[75]

The functioning of the German approach to employee representation on the supervisory boards of companies is best illustrated by reference to its most far-reaching model of 1951. Assume the supervisory board comprises eleven members.[76] Of these eleven members, five will be shareholder representatives and five must be employee representatives. The eleventh member is a neutral chairperson. That person has the casting vote without, however, representing either side. Two of the five employee representatives are works council nominees. To reflect the composition of the company's workforce at large, one of these works council nominees used to be a blue-collar employee, the other a white-collar employee. In 2001 this distinction between blue- and white-collar employees was abolished as it was considered dated and no longer appropriate. The remaining three employee representatives on the supervisory board are all union nominees. However, in order to avoid one faction systematically dominating proceedings in the supervisory board, the German legislature requires that one of the union nominees must be an independent, that is, neither a union official nor (even!) a company employee. Many labour law professors and (ex-) politicians have found their way onto boards in this fashion.

The supervisory board appoints the management board. Typically, in companies with a supervisory board of eleven members, the management board will comprise three members. Importantly, for the company's employees, one of these three members is known

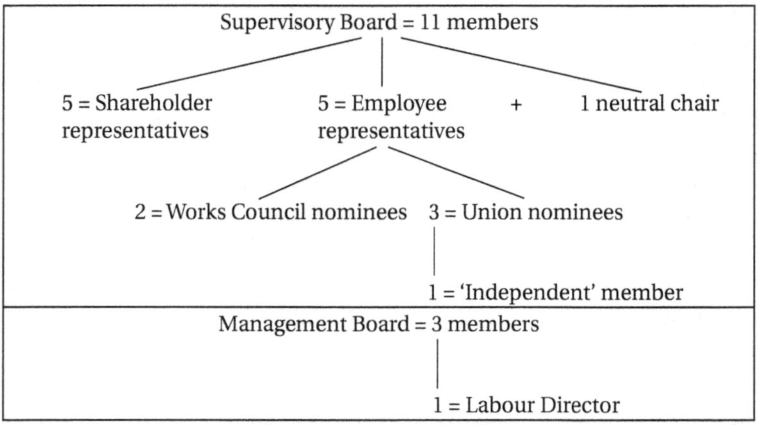

Figure 4.2: The German model of (equal) employee representation on company boards

as the labour director (*Arbeitsdirektor*). The labour director is in charge of personnel matters in the company. Because of the nature of this function, it is imperative that this member of the management board has the trust and confidence of all employees. Accordingly, the appointment and discharge of the *Arbeitsdirektor* requires the consent of all five employee representatives on the supervisory board. They effectively have veto powers in this regard.

The 1952 and 1976 models are variations of the 1951 model. Under the 1952 model the minority employee representatives on the supervisory board are elected by the workforce at large, either directly or upon nomination by the works council. As indicated already, under the 1976 model the chair is always a representative of the shareholders' meeting: this model therefore makes for quasi-equal employee representation at best.

The Dutch Model

Whereas the oldest form of employee representation on supervisory boards in Germany is a product of World War II and its immediate aftermath, in Dutch society discussions about industrial democracy during the 1960s culminated in the adoption of the so-called Structure Act (*Structuurwet*) of 1971.[77] The statute makes the establishment of a supervisory board compulsory for companies that meet certain thresholds in terms of financial capital and workforce numbers. The minimum number of employees required—in companies that have a works council in place—is a low (by German standards) 100.

A unique feature of the Dutch model is that no employees or union officials sit on the supervisory board as such. Instead the supervisory board co-opts its own members.[78] Both the works council and the general meeting of shareholders can suggest names for inclusion on the supervisory board, but the board is entitled to make up its own mind as to its composition. In any event, the works council and shareholders must be kept informed and—significantly—each party has veto rights. While the legislature has limited this right to veto co-optation decisions, it extends to concerns either party may hold about the suitability of particular individuals to carry out their duties as members of the supervisory board.[79] A formal veto can only be overturned by, initially, the Social-Economic Council (a national tripartite government advisory body) and, since 1987, the company division of the Amsterdam Court of Appeal (*Gerechtshof*). Once again, a figure may provide greater clarity.

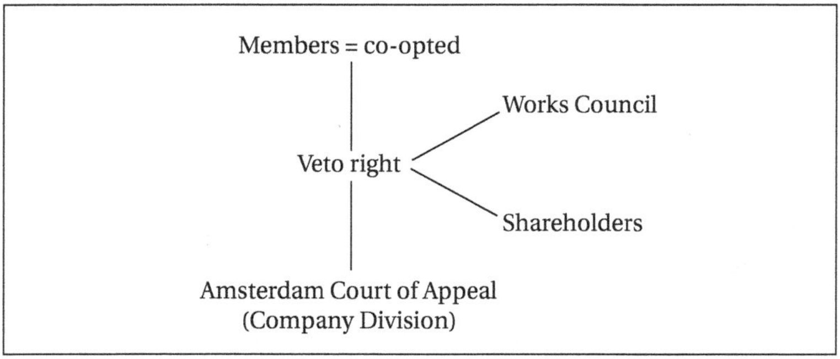

Figure 4.3: Dutch model of (minority) employee representation on company boards

Export Potential?

To date, institutionalised forms of employee participation remain essentially a continental European phenomenon. During the 1980s government studies were carried out in both Australia and New Zealand to determine their suitability for importation down under.[80] Intriguingly, the compulsory nature of the European schemes, along with their highly prescriptive nature, was found to constitute an insurmountable obstacle to their introduction on both sides of the Tasman Sea. Undoubtedly, these objections also carry some weight in the North American environment.

Perhaps the absence of a European-style, truly multi-party political system provides a further disincentive. In a two-party political system, the credibility and cross-party appeal of institutionalised employee participation is always going to be more difficult to establish.

Notes

1 This is a reference to Lord Wedderburn's call for autonomy from the English common law. See Wedderburn, 'Labour Law: From Here to Autonomy?', p. 1.

2 See Chapter 2.

3 In March 2007 an Employee Free Choice Bill was passed by the House of Representatives but subsequently filibustered in the Senate. The Bill sought to increase the effectiveness of the voluntary recognition system

by removing the right of employers to demand an election in the face of a card majority.

4 'There's Money in Mopping', pp. 38–40.

5 Section 9(b) of the National Labor Relations Act 1935.

6 A classic (contextual) discussion of the Board's shifting approaches to the determination of an appropriate bargaining unit can be found in Summers, Wellington and Hyde, *Labor Law. Cases and Materials*, pp. 603–68. Since the Reagan administration the activities of the Board have become more politicised: Brudney, 'Employee Majority Bargaining Systems: Comparing Developments in the United States and Australia'.

7 Section 9(c)(1) of the National Labor Relations Act 1935. An insightful account of the Board's approach to union recognition elections can be found in Getman and Blackburn, *Labor Relations. Law, Practice and Policy*, pp. 86–133.

8 Here it must be remembered that a union seeking to organise workers has no guaranteed access to the plant.

9 Section 9(c)(1)(B) of the National Labor Relations Act 1935.

10 Section 9(a) of the National Labor Relations Act 1935.

11 Section 9(c)(3) of the National Labor Relations Act 1935.

12 The contract-bar rule has only received indirect statutory recognition: Goldman and White, 'The United States of America', 2002 update, [434].

13 ibid.

14 ibid., [790].

15 Craver, 'The Relevance of the NLRA and Labor Organisations in the Post-Industrial Global Economy', p. 136.

16 Schedule 1 (Registration and Accountability of Organisations) of the Workplace Relations Act 1996 (Cth).

17 Section 13(1) of the Employment Relations Act 2000 (NZ).

18 Section 20 of Schedule 1 of the Workplace Relations Act 1996 (as amended).

19 Creighton and Stewart, *Labour Law*, p. 497.

20 Schedule 1 of the Workplace Relations Act 1996, Sections 19–20.

21 Creighton and Stewart, *Labour Law*, p. 495.

22 Gillard, *Introducing Australia's New Workplace Relations System*.

23 Section 14(1)(a) of the Employment Relations Act 2000 (NZ).

24 Section 14(1)(c) of the Employment Relations Act 2000 (NZ).

25 Chapter 1. Objects of Schedule and General Provisions.

26 Section 5(3) of Schedule 1.

27 ibid.

28 Section 5(1) of Schedule 1.

29 Division 3 of Schedule 1, Sections 21ff.

30 Section 19(1)(j) of Schedule 1.

31 Creighton and Stewart, *Labour Law*, p. 497.

32 Department of Foreign Affairs and Trade, *Workplace Relations in Australia*, About Australia Fact Sheet Series, p. 5.

33 Article 389, Paragraph 3, Treaty of Versailles.

34 Advisory Opinion No. 1, Concerning the Netherlands' Workers' Delegate to the Third Session of the International Labour Conference, 31 July 1922, [1922] *Permanent Court of International Justice*, Series B, 1.
35 Article 389, Paragraph 3, reads as follows: 'The Member States undertake to nominate non-government delegates and advisers chosen in agreement with the industrial organisations, if such organisations exist, which are *most representative* of employers or workpeople, as the case may be, in their respective countries.' (Emphasis added)
36 ibid. The full text of the Opinion can also be found in the section on Case Law (International Court of Justice) by R Blanpain (ed.), *International Encyclopaedia for Labour Law and Industrial Relations*, 2005 update, p. 9.
37 The statutory basis for these requirements can be found, *inter alia*, in the Act of 20 September 1948 concerning the Organisation of Industry Activities, the Act of 29 May 1952 on the Establishment of the National Labour Council, and the Act of 5 December 1968 concerning Collective Bargaining Agreements and Joint Committees.
38 Blanpain, 'Belgium', 2006 update, [556].
39 Act of 20 September 1948 concerning the Organisation of Industry Activities as amended by the Social Recovery Act of 22 January 1985.
40 *Algemeen Christelijk Vakverbond-Centrale des Syndicats Chrétiens.*
41 *Algemeen Belgisch Vakverbond-Fédération Générale du Travail de Belgique.*
42 *Algemene Centrale der Liberale Vakbonden-Centrale Générale des Syndicats Libres de Belgique.*
43 Blanpain, 'Belgium', 2006 update, [537].
44 Despax and Rojot, 'France', 1987 update, [52] and [335].
45 Weiss and Schmidt, 'Germany', 2000 update, [329].
46 ibid., [322].
47 The AFL was founded in 1886. During the late 1930s several of its member unions became frustrated with the lacklustre efforts of the AFL at organising employees on a more industrial (rather than craft or occupational) basis. In response they broke with the AFL and established a separate organisation under the indicative name of CIO. The AFL and CIO merged in 1955. The banner of AFL-CIO is still in place today.
48 Section 32 of the Employment Relations Act 2000 (NZ).
49 Section 4 of the Employment Relations Act 2000 (NZ).
50 Creighton and Stewart, *Labour Law*, p. 220–1.
51 Australian Labor Party, *Forward with Fairness. Labor's Plan for Fairer and More Productive Australian Workplaces*, p. 14.
52 Gillard, *Introducing Australia's New Workplace Relations System*, p. 10.
53 Wheeler, 'The Labor Movement in the 21st Century', p. 221.
54 Cella and Treu, 'National Trade Union Movements', p. 473.
55 Bramble, *Trade Unionism in Australia. A History from Flood to Ebb Tide*, p. 8; May, Walsh, Harbridge and Thickett, *Unions and Union Membership in New Zealand: Annual Review for 2002*, p. 3.

56 Rasking and Tegenbos, '138 miljoen voor vakbonden'.
57 Part IVA of the Workplace Relations Act 1996 (Cth).
58 Workplace Relations Amendment (Work Choices) Act 2005.
59 Workplace Relations Amendment (A Stronger Safety Net) Act 2007.
60 Directive 94/45/EC on the establishment of a European Works Council (or equivalent procedure) in 'Community-scale undertakings', *Official Journal* L 254/64. For a discussion, see Engels and Salas, 'Transnational Information and Consultation: The European Works Council Directive', p. 525.
61 Weiss, 'Modernising the German Works Council System: A Recent Amendment', p. 251.
62 Directive 02/14/EC, *Official Journal* L 080/29.
63 Royal Decree of 27 November 1973 concerning the Regulation of Economic and Financial Information to be made available to Works Councils, *Official Gazette*, 28 November 1973.
64 Act of 20 September 1948 concerning the Organisation of Industry Activities.
65 Biagi, 'Forms of Employee Representational Participation', pp. 507–9.
66 Jacobs, 'The Netherlands', 2004 update, [259].
67 Weiss, 'Modernising the German Works Council System: A Recent Amendment'.
68 Weiss, Simitis and Rydzy, 'The Settlement of Labour Disputes in the Federal Republic of Germany', pp. 85–6.
69 Weiss, 'Modernising the German Works Council System: A Recent Amendment'.
70 Biagi, 'Forms of Employee Representational Participation', p. 519.
71 The first proposals for the legal regulation of companies with a community dimension, the so-called *Societas Europaea* or European Company, date from the 1970s. A formal Regulation on the Statute for a European Company was adopted in 2001. The Regulation was supplemented by a Directive on the involvement of employees in this European Company: *Official Journal* L 294, 10 November 2001. For a detailed discussion, see Blanpain, *European Labour Law*, pp. 702–20.
72 The discussion below draws heavily from the chapter on labour law in my book *Fundamentals of European Civil Law and Impact of the European Community*, pp. 156–61.
73 This is the so-called Montan (*Montan–Mitbestimmungsgesetz*) Act. The 1951 legislation has since been amended on several occasions for the purpose of extending its application to holding companies, including holding companies with a minority interest in the industries of coal, iron or steel.
74 Works Constitution Act (*Betriebsverfassungsgesetz*) 1952.
75 Codetermination Act (*Mitbestimmungsgesetz*) 1976.
76 Actual numbers vary depending on the size of a company's workforce. Thus, for example, Volkswagen currently operates a supervisory board of twenty-one members. The principles outlined below are not affected by the actual size of the board, though.

77 Act of 6 May 1971 on the Structure of Public and Private Companies.

78 Jacobs, 'The Netherlands', 2004 update, [238]. Bakels and Opheikens, *Schets van het Nederlands arbeidsrecht*, pp. 226–31.

79 De Groot, *Netherlands Labour and Co-Determination Law in an EEC Perspective*, p. 239.

80 For Australia, see Department of Employment and Industrial Relations Working Environment Branch, *Industrial Democracy and Employee Participation—Policy Discussion Paper*. For New Zealand, see *Report of the Committee of Inquiry into Industrial Democracy*. The latter document is discussed in Vranken, 'An Australasian Approach to Industrial Democracy?', p. 81.

Chapter 5
Labour Courts

Setting the Scene

Labour courts occupy a special place in the overall court structure. The relative informality of proceedings in the labour court, the relative speed of deciding cases, and the relative specialisation of its judges, all assist plaintiffs in their quest for a remedy. In Europe, where the origins of this specialist court lie, particular significance attaches to these features of the labour court. Remember that employees there enjoy extensive statutory rights that over time have come to cover just about every aspect of the individual employment relationship.[1] For these rights to be meaningful, the availability of an appropriate enforcement mechanism is essential. Specialist labour courts provide such a mechanism.

This chapter will focus on two of continental Europe's best known labour courts: the French *conseil de prud'hommes* and the German *Arbeitsgericht*. While each may display certain differences in detail, both undeniably constitute courts of law. This means that their focus is squarely on judiciable disputes, that is, disputes that ultimately can be resolved through a process of formal adjudication rather than through negotiation, mediation, arbitration or a combination thereof. In other words, European labour courts stand for the application, interpretation and enforcement of pre-existing rights, not the creation of new ones.

This contrasts sharply with the scene on either side of the Tasman. The Arbitration Court established at the turn of the previous century in Australia and New Zealand, while its official name may have changed on more than one occasion in the course of its existence, never really amounted to the functional equivalent of a European labour court, nor was it ever intended to be. Of particular significance in this regard is the 1907 *Harvester* decision[2] in Australia. That decision, issued by Justice HB Higgins in the (then) Court of Conciliation and Arbitration, is generally regarded as having laid the foundation for the central court's 'dominance'[3] in settling wage claims, as well as determining a whole range of other terms and conditions of employment. Similarly, a 'fair-wage'[4] policy guided the operation of the Arbitration Court in New Zealand from its early years onwards and it has been said that by 1908 its control over wage disputes had become 'entrenched'.[5] It is therefore particularly intriguing to observe that New Zealand's shift away from industrial dispute resolution through compulsory conciliation and arbitration, unlike what happened in Australia, has produced an institutional result that today is much more in tune with the European system of labour courts. The current tandem of Employment Relations Authority and Employment Court, in particular, will be examined in the pages that follow. Conversely, while the role of the Australian Industrial Relations Commission was downgraded significantly under the Howard administration in recent years, no wholesale change of a similar magnitude has been reflected in either the office of the Employment Advocate or its successor, the Workplace Authority. The proposed office of Fair Work Australia, although the detail of the new legislation under the Rudd government remains somewhat sketchy at this stage, has been presented as 'a new independent umpire with teeth'. It is expected to operate with a new 'Inspectorate' to investigate breaches and enforce compliance with the newly to be introduced laws, including 'where necessary' through the courts. To this effect, 'specialist Fair Work Divisions' will be created in the Federal Court and the Federal Magistrates Court 'to hear matters that arise under the new laws'.[6]

Classification and Categories of Dispute

Although the manner in which disputes are classified may differ across national systems of labour law,[7] there is a major conceptual distinction between disputes of interest and disputes of right. Interest disputes are not really legal in nature. They do not involve any legal rights. The alternative label of economic disputes seems particularly apt as disputes of interest merely seek to create, that is, to establish, legal entitlements. A typical instance of an interest dispute concerns demands made upon one another by industrial parties during collective bargaining. Disputes of interest—about wage rises and related matters—are at the very core of the traditional jurisdiction of the Arbitration Court, in both Australia and New Zealand.

Once a collective bargaining agreement is in place, any disputes that arise about the interpretation or enforcement of the rights and, conversely, the obligations contained in the agreement qualify as rights disputes. In Europe an important additional source of rights disputes is triggered by the extensive statutory regime of employment rights bestowed upon individual employees. Thus the distinction between interest and rights disputes cuts across another distinction made in labour law systems, that is, the division of labour disputes into individual and collective disputes. Although a perfect correlation does not exist, individual disputes typically involve rights disputes, whereas collective disputes tend to centre around interest disputes.

It has been suggested at one time that the distinction between interest and rights disputes is more important than the qualification of disputes as either individual or collective.[8] Such a generalisation is not particularly useful. As the discussion below makes clear, the jurisdiction of the labour court may hinge on it. And, of course, any overlap is necessarily incomplete. While the labels of interest and rights disputes refer to the nature of the dispute between the parties, the qualification of a dispute as either individual or collective alludes to the type of parties that are in dispute. Only, the involvement of a single employer on the side of business does not prevent the classification of a dispute with the collective representative of the employee as collective in nature.

Dismissal disputes represent a typical instance of individual disputes over pre-existing rights. In some non-European systems of labour law, rights disputes between individual employees and their employer—whether the former act with or without union assistance—are known as 'personal grievances'. This term has been an integral feature of the New Zealand system of labour law since the early 1970s when the legislature sought to deflect strike action associated with dismissal disputes. The personal grievance procedure in New Zealand has been modelled on the grievance procedure that operates under the National Labor Relations Act in the United States since 1935.[9]

Specialist institutions for the resolution of labour disputes are typically creatures of the legislature. The type and nature of the institution tends to be a reflection of the broader system of labour law it serves. Thus, in Australia and New Zealand, the jurisdiction of the Arbitration Court—the conciliation and arbitration of collective disputes of interest—has been shaped by the centralist, collectivist and economic focus of the traditional system of industrial relations in these countries. The peaceful resolution of collective (interest) disputes, without the need for either party to resort to strike action or lock-out, preoccupied the mind of the legislature on both sides of the Tasman throughout much of the twentieth century. Conversely, (individual) disputes over rights epitomise the core jurisdiction of the European-style labour court wherever statutory employment rights form a central feature of the overall system of labour law. Interestingly, in this regard, the relatively late arrival of industrial tribunals in Great Britain coincided with the 'discovery' of individual employment rights by the legislature during the 1960s.[10] Law enforcement, rather than rights creation, is also a primary function of the National Labor Relations Board in the United States.

European-Style Labour Courts

Autonomy and Specialisation in Labour Law

In Chapter 2 reference was made to the ongoing debate among scholars about autonomy and specialisation in labour law. The focus there was on the substantive rules of labour law. Let us now shift our attention to the procedural dimension of labour law. Lord Wedderburn, in particular, has argued that the latter may be even more important than the former. While Wedderburn's observations were made from the perspective of British labour law, their validity need not be so limited. Lord Wedderburn put it rather eloquently as follows:

> The issue upon which we have stumbled here goes not only, or not so much, to the substance of a reformed labour law, but to its application and procedures.[11]

The point he makes is that the adoption of special labour laws to strengthen the legal position of the employee *vis-à-vis* the employer additionally requires the creation of a specialist enforcement body. Without it, goes the argument, the spirit in which the substantive labour laws need to be applied, for purposes of maximum efficacy, may be at risk. In particular, the ordinary courts of law are said to be prone to interpret any special labour laws rather too narrowly, that is, by reference to the general rules of contract and tort. A related argument in favour of a specialist labour court is that its establishment allows for the resolution of labour disputes in a manner that is less rigid, less time-consuming and less formal than civil litigation overall.[12]

A comprehensive study of dispute-resolution mechanisms has found that labour courts represent the most commonly used mechanism for the settlement of disputes over rights in matters of labour law.[13] This is particularly true for Western Europe, where the adjudication of labour disputes is left to the regular courts in only a few countries.[14] Further, unlike the situation in the United States, the adjudication of labour disputes is deemed to concern the public order of the state. To bypass the labour court by means of private arbitration therefore is not an option in Europe.[15]

Labour courts owe their origin to the probiviral court or *conseil de prud'hommes* (literally, council of wise men), established in the French city of Lyon pursuant to a Napoleonic law of 1806. The basic premise underlying their creation was to have certain employment disputes settled quickly and cheaply by a small committee comprising representatives of employers and employees.[16]

Various criteria can be used to examine the degree of specialisation in the European labour courts. The discussion below focuses on the composition and structure of labour courts, their jurisdictional scope, court access and representation. A few observations about actual proceedings in the European-style labour court will be made as well.

Composition and Structure

While their composition tends to be tripartite elsewhere in Europe, labour courts in France continue to be bipartite, comprising a representative from the employers and from the employees. A professional judge (*juge départiteur*) is only added to the bench when necessary to break a deadlock. Historically, this emphasis on the lay element was intended to ensure that cases are heard in the first instance by the parties' peers.[17] The employer and employee members are elected for a renewable term of five years. The chair alternates between an employer and an employee member. In addition to enjoying special dismissal protection, employee members on the *conseil de prud'hommes* receive training, paid for out of public funds, to equip them for their task. Any such training typically occurs during working hours. The employer cannot withhold pay for any hours lost.[18]

Speed, affordability and informality typify proceedings of the labour court throughout Europe and the same holds true for the French labour courts. Although appeals are heard by the ordinary appellate courts, the latter sit in specialist panels. Labour matters, along with social security claims, are referred to a social chamber (*chambre sociale*) within the appellate courts. Tellingly, this social chamber is composed exclusively of professional judges, who are not bound by the findings of the *conseil de prud'hommes* at first instance.

Although the roots of the German system of labour courts also date back to the nineteenth century, the real starting point in Germany was the Labour Courts Act of 1926. The current statutory framework is contained in the *Arbeitsgerichtsgesetz* of 1953, as amended in 1979.[19] When compared to the *conseil de prud'hommes* in France, the contemporary significance of the German labour court is beyond doubt and arguably surpasses that of its French counterpart. In effect, Weiss and Schmidt suggest that the role of the labour court goes beyond mere dispute adjudication: in the development of German labour law it parallels that of the legislature.[20] A most famous instance of judicial law-making in this regard is the legal regulation of industrial action. The various prerequisites for the conduct of lawful strikes, in particular, are the product of judicial creativity in the German labour court. They include the principle of social adequacy (*Sozialadäquanz*) required to justify industrial action as well as, most famously, the principle of proportionality (*Verhältnismässigkeitsprinzip*).[21] Case law regulates the contents of the latter principle in a fairly detailed fashion. Thus, strikes must respect the peace obligation (*Friedenspflicht*).[22] They must be fair and can only be used as a means of last resort. Further, they must be preceded by a secret ballot of union members.[23] This last aspect of the proportionality requirement especially has proved somewhat controversial in recent times in an Australian labour law setting.[24] Be this as it may, the Rudd administration foreshadows no change on this score. On the contrary, 'tough' rules on industrial action, including a secret ballot of employees and three days advance notice, are said to be an important feature of the newly to be introduced legislation.[25]

The relative prominence of the labour court in German labour law can be explained, at least in part, by the provision for a specialist court structure beyond the initial (trial) stage of any litigation. In Germany an advanced degree of specialisation indeed exists at all levels of the judicial hierarchy. Specifically, Germany has three stages of labour courts and the tripartite court composition is maintained at each stage. At the top of the pyramid sits the Federal Labour Court (*Bundesarbeitsgericht*). It hears cases in panels comprising three career judges and two lay members. While these lay members are appointed rather than elected, they are not answerable to the organisations that have nominated them. As in France, lay members are not to represent the interests of any party to the dispute either. In practice, since the Federal Labour Court deals exclusively with questions of law, the professional members inevitably carry more weight than in the lower courts.[26] Both the labour court in the first instance and the intermediate labour court are state courts that operate at the level of the various states (*Länder*) only.

Occasionally, a further appeal lies from the Federal Labour Court to the Federal Constitutional Court (*Bundesverfassungsgericht*). Technically, this can only happen on points of constitutional law. The popularity of constitutional challenges in Germany is said to have been on the rise in recent years.[27]

Jurisdiction

As for their powers, labour courts are exceptional or extraordinary courts. They can only hear cases for which their competence has been expressly recognised under the enabling legislation. In France the emphasis is clearly on the resolution of individual employment disputes. In part, this reflects the pre-union origin of the *conseil de prud'hommes*.[28] Arguably, a more contemporary justification for the individual focus in the jurisdiction of the French labour court lies in the importance attached to the protection of individual rights in the French legal system overall. Needless to say, in practice the distinction between individual and collective disputes can prove more apparent than real at times. In its simplest manifestation, a labour dispute is individual when it concerns a single employer and a single employee. Typically, this type of dispute arises out of an individual employment contract and addresses issues of rights only. However, French labour courts tend to interpret the concept of an individual dispute broadly. The consideration that terms and conditions of employment in an individual contract frequently are the result of collective bargaining is certainly not viewed as constituting a bar to the jurisdiction of the labour court. While it may be argued that any such 'individual' disputes inevitably, albeit indirectly, involve the application and interpretation of the originating collective instrument, the relevant terms of the collective agreement are legally deemed to have become incorporated within the individual contract of employment.

Technically, the legal construct of incorporation or, better perhaps, individualisation is restricted in its application to the normative part of collective agreements in Europe. Legal scholarship, at its most advanced in Germany, divides the contents of collective agreements into normative and obligatory components. The normative component in turn is divided further into individual-normative and collective-normative parts. Provisions pertaining to the obligatory part exclusively concern the relationship between the contracting parties themselves. Individual employees remain legally unaffected by the obligatory part as they only come to collective agreements indirectly, that is, via the negotiating union. Individual employees therefore do not derive any direct rights nor do they incur direct legal obligations from the contents of this obligatory or contractual component of collective agreements. An illustration is the implied duty to maintain the sanctity of the agreement during the period of its currency. Normative provisions, on the other hand, spell out norms or legal rules for the relationship between employer and employee. They therefore tend to be of direct legal relevance to individual employees. Even then, any normative provisions that merely pertain to the workforce overall, or that seek to regulate the employment relationship purely in the abstract, are labelled collective-normative in nature. Examples are provisions that detail the requirements for the establishment of a union delegation or the selection of employee representatives at the workplace. Generally speaking, collective-normative provisions, as distinct from individual-normative provisions, do not trigger enforceable rights for individual employees. Provisions dealing with wages or other conditions of employment such as sick leave, holiday entitlements, redundancy, on the other hand, belong squarely to the individual-normative part of the collective agreement. They are directly enforceable in the labour court by any individual employees that fall within the personal scope of application of the agreement.[29]

The overwhelming majority of cases that come before the French labour courts involve claims by individual employees whose individual employment contract has come to an end. This is also the case in neighbouring Belgium.[30]

As in France, the German labour courts can only entertain legal disputes, that is, disputes over rights. However, their jurisdiction expressly extends to both individual and collective disputes, thus avoiding problems regarding the cataloguing of disputes experienced in France. To be clear, the bulk of cases before the German labour courts still concern the employment relationship between individual employees and their employer. The importance of collective disputes before the German labour courts must be judged in qualitative rather than quantitative terms. Significantly, apart from regulating the power relationship between the parties in industrial conflict as indicated already (strike action!) or, more generally, regulating the process of collective bargaining itself, case law in Germany has helped shape the operation of the works councils.[31]

Even so, not even the jurisdiction of the German labour courts is genuinely comprehensive. The most notable exclusion in this regard concerns disputes involving the employee representatives on supervisory boards. As long as the legal regulation of supervisory boards continues to be viewed as an integral part of corporate law instead of labour law, dispute adjudication is destined to remain the domain of the ordinary courts of law *par excellence*.[32]

The relationship between the specialist labour court and the ordinary courts of law is not usually a matter for concern in Europe. The ordinary or general courts of law by and large accept the special jurisdiction of the labour court. Besides, specialisation is a feature of the European civil law that extends to areas beyond labour law.[33] Occasionally, the general rather than specialist court is approached by employers when seeking to bring an end to alleged unlawful strike action. Injunctions and court orders for damages make rather blunt weapons, though, and they are rarely pursued fully. Applications for interim relief or even a mere threat of court action tend to be more effective bargaining strategies available to parties who must continue to deal with one another long after the particular dispute that triggered the application for court intervention has ended.

Court Access and Representation

As indicated already, whatever competence the French labour courts have in dealing with collective matters derives squarely from the broad interpretation given to the notion of individual dispute. Their jurisdiction in collective disputes represents the proverbial exception to the general rule. In France the proper plaintiff is the individual, whether employee or employer. While legal representation is not uncommon nowadays, especially as regards the employer party, in French litigation there is a distinct emphasis on appearance in person. An explanation for this state of affairs is sometimes sought in the traditional dual mission of labour courts. An attempt at conciliation compulsorily precedes the exercise of any formal powers of adjudication. To this effect separate Boards of Conciliation (*bureaux de conciliation*) and Judgment Boards (*bureaux de jugement*) operate within the French system of labour courts. Conciliation works best when the parties appear in person. However, to avoid the conciliation stage being treated in a perfunctory way, conciliation boards are legally empowered to issue certain orders, even if the defendant fails to show.

Judges serving as conciliators in a particular case may not participate in the subsequent judgment session. Parties need not appear in person during the judgment part of the court proceedings.

In Germany, employees and employers have 'standing' to appear before the labour court. So too do their collective representatives (who can bring proceedings in their own right) and even works councils (for disputes involving aspects of the Works Constitution legislation). As in France, though, the primary plaintiff before the German labour court is the individual employee.[34] Every case before the German labour court starts with a conciliation session (*Gütetermin*) heard by the chairperson sitting alone. The separation of the conciliation and adjudication stages in proceedings before the German labour courts is less strict than in France. Weiss and Schmidt comment that the chair tends to indicate his (or her) opinion as to the legal position of the parties, should the case go on to the full trial stage, and this practice has considerable influence on the parties' willingness to compromise.[35]

Legal counsel is required at the appellate stages of the court case in Germany. While the state appeal courts hear cases *de novo*, the Federal Labour Court—to be approached only if leave is granted—entertains appeals on points of law only.

The labour court is not the only option available to German employees wishing to air grievances. When employees feel they have been treated unfairly, or have otherwise been put at a disadvantage by the employer (or by a fellow employee), they can complain to the works council. Approaching the works council is either an alternative to going to the labour court or it can be a first step, prior to bringing formal court proceedings. Should the works council decide to take up the matter with the employer but the parties fail to agree about the handling of the complaint, the works council can approach the Arbitration Committee. This committee operates at the place of work. It is either a standing body or it can be established on an *ad hoc* basis. It comprises equal numbers of representatives from both sides plus a neutral chair.[36] If the matter is in the nature of a dispute of interest, the decision of the Arbitration Committee has the force of a recommendation only. On the other hand, if it involves a rights dispute, the committee's decision is legally binding—subject to a challenge in the labour court on the ground that the committee exceeded its jurisdiction.

The statutory basis for the above complaints procedure before the works council is the Works Constitution Act of 1972.[37] The procedure has the advantage of keeping grievances in house. And yet, Weiss and Schmidt have found that, in practice, this manner of resolving disputes is rarely used.[38] In one sense, this reinforces the significance of the labour courts as the primary vehicle for the resolution of employment disputes in Germany. By the same token, it confirms an understandable reluctance among employees generally to resort to open disputation with their employer while the employment relationship remains in existence.

Proceedings in the Labour Court

While proceedings in the labour court are based on the same general principles as those applicable in the ordinary courts of law, the legislation on labour courts seeks to facilitate simplicity and expeditiousness while also keeping down the cost of litigation for the parties. Overall, albeit on a largely impressionistic level, the feeling prevails that the European type of labour court may have lost some of the initial informality in its proceedings.[39] Further, in some instances the workload of the labour court has significantly increased over time. Figures for Germany, in particular, show that the number of cases brought before the state labour courts almost doubled in the immediate aftermath of unification between East and West Germany, even though the new *Länder* statistically only add an extra 25 per cent to the total working population of that country. Inevitably, this has resulted in an increase in the time required to decide cases.[40] In France, special regulations allow for extra urgency to be accorded to certain types of labour disputes, in particular litigation involving dismissals on economic grounds.[41]

Everything in life is relative. When compared to civil litigation in the ordinary courts of law, labour courts remain a quick and cheap mechanism for adjudicating employment disputes. And, while the complexity of some of the cases before the court may have increased, so has the expertise displayed by the court personnel. All up, labour courts are a fully accepted, non-controversial part of the judicial landscape in continental Europe.

The 'Labour' Court in Australia and New Zealand

A Problem of Comparability

The Australasian counterpart of the European-style labour court is the Arbitration Court. This label is a convenient shorthand for the succession of specialist courts and tribunals, with differing names, established under labour legislation on both sides of the Tasman in the course of the past hundred years or so. A hands-on comparison remains problematic, though. The Arbitration Court can be regarded as the functional equivalent of the labour court in Europe, in that both courts symbolise a state commitment to providing a public institution for the peaceful resolution of industrial disputation. However, at its core, the meaning of the very notion of industrial dispute in Australia or New Zealand is radically different from the type of labour dispute that triggers the jurisdiction of the European labour court. To use the classification device discussed at the start of this chapter, the type of dispute before the European labour court concerns individual rights. By contrast, the traditional dispute before the Australasian Arbitration Court is collective in nature and involves economic interests rather than established rights. The ramifications are major and can only be appreciated fully when placed in their proper historical context. New Zealand labour law, in particular, illustrates this point well.

New Zealand: From Court of Arbitration to Labour Court

The earliest history of the Arbitration Court in New Zealand resembles that of its Australian counterpart, to be discussed later in this chapter. It certainly has little in common with the European-style labour court. A suitable starting point is provided by the Industrial Conciliation and Arbitration Act 1894 (NZ). The purpose of the Act was reflected in its title as follows:

> An Act to encourage the formation of industrial unions and associations and to facilitate the settlement of industrial disputes by conciliation and arbitration.

To give effect to its statutory objective, the Act provided for the establishment of multiple Boards of Conciliation as well as a single, central Court of Arbitration. Each Board of Conciliation was to consist of equal numbers of elected (or, failing this, government-appointed) employer and union representatives. Together the Board members were to choose an impartial chairperson who would have a casting vote. While individual employers had standing to appear before the

Board, individual employees did not. Any inference of union monopoly in terms of bringing employee claims before the Board, however, needs to be tempered by the consideration that, at least initially, it sufficed for seven workers in an industry to form themselves into an industrial union and register as such under the Act.[42]

The focus in these Boards of Conciliation was very much on the resolution of interest disputes. Even so, any claims arising under an existing industrial instrument, that is, an award or collective agreement, clearly fitted the definition of 'industrial matters' to which the Act applied.[43] It follows that neither the distinction between individual and collective disputes nor, more importantly perhaps, the difference between interest and rights disputes appears to have been particularly rigid at the outset. Certainly, the activities of the Board were not meant to be restricted by the way in which matters were referred to it. To this effect the 1894 Act stated that:

> Every Board shall, in such manner as it shall think fit, carefully and expeditiously inquire into and investigate *any industrial dispute of which it shall have cognisance, and all matters affecting the merits of such dispute or the right settlement thereof*...[44]

The New Zealand legislature envisaged that proceedings in the Boards of Conciliation would be informal.[45] Even so, the behaviour by the Board members and the parties themselves inserted an element of formalism to the Boards' operation. Woods stresses in this respect that Boards were given no real guidance as to how proceedings should be conducted.[46] Thus, Boards were officially entrusted with the same powers to summon witnesses and hear evidence as the Arbitration Court.[47] This is said to have resulted in 'some predisposition towards a copying of the more formal procedure of the Court'.[48] Further, the parties were allowed to be represented by an agent, although representation by a solicitor required the agreement of both sides to the dispute. Finally, Board decisions had to be reached by a majority of its members. Woods observes that this feature, in particular, encouraged a tendency among the parties to 'state' their case rather than discuss it.[49]

Boards were given a strict timeframe for resolving disputes, typically two months from the date of initial referral.[50] Unresolved disputes, including decisions that left one party unsatisfied, were referred to the Court of Arbitration at the initiative of either the Board itself or the aggrieved party. The Court was presided over by a professional judge (taken from the ranks of the Supreme Court). In addition, there were two lay members, appointed to represent employers and organised labour respectively.[51]

The Court of Arbitration could set its own procedure. It was allowed to hear any evidence it deemed appropriate, whether legally admissible or not. As in the case of the Boards, legal representation was only permitted if both parties agreed to it.[52] The Court had to decide the case within a month of the initial hearing. The Court was empowered to give a final determination in any matter referred to it 'in such manner as [it] shall find to stand with equity and good conscience'.[53] This is the origin of the so-called equity and good conscience powers of the Labour (and, subsequently, Employment) Court that would come to the fore in later years.

Technically, any decision, to be reached by majority and referred to as an award, only became enforceable upon being filed with a court of general jurisdiction, the Supreme Court.[54]

The parties did not readily fall into line with the institutional set-up envisaged by the 1894 legislature. The main problem seems to have been the Boards of Conciliation. Many employers simply 'refused to co-operate' with the Boards, while many unions, for their part, considered that the Arbitration Court was 'more effective' in dealing with disputes over wages and this realisation in turn affected organised labour's commitment to the conciliation machinery.[55] In recognition of this reality, a 1901 amendment to the 1894 legislation effectively allowed either party to bypass the Boards and submit a dispute to the Court for arbitration instead.

Conciliation as a compulsory first step in the resolution of industrial disputes was re-introduced in 1908, if only in an attempt to address issues of work overload by the Arbitration Court, including any associated delays in hearing cases. However, the prominence of the Arbitration Court in matters of wage fixation continued unabated. In 1970 the legislation was amended for the specific purpose of introducing a personal grievance procedure, as well as a model clause for dealing with disputes of rights. To be fair, the development of procedures for the resolution of matters which today are called rights disputes predates the 1970 amendment.[56] The 1970 amendment then made it compulsory for awards and agreements to contain a clause outlining the steps to be taken for dealing with problems concerning the interpretation of these instruments during their lifetime, including 'matters dealt with in the instrument and not clearly and specifically disposed of by the terms of the instrument'.

Truly innovative, from a New Zealand perspective at least, was the introduction of a personal grievance clause pursuant to the 1970 legislation. At the time the country was experiencing considerable social unrest, which often took the shape of strike action, caused by disputes over dismissals. The statutory procedure adopted for tackling allegations that an employee's employment had been terminated unfairly or that an employer had taken some action short of dismissal but nonetheless disadvantageous to the employee's employment, is said to have been inspired by the grievance procedure operating under the National Labor Relations Act 1935 in the United States.[57]

The separate procedures for rights disputes and personal grievances were consolidated in the Industrial Relations Act 1973. Significantly, however, the 1973 Act entrenched the formal distinction between economic (wage or interest) disputes and legal (whether collective or individual) disputes in New Zealand. It did so by abolishing the Arbitration Court and replacing it with two new institutions: an Industrial Commission and an Industrial Court. Ironically, both bodies were discontinued a few years later in 1977, in favour of a resurrected (unitary) Arbitration Court. However, by that time the fate of the rather amorphous and all-encompassing notion of industrial dispute had already been sealed. The distinction between interest disputes and rights disputes with, as regards the latter, the acknowledgement of a special sub-category of personal grievances, had firmly entered the New Zealand psyche, not to be challenged again.

The Contemporary Employment Court in New Zealand

Personal Grievance Handling

The contemporary Employment Court has its direct antecedents in the Labour Relations Act 1987. This statute replaced the Industrial Relations Act 1973 and was the product of a thorough review of New Zealand's traditional approach to the regulation of industrial relations. The review was carried out by a newly elected Labour government under the formidable (if somewhat eccentric) leadership of David Lange. In recognition of the need for specialisation in terms of institutional set-up, the Labour Relations Act acknowledged the merits of having separate bodies to deal with different types of disputes.[58] Revealingly, the legislature replaced the old label of 'industrial dispute' by a more contemporary notion of 'labour dispute'. The significance of this move goes beyond mere symbolism. On one level, the Act affirmed the distinction between disputes about the negotiation of awards or (collective) agreements, and disputes about the enforcement of these industrial instruments. On another and arguably more significant level, the Act crystallised a shift in focus, swapping a primary concern with economic disputation for addressing disputes suitable for adjudication in a (specialist) court of law. As regards the latter, the historical emphasis on collectivism in New Zealand's system of industrial relations—typified by the privileged role of (registered) unions—was lessened, albeit cautiously at first. This is the significance of the newly created Labour Court and its express jurisdiction to adjudicate disputes of rights as well as disputes in the nature of personal grievances.

New Zealand's evolving approach to personal grievance handling, in particular, deserves closer attention. To fully appreciate the current state of affairs, it must be borne in mind that the Labour Relations Act itself was replaced by an Employment Contracts Act in 1991 which in turn has had to give way for the current Employment Relations Act, adopted in 2000. The Industrial Relations Act 1973, the immediate predecessor of the Labour Relations Act 1987, defined personal grievance to mean any grievance that individual employees might have against their employer because of a claim that they were either unjustifiably dismissed or the subject of detrimental employer action short of dismissal, 'not being an action of a kind applicable generally to workers of the same class employed by the employer'.[59] The part as quoted reflected a legislative intent to distinguish the treatment of disputes over individual rights from rights disputes that are collective in nature.[60] For individual employees to be granted legal standing to bring their claims directly before the Court, claimants were required to show that the union had failed to act, or had failed to act promptly, upon their grievance.[61] Even then, the Court allowed the union considerable discretion in deciding whether or not to take up any particular grievance its members cared to bring to its attention.[62]

At the time a narrow approach to the availability of the personal grievance procedure could hardly be considered an anomaly, especially since access to statutory mechanisms for the resolution of industrial disputes and, most notably, the Arbitration Court, was traditionally seen as the *quid pro quo* for union registration. Any union fears of losing control over the interpretation of industrial instruments it had helped to bring about were sought to be alleviated by the consideration that, as a rule, the legislative provision for a personal grievance procedure was not meant to result in individual employees acquiring direct access to the Arbitration Court. It also helps explain why, under the 1973 Act, the personal grievance procedure was available on the double condition of award coverage and union membership. Inevitably, this meant that several groups of employees[63] could be forced to seek redress in the ordinary courts of law where only limited protection was available at common law. This could prove problematic, especially in situations involving wrongful dismissal.[64]

Intriguingly, pursuant to the 1987 Act, the Labour government of the day discontinued the restriction of the personal grievance procedure to disputes affecting single employees. Instead, personal grievances were henceforth defined by reference to their subject matter, rather than the number of employees affected by the employer's action.[65] This also remains the case under current law.[66] Full and direct access by individual employees to the specialist court was not achieved immediately, though. Under the Labour Relations Act availability of the personal grievance procedure was no longer dependent on coverage by an award or collective agreement. However, except in certain limited circumstances,[67] it remained a benefit of union membership. Furthermore, access to the Labour Court was made subject to leave being granted by the Court itself.[68]

It took a conservative National government to see the process started under Labour to its logical conclusion. The Employment Contracts Act 1991 removed any open reference to unions throughout the entire statute. The Labour Court was replaced with a two-tier specialist structure, available to employees regardless of their union membership status. Jurisdiction to adjudicate personal grievances went to an Employment Tribunal in the first instance,[69] with appeals to be heard by an Employment Court.[70] Neither the Tribunal nor the Court featured lay members in their make-up.

Once a Labour government regained office, the anti-union legislation was abolished and the current Employment Relations Act 2000 was substituted for the 1991 Act. The Tribunal was renamed the Employment Relations Authority, while the Employment Court kept its label. Significantly, access to both institutions was not affected by the 2000 legislature. It thus remains open to all employees in New Zealand.

Under the Employment Relations Act 2000 the official procedure for the handling of personal grievances operates as follows: any employee with a personal grievance is expected to raise the matter with the employer first.[71] If the matter cannot be resolved in this manner, the employee can approach the Employment Relations Authority. The Authority comprises government-appointed officials who can hear cases while sitting alone.[72] The Authority has exclusive jurisdiction to make determinations about employment relationship problems generally, including personal grievances.[73] The legislature refers to the Authority as an investigative body. Its brief is to focus on the substantive merits of each case, 'without regard to technicalities'.[74] The Authority is free to set its own procedure. It may take into account such evidence and information as 'in equity and good conscience' it thinks fit, and 'whether strictly legal or not'.[75] Remedies available to the Authority include reinstatement (in the employee's former position),[76] re-employment (in a position no less advantageous to the employee), reimbursement (of any wages or other money lost), as well as the payment of compensation by the employer.[77] As regards the latter remedy, specific mention is made of compensation for 'humiliation, loss of dignity, and injury to the feeling of the employee'.[78] This remedy caters for dismissals that may prove sound in substantive terms yet are deemed procedurally unfair because of the manner in which the dismissals have been carried out.[79]

The Authority operates independently of the Court.[80] However, if one party is dissatisfied with the Authority's determination, the matter can be referred to the Employment Court. Those challenging the Authority's decision may seek a complete rehearing of the case *de novo*. Alternatively, the appeal can be limited to specific questions of fact or law.[81] Further, any party to the dispute may ask the Authority or the Court to have the matter heard in the Court without the Authority investigating the personal grievance first. Obviously, good reasons must attach to any such request if it is to succeed. The need to address an important principle of law so qualifies, as does the need for urgency in the public interest.[82] Finally, the Authority itself may also refer a question of law to the Court for its opinion at any stage during the investigation of the personal grievance. In that case proceedings before the Authority are suspended pending the Court's opinion.[83] This procedure bears a strong resemblance to the so-called preliminary ruling technique that governs the relationship between the European Court of Justice and the national courts in the legal order of the EU.[84]

The Employment Court is a continuation of the Court by the same name established under previous (1991) legislation.[85] It consists of three professional judges who must all be lawyers with a minimum of seven years experience as a barrister or solicitor.[86] As a rule, the jurisdiction of the Employment Court is exercised by a professional judge sitting alone.[87]

In resolving employment disputes generally, the 2000 legislature recognises that access to information and mediation services is more important than adherence to rigid, formal procedures.[88] In this spirit the Court must consider the use of mediation before it proceeds to hear the merits of any case brought before it.[89] The actual proceedings in the Employment Court continue to place emphasis on substance over form. Its jurisdiction must be exercised 'as in equity and good conscience it thinks fit'. In the same vein, the Court is free to accept evidence it deems appropriate, 'whether strictly legal evidence or not'.[90] Of course, this does not place the Employment Court above the law. First, the role of the Court is limited to determining what the rights and obligations of the parties are, and does not extend to the creation of any new terms and conditions of employment.[91] Second, appeals on points of law are heard by a court of general jurisdiction, the Court of Appeal.[92] The Court of Appeal may refer the case back to the Employment Court for reconsideration.[93] In any event, in determining an appeal, the Court of Appeal must have regard to the special nature and jurisdiction of the Employment Court.[94]

Relationship with the Court of Appeal

The relationship between the specialist court and the supervisory court of general jurisdiction is fascinating, not only because it is revealing about the connection between labour law and general law in employment matters, but also because it sheds light on the extent of specialisation in contemporary New Zealand labour law. In 1987, the year in which the Labour Relations Act was adopted and the Labour Court was substituted for the Arbitration Court, Sir Ivor Richardson gave an address at the Industrial Relations Centre of Victoria University in Wellington. At the time Richardson was a distinguished judge of the New Zealand Court of Appeal and later would become its president. Sir Ivor began his speech as follows:

> [I]n the lives of productive enterprises and in the lives of workers alike, the employment of labour needs to be seen as a continuing relationship. As in other human relationships, there will be highs and lows, there will be tensions and hiccups. They have to be resolved in a way that will allow that continuing relationship to endure for the common good.[95]

His Honour then proceeded to list three reasons why courts of general jurisdiction are not well suited for that kind of conflict resolution role.

> The first is the adversary method of conflict resolution which is the traditional way in which disputes are resolved in the courts of general jurisdiction. By definition it focuses on the dispute itself rather than on a continuing relationship: it pits one side against the other and there is no built-in encouragement to find common ground, let alone a central role for mediation and conciliation. The second is that the field of industrial relations calls for the development of broad expertise and experience. It requires specialised judges who become steeped in the field and who work with those from union and employer ranks who, through their own background and experience, have the confidence of their organisations. Such tribunals are likely to be more sensitive instruments for resolving these

> disputes. The third and associated reason is that *the orderly resolution of industrial conflict in an ongoing relationship is not simply a matter of applying legal principles* and attempting to discover on examination who is right and who is wrong. Such questions are often not susceptible to that kind of cold analysis in a forum far removed from the reality of industrial life and industrial strife. Bringing in the law and the regular court processes may simply exacerbate the human drama going on behind an industrial dispute.[96]

When reviewing the relevant case law, frequent references appear in the judgments of the Court of Appeal to the expertise of the specialist court—as instructed by the legislature. This inevitably colours the approach to deciding cases in the Court of Appeal. Particularly representative are dismissal cases. In *Auckland City Council v Hennessy*,[97] for instance, the Court of Appeal concurred with the opinion of the (then) Arbitration Court that the term 'unjustifiably' in the labour legislation could not be confined to matters of substantive justification for the termination action. Thus an employer carrying out an inquiry prior to the decision to terminate the employment relationship must do so, to paraphrase Richardson, 'in a fair and reasonable manner'.[98] A few years later, the Court of Appeal suggested that fair and reasonable treatment is so generally expected today of any employer that the law has come to recognise it as an ordinary obligation in contracts of service. Cooke J in *Marborough Harbour Board v Goulden*[99] put it as follows:

> Turning to the application to this case of principles to be found in the modern authorities, we think that the position has probably been reached in New Zealand where there are few, if any, relationships of employment, public or private, to which the requirements of fairness have no application whatever. Very clear statutory or contractual language would be necessary to exclude this elementary duty.[100]

Any deference to the jurisdiction of the specialist court can never be a blank cheque, though. Since the Richardson address, the cautious, almost hands-off approach of the Court of Appeal *vis-à-vis* the Labour

Court and its predecessor, the Arbitration Court, has been replaced with a greater willingness to intervene in the domain of the Employment Court. In part, an explanation for this shift may lie in the more adventurous stance adopted by the contemporary Employment Court and perhaps even in the personality of some of its members. No doubt, the radical change in statutory framework governing New Zealand labour law during the 1990s, especially the substitution of the Employment Contracts Act 1991 for the Labour Relations Act 1987, also played a role.[101] The discussion below focuses on two cases that illustrate, particularly well, the tightening in the relationship between the Court of Appeal and the specialist court. They are the Court of Appeal decisions in *Hagg*[102] and *Aoraki*.[103]

Hagg concerned the personal scope of application of the protective labour legislation, more specifically access to the personal grievance procedure pursuant to the Employment Contracts Act 1991. Mr Hagg had been employed as a lecturer under successive fixed-term contracts. He argued that his employment had been unjustifiably terminated after five and a half years, upon expiry of the third contract, notwithstanding a subsequent employer invitation for Mr Hagg to apply for a further limited-term appointment to a relieving position. The Employment Court invoked its 'equity and good conscience' powers and ruled that the employer's conduct had been unfair in the circumstances. The Court of Appeal disagreed. It drew attention to the statutory requirement for the Employment Court to exercise its jurisdiction in accordance with the law. Any special powers the Employment Court might possess under enabling legislation, did not allow it to misconstrue the statutory concept of unjustifiable dismissal. The majority held that to allow a temporary employment contract to expire did not amount to a dismissal, let alone an unjustifiable dismissal.

Several observations are called for. First, the decision in *Hagg* was delivered by its then president, Sir Ivor Richardson. Second, the case was decided by reference to the ordinary principles of contract law. The Court of Appeal was quite specific in ruling that no different or special set of rules apply to the interpretation of employment contracts as compared to contracts in general. To be fair, the Court of Appeal acknowledged that employment contracts can involve an inequality in bargaining power of the parties. It even expressed sympathy for the weaker party. However, the Court of Appeal was equally adamant that, in the absence of unambiguous parliamentary intention to address the specific issue of employer abuse of successive fixed-term contracts, its own hands were tied.[104]

It remains unclear whether the response by the legislature in the Employment Relations Act 2000 adequately addresses the problem as articulated in *Hagg*. That Act allows the use of fixed-term employment for genuine (operational) reasons only. Its use is expressly disallowed where the purpose is either to 'exclude or limit' statutory employee rights or even to establish 'the suitability of the employee for permanent employment'.[105] In June 2008 the government proposed an amendment to the 2000 legislation in an apparent attempt at clarifying the rights of casual and temporary employees. Specifically, the Department of Labour is to develop a so-called Code of Employment Practice for Casual and Non-Standard Employment. At present, only the Employment Relations Authority and the Employment Court have jurisdiction to decide whether an employee has a fixed-term contract or is actually a permanent employee. The proposed amendment to the Employment Relations Act extends this power to labour inspectors, 'giving employers and employees a simpler process for confirming their status'.[106]

On one reading of the case, the decision in *Hagg* stands for a declaration of faith in the principles of general contract law. The perceived need by the Court of Appeal to uphold an undeniable shift in philosophy by the legislature, as reflected in the substitution of the 1991 Act for the 1987 statute, may provide the real reason for its uncompromising stance regarding the interpretation of terms in employment contracts. The decision in *Aoraki*, issued a few years later, confirms this assessment.

Aoraki is a company that develops computer software. In 1995 a proportion of the workforce was made redundant for reasons of company restructuring in the face of financial difficulties. One of the people declared redundant was McGavin, a marketing manager who had been with the firm for some ten years. A dispute arose about the size of the financial compensation package. The Employment Court upheld McGavin's claim of unjustifiable dismissal. It ruled that the dismissal was justified in substantive terms as it had been founded on genuine commercial grounds. However, while the Court accepted that the redundancy situation was real, it considered that the manner in which the subsequent dismissal had been handled displayed aspects of procedural unfairness. Specifically, the company was said to have failed to act in a fair and reasonable manner in the determination of Mr McGavin's redundancy compensation package. The company had also failed to consult with him, had failed to provide counselling services available to other employees, and had denied him the opportunity to discuss the reasons for the redundancy.

In quashing the judgment of the Employment Court, the Court of Appeal in *Aoraki* embarked upon a detailed analysis of the Employment Contracts Act. The 1991 legislation was said to represent 'a substantial departure from the collectivist principles of the previous industrial relations legislation in favour of a model of free contractual bargaining'.[107] The Court of Appeal acknowledged that the legislature had not fully equated employment contracts with ordinary commercial contracts for the supply of services. The 1991 legislation had not abolished the personal grievance procedure. But the context in which the procedure was to be applied had changed sharply. The increased emphasis by the statute-maker on contractual freedom was too significant to be ignored. Ultimately, the responsibility of the courts was to give effect to the intent of Parliament, notwithstanding the 'tension' that 'inevitably' existed between a contractual approach to employment issues and the 'social and economic concerns inherent in the relationship' between employer and employee.[108] The extent to which any subsequent shift in legislative intent as reflected in the Employment Relations Act 2000 might be seen as a cause for renewed optimism will be explored more fully in Chapter 7.[109]

The Anomaly of a Non-Existent Labour Court in Australia

Australia never had a European-style labour court, nor does it have one today. Throughout most of the twentieth century the core specialist institution in the federal system of industrial relations was, to use its original name, the Commonwealth Court of Conciliation and Arbitration.[110] This body was not a court in the conventional sense of the word. Its jurisdiction covered not just, and not even primarily, legal disputes over pre-existing rights but rather its powers extended, most importantly, to entertaining economic disputes of interest. As a practical matter, the primary function of the Commonwealth Court was to 'guide' negotiations over wages and other conditions of employment. Formal adjudication, for purposes of interpreting and enforcing the outcome of these negotiations, traditionally took second place and, even then, invariably the focus remained confined to the award parties, that is, registered unions and employers. Employment disputes between individual employees and their employer were only addressed indirectly at best.

In 1956 the High Court of Australia ruled that a concentration of judicial and quasi-legislative functions in one single body was unconstitutional.[111] The decision, known as the *Boilermakers* case, forced the federal legislature to redistribute the powers of the Commonwealth Court among separate institutions. Jurisdiction to resolve disputes about the creation of new terms and conditions of employment—that is, wage disputes—stayed with a revamped Commonwealth Conciliation and Arbitration Commission (instead of Court). Under the Industrial Relations Act 1988 and, thereafter, the Workplace Relations Act 1996 this body was renamed the Australian Industrial Relations Commission. The judicial function, by contrast, was transferred to a newly established Commonwealth (later: Australian) Industrial Court.

Academic commentators in Australia have queried the wisdom of the High Court decision in *Boilermakers*. They point out that, at times, the distinction between judicial and non-judicial powers in matters of industrial relations can be quite arbitrary.[112] However, as discussed earlier in this chapter, the distinction is firmly established in legal systems elsewhere. And, in any event, the provision of separate institutions for each type of function continues to be a feature of Australian labour law to date. Ironically, the proposed introduction, by 1 January 2010, of a 'new', one-stop shop in the form of Fair Work Australia may seem a retrograde step of sorts.[113] Not surprisingly, perhaps, it is the Commission that traditionally has received most attention in academic (including legal) writings.[114] The focus on the Industrial Court below seeks to remedy this state of affairs somewhat.

When first established in 1956 the Industrial Court was composed of a chief judge and two further judges.[115] All members on the bench were stipulated to be professional judges, with a minimum of five years seniority as barrister or solicitor.[116] The jurisdiction of the

Court was to be exercised by not fewer than two judges, but the legislature allowed for disputes about the interpretation of awards to be heard by a single judge sitting alone.[117] The main task of the Court was the enforcement of awards and the supervision of internal union affairs, including complaints about the treatment of individual members by the union organisation.[118] In the view of at least one commentator, the contemporary relevance of the case law of the (now defunct) Court is limited.[119]

Until the 1970s the lower courts of general jurisdiction were typically state-based. A major change in the overall structure of the federal judiciary occurred with the passage of the Federal Court of Australia Act 1976 (Cth). As its title suggests, the 1976 Act created the Federal Court of Australia. At the outset the Federal Court was divided into two divisions: a general division and an industrial division.[120] The Industrial Court was abolished and its jurisdiction transferred to the new Federal Court (Industrial Division).

While the 1976 legislature did not prevent judges from being assigned to only one division, appointments are to the Federal Court as such. This set-up is rather different from the specialist labour judiciary in Europe or indeed New Zealand. It also compromises somewhat any initial beliefs by the drafters of the 1976 Act that a separate industrial division within the Federal Court would allow for the work of the previous Industrial Court to be continued and the specialist nature of the labour jurisdiction to be maintained.[121] The Hawke Labor government sought to tackle the issue head-on in the Industrial Relations Bill 1987. The Bill had been drafted in response to the findings of a committee established to carry out an overall review of Australia's system of industrial relations and its operation. This review, unlike the one conducted almost simultaneously under prime minister Lange in New Zealand, did not lead to calls for radical change.[122] Even so, the Hancock Report—named after the committee's chair and professor of economics, Keith Hancock—did recommend the establishment of a genuinely separate Labour Court to replace the Industrial Division of the Federal Court. Under the Industrial Relations Bill 1987 all judges of the proposed Labour Court would be required to possess the normal qualifications for judicial office. Significantly, they were also expected to have 'skills and experience in the field of industrial relations'.[123] Thus the legislature sought to acknowledge the merits of having judicial appointees with special expertise in dealing with 'the unique requirements of the industrial relations system' so as to better 'promote consistency and understanding in the application, interpretation and enforcement of the law'.[124]

No provision was made for direct, general access by individual employees to the proposed Labour Court. Instead, under clauses 188–191 of the Industrial Relations Bill 1987, employees wishing to challenge the fairness of a dismissal decision had to approach the Commission for redress in the first instance. That unfair dismissal was accepted as an industrial relations issue at all was itself a recent phenomenon. Unfair dismissal protection clauses only became a standard feature in federal awards in the aftermath of the so-called TCR (Termination, Change and Redundancy) case of 1984.[125] Under the 1987 Bill, should a conciliation attempt by the Commission fail, the matter could be referred to the Labour Court which had powers to make reinstatement orders in appropriate cases.[126]

In the end, the legislature dropped the idea of a Labour Court from the final text of the Industrial Relations Act 1988 (Cth). Interestingly, a few years later the 1988 Act was amended to allow for the establishment of an Industrial Relations Court of Australia after all.[127] However, the existence of the new body was short-lived. Following a change of government, the Industrial Relations Act 1988 had to make way for the Workplace Relations Act 1996 (Cth). The 1996 Act abolished the Industrial Relations Court and transferred its jurisdiction back to the Federal Court of Australia. The 1996 legislature did not favour a return of labour disputes to a specialist industrial division within the Federal Court, though. By way of minor (although, in practical terms, not necessarily unimportant) concession to individual employee claimants, under the Workplace Relations Act there is no automatic obligation to pay the costs of the other party should a claim prove unsuccessful.[128]

Intriguingly, few if any tears were shed to 'mourn' the demise of the Industrial Relations Court.[129] While some commentators might have liked the 1996 legislature to have restored the Industrial Division of the Federal Court,[130] others have argued that, in practical terms, the two-division structure of the Federal Court had already become superfluous by the early 1990s.[131]

Fair Work Australia

The story does not end here. In the lead-up to the 2007 federal elections the Labor Opposition released its plan for a new industrial relations system.[132] Under this plan the Australian Industrial Relations Commission, once again, will be replaced by a 'new umpire', called Fair Work Australia. In part, this new body signals a return to the days before *Boilermakers*, in that Fair Work Australia will encapsulate both judicial and non-judicial functions under a single umbrella institution. It has been foreshadowed that Fair Work Australia will be responsible for a wide-ranging mix of functions as follows:

- Assisting parties to resolve workplace grievances
- Resolving (unfair as well as unlawful) dismissal claims
- Facilitating collective bargaining
- Enforcing a new statutory duty of good faith bargaining
- Adjusting minimum wages and award conditions
- Monitoring compliance with any applicable labour laws
- Regulating registered industrial organisations.[133]

The above list of functions is sufficiently broad to ensure the involvement of the new body in all aspects of labour law, whether these concern the creation of new terms and conditions of employment, the interpretation of existing terms of employment that are in place, or—significantly—the investigation and enforcement of employment terms and labour laws generally. To accommodate any constitutional requirements about the separation of powers, the exercise of the judicial function is proposed to be allocated to a 'separate division' within Fair Work Australia that is to be 'independent' of the industrial relations parties themselves.[134] A policy implementation plan, released in August 2007, adds that 'the separate judicial division of Fair Work Australia will need judicial members and those judicial members will be appointed in accordance with current processes'.[135]

Notes

1 See Chapter 2.
2 *Ex Parte HV McKay* (1907) 2 CAR 1.
3 Creighton and Stewart, *Labour Law*, p. 51.
4 Woods, *Industrial Conciliation and Arbitration in New Zealand*, p. 62.

5 Department of Labour, *Industrial Relations: A Framework for Review*, vol. 2, p. 114.
6 Gillard, *Introducing Australia's New Workplace Relations System*, p. 9.
7 Gladstone, 'Settlement of Disputes over Rights', p. 644.
8 Camerlynck and Lyon-Caen, *Droit du Travail*, p. 704, cited in Despax and Rojot, 'France', 1987 update, [683].
9 Department of Labour, *Industrial Relations*, p. 146.
10 Gladstone, 'Settlement of Disputes over Rights', p. 644.
11 Wedderburn, 'Labour Law: From Here to Autonomy?', p. 16; 'Labour Law: Autonomy from the Common Law?', p. 237.
12 See, generally, Vranken, 'Specialisation and Labour Courts: A Comparative Analysis', p. 497.
13 Aaron, Chapter 16, 'Labour Courts and Organs of Arbitration', p. 5.
14 The most conspicuous instance is the Netherlands.
15 In the absence of a European-style system of labour courts, private arbitration—paid for by the parties themselves rather than through the public purse—is a popular alternative in the United States.
16 International Labour Organization, *Labour Courts, An International Survey of Judicial Systems for the Settlement of Disputes*, p. 3, cited in Kassalow, *Trade Unions and Industrial Relations: An International Comparison*, p. 169.
17 Equal representation of employers and employees in France was not achieved until 1848: Act of 27 May 1848. The main statutory provisions on the contemporary labour court are contained in the Labour Code (*Code du travail*). From 1 March 2008 onwards, they can be found in Book 4 of the French Code.
18 Javillier, *Droit du travail*, pp. 66–7.
19 Weiss and Schmidt, 'Germany', 2000 update, [265].
20 ibid., [72].
21 ibid., [401]. A principle of proportionality also features, more generally, at the level of EU law.
22 ibid., [360].
23 ibid., [402].
24 See the critical discussion in Orr and Murugesan, 'Mandatory Secret Ballots Before Employee Industrial Action', p. 272.
25 Gillard, *Introducing Australia's New Workplace Relations System*, p. 6.
26 Weiss and Schmidt, 'Germany', 2000 update, [273].
27 ibid., [275]. Another federal system where the constitutional dimension of labour law traditionally features heavily is, of course, Australia.
28 Kassalow, *Trade Unions and Industrial Relations*, p. 155.
29 For an application beyond German labour law of the distinction between obligatory and normative provisions and, within the category of normative provisions, between collective and individual normative provisions, see Vranken, *De collectieve arbeidsovereenkomsten in België van 1974 tot 1980. Evolutie en juridische evaluatie*, pp. 357–88.
30 For Belgium, Blanpain adds, tongue in cheek, that somehow the ability to sue one's employer while the employment relationship is still in place

does not seem particularly appealing to the average employee! See Blanpain, 'Belgium', 2006 update, [62].

31 Weiss and Schmidt, 'Germany', 2000 update, [503]. See Chapter 4 for a more detailed discussion of works councils.

32 Disputes about expulsion from union membership are also heard by the ordinary courts in Germany: Weiss and Schmidt, 'Germany', 2000 update, [549]. Employee representation on supervisory boards of companies is discussed more fully in Chapter 4.

33 Vranken, *Fundamentals of European Civil Law*, pp. 58–62.

34 Weiss and Schmidt, 'Germany', 2000 update, [284].

35 ibid., [291].

36 If parties cannot agree on who is to be the chair, the labour court decides. Often a career judge from the labour courts ends up chairing the Arbitration Committee: ibid., [486].

37 Sections 84–86 (*Betriebsverfassungsgesetz*).

38 Weiss and Schmidt, 'Germany', 2000 update, [311].

39 Vranken, 'Specialisation and Labour Courts', p. 513.

40 Intriguingly, the same is not true for the Federal Labour Court: Weiss and Schmidt, 'Germany', 2000 update, [306] and [308].

41 Javillier, *Droit du travail*, p. 65.

42 Woods, *Industrial Conciliation and Arbitration in New Zealand*, p. 44.

43 Section 2 of the Industrial Conciliation and Arbitration Act 1894 (NZ).

44 Section 43 of the Industrial Conciliation and Arbitration Act 1894 (NZ) (emphasis added).

45 Woods adds that provision was not even made for Board members to be paid: *Industrial Conciliation and Arbitration in New Zealand*, p. 45.

46 ibid., p. 46.

47 Section 43 of the Industrial Conciliation and Arbitration Act 1894 (NZ).

48 Woods, *Industrial Conciliation and Arbitration in New Zealand*, p. 45.

49 ibid., p. 46.

50 Section 44 of the Industrial Conciliation and Arbitration Act 1894 (NZ).

51 Section 48 of the Industrial Conciliation and Arbitration Act 1894 (NZ).

52 Section 53 of the Industrial Conciliation and Arbitration Act 1894 (NZ).

53 Section 61 of the Industrial Conciliation and Arbitration Act 1894 (NZ).

54 Section 75 of the Industrial Conciliation and Arbitration Act 1894 (NZ).

55 Department of Labour, *Industrial Relations*, p. 114.

56 The government's so-called green paper traces its antecedents to the 1930s: ibid., p. 144.

57 ibid., p. 146.

58 The Labour Relations Act 1987 replaced the Arbitration Court with an Arbitration Commission ('to hear and determine disputes of interest': Section 260(1)(b)) and a Labour Court ('to hear and determine any question connected with the construction of any award or agreement': Section 279(1)(g) and also 'to hear and determine personal grievances': Section 279(1)(i)).

59 Section 117(1) of the Industrial Relations Act 1973 (NZ).

60 Department of Labour, *Industrial Relations*, p. 159.

61 Section 117(3)(A) of the Industrial Relations Act 1973 (NZ).

62 Vranken, 'Specialisation and Labour Courts', p. 521.

63 The Department of Labour's 1985 green paper listed the following groups of workers: those who had gained an official exemption from compulsory union membership; managerial or supervisory staff not represented by a union; those whose wages were above the salary bar specified in the relevant award; those who were not covered by an award or agreement (including home workers); those who did not fall within the definition of 'worker' (such as contractors): Department of Labour, *Industrial Relations*, pp. 159–60.

64 The continued application in New Zealand of the so-called *Addis* rule meant that the common law remedies for dismissal were distinctly unsatisfactory from an employee perspective. The *Addis* rule is a reference to a 1909 decision in the House of Lords. Under the rule as articulated in *Addis*, compensation is limited to a sum equivalent to the wages earned if a proper (but invariably short) term of notice had been observed by the employer. Loss of status, distress or humiliation suffered by the employee typically were precluded from compensation: *Addis v Gramophone Co Ltd* [1909] AC 488.

65 Section 210(1) of the Labour Relations Act 1987 (NZ).

66 Section 103 of the Employment Relations Act 2000 (NZ).

67 See the list of circumstances in Section 218 of the Labour Relations Act 1987 (NZ).

68 Section 218(1) of the Labour Relations Act 1987 (NZ).

69 Section 79(b) of the Employment Contracts Act 1991 (NZ).

70 Section 104(1)(a) of the Employment Contracts Act 1991 (NZ).

71 Section 114 of the Employment Relations Act 2000 (NZ).

72 Section 166(2) of the Employment Relations Act 2000 (NZ).

73 Section 161(1)(e) of the Employment Relations Act 2000 (NZ).

74 Section 157(1) of the Employment Relations Act 2000 (NZ).

75 Section 160 of the Employment Relations Act 2000 (NZ).

76 The legislature lists reinstatement as the primary remedy in situations of unjustifiable dismissal: Section 125 of the Employment Relations Act 2000 (NZ).

77 Section 123 of the Employment Relations Act 2000 (NZ).

78 Section 123(c)(i) of the Employment Relations Act 2000 (NZ). This is a direct reaction to the old rule in *Addis* (see *Addis v Gramophone Co Ltd* [1909] AC 488).

79 Szakats and Mulgan list the following requirements for the procedural fairness of dismissals: (i) warning and a request for the employee to improve conduct and performance; (ii) opportunity for the employee to give an explanation as to the alleged misconduct prior to the actual dismissal; (iii) full investigation of the facts at the basis of the dismissal decision prior to the actual termination of the employment relationship: *Dismissal and Redundancy Procedures*, p. 82.

80 The Act states expressly that 'it is not a function of the Court to advise or direct the Authority in relation to the exercise of its investigative role,

powers, and jurisdiction': Section 188(4) of the Employment Relations Act 2000 (NZ).

81 Section 179 of the Employment Relations Act 2000 (NZ).

82 Section 178 of the Employment Relations Act 2000 (NZ).

83 Section 177 of the Employment Relations Act 2000 (NZ).

84 The legal order of the EU is discussed in Chapter 6.

85 Section 186(2) of the Employment Relations Act 2000 (NZ).

86 Sections 197 and 200 of the Employment Relations Act 2000 (NZ).

87 Sections 208 and 209 of the Employment Relations Act 2000 (NZ).

88 Section 101(a) of the Employment Relations Act 2000 (NZ) (object clause).

89 Section 188(2) of the Employment Relations Act 2000 (NZ).

90 Sections 189 (equity and good conscience) and 203 (proceedings not to be questioned) of the Employment Relations Act 2000 (NZ).

91 Section 101(d) of the Employment Relations Act 2000 (NZ) (object clause).

92 Any such appeal requires leave from the Court of Appeal: Section 214 of the Employment Relations Act 2000 (NZ). Prior to the Supreme Court Act 2003 (NZ) the Court of Appeal was effectively the top court in New Zealand. While not abolishing the Court of Appeal itself, the 2003 Act establishes a new court of final appeal, the Supreme Court of New Zealand. The Supreme Court came into being on 1 January 2004. It replaces the Judicial Committee of the Privy Council located in London. As the practical relevance of the Privy Council for New Zealand labour law has been limited in recent years, it can similarly be speculated that the role of the new Court in employment litigation will be marginal as well.

93 Section 215 of the Employment Relations Act 2000 (NZ).

94 Section 216 of the Employment Relations Act 2000 (NZ).

95 Richardson, 'The Role of the Courts in Industrial Relations', p. 113.

96 ibid., p. 114 (emphasis added).

97 (1982) ACJ 699 (CA).

98 Richardson, 'The Role of the Courts in Industrial Relations', p. 117.

99 (1985) 2 NZLR 378.

100 ibid., at 383.

101 Vranken, 'The Role of Specialist Labour Courts in an Environment of Substantive Labour Deregulation: A New Zealand Case Study', p. 303.

102 *Principal of Auckland College of Education v Hagg* [1997] 2 NZLR 537 (CA).

103 *Aoraki Corporation Ltd v McGavin* [1998] 3 NZLR 276 (CA).

104 In practical terms, this meant that any problems of bargaining inequality between the parties to an apparently temporary employment relationship had to be dealt with through application of 'the well-settled principles concerning sham or non-genuine aspects of contracts and the variation of contracts': [1997] 2 NZLR 537 at 554.

105 Section 66 of the Employment Relations Act 2000 (NZ). Probationary arrangements are regulated in a separate provision (see Section 67 of the Act).

106 Mallard, Minister for Labour, 'Stronger Protection for Casual and Temp Workers'.
107 [1998] 3 NZLR 276 at 286.
108 ibid., at 287.
109 One commentator suggests that the 2000 legislature has sought to restrict the role of the Court of Appeal in employment matters. This legislative intent is meant to be reflected in Section 214(3) which directs the Court to grant leave to appeal in cases that raise legal issues of 'general or public importance'. However, that same statutory provision also allows for maximum judicial discretion in considering applications for leave 'for any other reason'. See Anderson, 'Just a Jump to the Left?', p. 82.
110 Conciliation and Arbitration Act 1904 (Cth).
111 *R v Kirby; ex parte Boilermakers' Society of Australia* (1956) 94 CLR 254.
112 Creighton and Stewart, *Labour Law*, pp. 118–20.
113 The Rudd reforms are discussed further below.
114 A notable exception is McCallum, 'A Modern Renaissance: Industrial Law and Relations under Federal Wigs 1977–1992', p. 401.
115 Section 26 of the Conciliation and Arbitration Act 1904 (Cth) as amended by Section 10 of the Conciliation and Arbitration Act 1956 (Cth).
116 Section 28 of the Conciliation and Arbitration Act 1904 (Cth) as amended by Section 10 of the Conciliation and Arbitration Act 1956 (Cth).
117 Section 32 of the Conciliation and Arbitration Act 1904 (Cth) as amended by Section 10 of the Conciliation and Arbitration Act 1956 (Cth).
118 The powers of the Court are listed in Section 37 of the Conciliation and Arbitration Act 1904 (Cth) as amended by Section 10 of the Conciliation and Arbitration Act 1956 (Cth).
119 McCallum, 'A Modern Renaissance', p. 405.
120 Section 13 of the Federal Court of Australia Act 1976 (Cth).
121 McCallum refers to the second reading speech by the Attorney-General in *Hansard*, 21 October 1976, vol. 101 2110, 2112: McCallum, 'A Modern Renaissance', pp. 406–7.
122 *Report of the Committee of Enquiry into Australian Industrial Relations Law and Systems.*
123 Clause 49(b) of the Industrial Relations Bill 1987.
124 Ralph Willis, Minister for Industrial Relations, second reading speech, *Hansard*, 14 May 1987, vol. 155 3164 at 3167, cited by McCallum, 'A Modern Renaissance', p. 430.
125 This was a decision by the Full Bench of the Australian Conciliation and Arbitration Commission in response to a test case mounted by the Australian Council of Trade Unions. The ACTU's purpose in bringing the case was to obtain 'fundamental improvements in employment security in this country in the relationship between employers and employees': (1982) 24 AILR 487. The decision itself can be found at (1984) 294 CAR 175.
126 See the discussion by McCallum, 'A Modern Renaissance', pp. 429–31.
127 Industrial Relations Reform Act 1993 (Cth).

128 Section 347 of the Workplace Relations Act 1996 (Cth). Note that this provision does not distinguish between employee or employer litigants.
129 Creighton and Stewart, *Labour Law*, p. 134.
130 ibid.
131 McCallum, 'A Modern Renaissance', p. 407.
132 Australian Labor Party, *Forward with Fairness. Labor's Plan for Fairer and More Productive Australian Workplaces.*
133 ibid., p. 17.
134 ibid.
135 Australian Labor Party, *Forward with Fairness. Policy Implementation Plan*, p. 25.

Chapter 6
The International Dimension of Labour Law

Universal Organisations: The International Labour Organization

It has been argued that international labour law is almost as old as labour itself.[1] While this may be somewhat of an exaggeration, especially when the notion of labour is interpreted broadly so as to include agricultural work,[2] a close nexus does exist between the development of international labour standards and the advent of industrialisation. From the outset, it was felt that the success of any efforts at establishing employee protective rules within a particular country risked being compromised if these could not be supported (or, at a minimum, not undermined) through parallel standards adopted elsewhere. Once competition by nations with less-developed conditions of work came to be viewed as unfair, the foundation was laid for the main global actor in the field of international labour law today, the International Labour Organization (ILO).[3]

The ILO was officially established in 1919. Its creation formed part of the peace settlement reached at the end of World War I.[4] The Preamble of the ILO Constitution expresses the link between combating warfare, poor economic conditions and social injustice in the following terms:[5]

Whereas universal and lasting peace can be established only if it is based upon social justice;

And whereas conditions of labour exist involving such injustice, hardship and privation to large numbers of people as to produce unrest so great that the peace and harmony of the world are imperilled; and an improvement of those conditions is urgently required: as, for example, by the regulation of the hours of work, including the establishment of a maximum working day and week, the regulation of the labour supply, the prevention of unemployment, the provision of an adequate living wage, the protection of the worker against sickness, disease and injury arising out of his employment, the protection of children, young persons and women, provision for old age and injury, protection of the interests of workers when employed in countries other than their own, recognition of the principle of equal remuneration for work of equal value, recognition of the principle of freedom of association, the organisation of vocational and technical education and other measures;

Whereas also the failure of any nation to adopt humane conditions of labour is an obstacle in the way of other nations which desire to improve the conditions in their own countries;

The High Contracting Parties, moved by sentiments of justice and humanity as well as by the desire to secure the permanent peace of the world, and with a view to attaining the objectives set forth in this Preamble, agree to the following Constitution of the International Labour Organisation.

Further factors, peculiar to the time period, that undoubtedly helped focus the minds of the Allied forces when drafting the social component of the Treaty of Versailles include a growing movement towards internationalisation by organised labour itself and the anti-establishment uprising through the Russian Revolution of 1917.[6]

The fairly extensive list of social concerns in the ILO Preamble displays a surprising degree of contemporary relevance, especially when viewed against the backdrop of a progressive reduction in the number of allowable award matters during the period of the Howard government. The social concerns listed in this 1919 document certainly ring familiar when studied in conjunction with the much more recent Community Charter on Fundamental Social Rights of Workers (1989) or the Charter of Fundamental Rights of the European Union (2000).[7] Today, the ILO is one of the better known specialised agencies of the United Nations. It is also a genuinely universal organisation, with a membership of not quite 200 countries (including Australia as a founding nation) across the globe and with an even larger body of laws.[8] The main legal instruments at the disposal of the ILO are conventions and recommendations. Whereas the former are in the nature of treaties—that is, they intend to create obligations for any ratifying member states, recommendations 'merely' provide guidelines for national policy formulation. However, in terms of legal enforceability, both instruments must be labelled as soft law only. Compliance, as is typical in areas of international law generally, depends heavily on moral pressure brought about by international public opinion.

Being universal has proved the biggest asset as well as a handicap for the ILO. By being a truly worldwide organisation, the tripartite structure of its component institutions gives an opportunity for the representatives of government, employees and business to meet and confer on a range of issues that transcend national boundaries. Thus, it is an ideal forum for tackling genuinely fundamental social issues, such as basic labour rights and freedoms. Convention No. 87 on Freedom of Association and Protection of the Right to Organise, adopted in 1948, and Convention No. 98 on the Right to Organise and Collective Bargaining, adopted in 1949, illustrate this point rather well. Convention No. 87, in particular, has provoked heated debate from time to time. While the Convention does not expressly grant a right to strike, the case law of the various ILO supervisory bodies nonetheless treats it as inherent to the right of unions to organise workers and defend their interests through, most notably, collective bargaining. Thus a logical link exists between Conventions No. 87 and No. 98.[9] The availability of a right to strike is also what traditionally distinguishes systems of collective bargaining from systems that rely on compulsory conciliation and arbitration for the resolution of industrial disputes.[10]

On other hand, the sheer size of the ILO makes for an unwieldy organisation and this has a negative impact on its effectiveness in terms of rule formulation. By and large, international labour laws have not played a major role in the development of domestic labour law in Australia.[11] The need to compromise reduces the practical relevance of the ILO, especially for the Western advanced nations among its members. Yet it would be wrong to dismiss the ILO out of hand. Recommendation No. 119 of 1963 concerning Termination of Employment at the Initiative of the Employer provides a most pertinent case in point. In essence, the Recommendation stands for the proposition that an employee's employment should not be terminated by the employer unless there is 'a valid reason'. While the Recommendation deliberately refrains from providing an exhaustive definition, a valid reason is stipulated to arise from either the conduct of the employee, or the capacity of the employee to perform the work, or 'the operational requirements' of the business. Recommendation No. 119 has subsequently provided the basis for the adoption of Convention No. 158 on Termination of Employment together with a supplementary Recommendation No. 166, both adopted in 1982. These were the international instruments that inspired the Australian Council of Trade Unions (ACTU) to bring its (successful) TCR claim in 1984.[12] By the same token, Convention No. 158 did not deter the Howard government from removing the legal entitlement to question the fairness of dismissal decisions in 'small' companies with a workforce of up to 100 workers.[13]

Regional Organisations: The European Union

Perhaps small makes beautiful after all. The relevance of supranational initiatives for advanced nations can increase when the focus is limited to the regional domain. The legal order of the EU is a qualified success story in this regard.

Historical Antecedents

The legal basis of the EU dates from 1957. This was the year in which the Treaty of Rome establishing the European Economic Community (EEC) was signed by France, Germany, Italy and the Benelux countries of Belgium, the Netherlands and Luxembourg. The Treaty of Rome paid little, if any, attention to social policy—let alone labour law. As suggested by its title, the central focus of the EEC Treaty was on economic issues and, more specifically, the integration of the national markets in the above countries. While the concept of common market is nowhere defined in the 1957 Treaty text, it was envisaged that it would go beyond a mere free-trade arrangement along the lines of the North American Free Trade Agreement (NAFTA) or Asia-Pacific Economic Cooperation (APEC). To this effect a common (external) tariff was to be applied in the relationship between the member states and third countries in addition to the abolition of all barriers to intra-Community trade. As regards the development of a social policy for Europe, the prevailing idea at the time was that this would be the inevitable byproduct of any economic integration of the six founding member states to be achieved first. To fully appreciate the logic behind this type of reasoning, we will look at some core events in the immediate aftermath of World War II.

To be fair, the history of the European integration movement arguably predates 1945. The expression 'United States of Europe' is said to have been used first in 1849 by a novelist and poet from the French romantic period, Victor Hugo. The timeframe is interesting and somewhat ironic as by that stage the contemporary codification movement was in full swing throughout continental Europe.[14] The legal construct of codification served as a political tool and a symbol of nation-building in nineteenth-century Europe. It thus reflected a desire by countries to differentiate themselves from one another rather than, in legal terms, go back to the bygone era of Roman law as the 'common law' (*ius commune*) of Europe.

Less romantic but equally ineffective was the pan-European movement led by Count Coudenhove during the first half of the twentieth century. Coudenhove was the son of an Austrian-Hungarian diplomat who sought to respond to the 'bolshevist threat' from Russia. Ultimately, though, it was World War II that triggered real change in the attitudes of national leaders in Western Europe. In 1946 Winston Churchill formulated his plan for 'a kind of United States of Europe' during a speech delivered at the University of Zurich in Switzerland. Churchill was in (political) opposition at the time. No doubt this allowed him to express himself more freely. Europe, especially the Continent, was in rather a mess. Economically, large parts of the 'freed' as well as 'defeated' countries found themselves literally in ruins because of the war. The political and military scene did not provide much basis for optimism either. In short, Western Europe had come out of the war severely weakened. There was little time to regain strength as the 'real' war would soon be followed by a 'cold' war and, linked to this, a growing fear of Russian expansionism. In effect, the so-called Allied forces did not stay united for long. It will be recalled that in 1949 the French, British and American zones of occupied Germany formed the BRD (*Bundesrepublik Deutschland*: West Germany) whereas the Russian zone became known as the DDR (*Deutsche Demokratische Republik*: East Germany). One year later, in 1950, the war in Korea started. Unless it somehow managed to pull itself together, a near perfect scenario thus existed for Europe to become ever-more dependent on the United States.

Not all was negative about the growing dominance of the United States in Europe. Undoubtedly, in economic terms, Europe has benefited greatly from financial assistance provided through the 1947 Marshall Plan. The Marshall Plan, named after the then US Secretary of State in reference to a speech made at Harvard University, laid the basis for the establishment of the Organisation for European Economic Co-operation (OEEC) in 1948 which, in turn, acted as the forerunner of the current Organisation for Economic Co-operation and Development (OECD) set up in 1961. Further, in political and military terms, the establishment of the North Atlantic Treaty Organization (NATO) has been referred to as 'the umbilical cord that kept Western Europe attached to the United States long after the period of US economic dominance was over'.[15] Against this backdrop calls grew for a Europe sufficiently strong to be able to stand on its own feet. Churchill did not see a need for Britain itself to become a part of the European integration effort, though. Only when no risk of abandoning national sovereignty arose was the United Kingdom prepared to come on board. It certainly helps explain that country's readiness to join in the formation of the Council of Europe in 1949.

The Council of Europe is not to be confused with the European Council in the context of the EU, discussed later. Because of its reliance on intergovernmental co-operation rather than a transfer of national sovereignty by the participating states, the Council of Europe has proved largely ineffective. A notable exception perhaps is the European Convention of Human Rights and Fundamental Freedoms

(1950).[16] The European Convention focuses on civil and political rather than social or labour rights, however. The latter type of entitlements was addressed in a separate European Social Charter of 1961, as revised in 1996.

Of more direct relevance than Churchill's Zurich speech was a declaration by the French Minister for Foreign Affairs, Robert Schuman, in 1950. Schuman called for a partnership between France and Germany (and any other country that cared to join) as regards the heavy industries of coal and steel. Clearly, the idea was to prevent another war by Germany by removing national control over industries that had played such a pivotal role in the war effort previously. Pursuant to the European Coal and Steel Community Treaty (ECSC), signed in Paris in 1951, France, Germany and four other countries (the Benelux countries plus Italy) agreed to transfer national sovereignty to a joint High Authority. The financial independence of this High Authority was secured through a levy on the production of coal and steel within the newly established Community. Because of its limited (fifty-year) timeframe, the ECSC is no longer in operation today. However, the experimental supranational model of the ECSC treaty was used in the much broader based (in terms of subject matter) and open-ended (in terms of timeframe) 1957 treaty establishing the European Economic Community among the same six signatory countries. A third Community treaty, on the peaceful use of atomic energy (Euratom), completed the 1957 picture as follows:

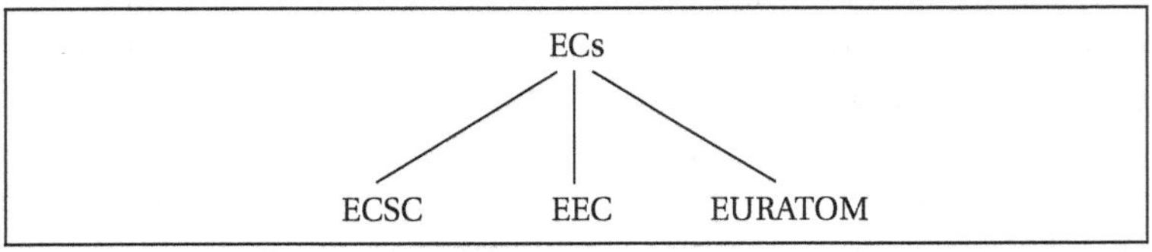

Figure 6.1: Trinity of European Communities

The European Economic Community and Beyond

Economic Integration First

Article 2 of the EEC Treaty contains the stated aims and objectives of the European Economic Community. While it lists a mixture of economic and political objectives, there is no direct reference to social integration. The 1957 text of Article 2 reads as follows:

> The Community shall have as its task, by establishing a common market and progressively approximating the economic policies of Member States,
>
> - to promote throughout the Community a harmonious development of economic activities,
> - a continuous and balanced expansion,
> - an increase in stability,
> - an accelerated raising of the standard of living
> - and closer relations between the States belonging to it.

The 1957 Treaty contains a separate Title with the official heading of Social Policy.[17] However, that Title comprises six short 'social provisions' only. Most significant, at least in historical terms, is Article 119 on equal pay for equal work between men and women. But, even this provision lay largely dormant during the first, neo-liberal phase of the European integration movement. Also worth noting is the creation of a European Social Fund for the specific purpose of increasing the geographical and occupational mobility of workers within the Community.[18] The so-called free movement of persons (including, but not limited to, workers) constitutes one of four freedoms that together form a core pillar upon which the Community is founded.[19]

A turning point came in the early 1970s. In a Solemn Declaration dated 1972 the Six Heads of State and/or Government openly acknowledge that, henceforth, progress in social policy is just as important as advances in the economic policy domain. The 1972 Declaration led to the adoption of a 'Social Action Plan' in 1974. It in turn triggered a series of European laws on equal pay (1975), equal treatment (1976), as well as the protection of employee-acquired rights in instances of, respectively, collective redundancy (1975), transfer of undertaking (1977), and even employer insolvency (1980).[20] Because of the prolific nature of legislative activity during the second half of the 1970s, this period has been labelled the 'golden era' (*l'âge d'or*)[21] of social harmonisation. Even so, in substantive terms, the focus of the legislature was very much on damage control rather than on proactively bringing about a European social dimension. All but the first two European laws above are reactionary, in that they seek to soften the social implications of economic and business rationalisation facilitated and, at times, necessitated by the drive towards market integration.

By the start of the 1980s the social policy dimension of the EEC had run out of puff. Arguably, no particular significance attaches to this state of affairs as all other aspects of the European integration effort had come under severe pressure as well. In any event, the then president of the European Commission,[22] Jacques Delors, almost singlehandedly reinvigorated the integration debate. Under his stewardship an amendment to the Treaty of Rome was adopted in 1986. Known as the Single European Act (SEA), it reflected a back-to-basics approach by setting a new date for the completion of the common market, renamed the (single) internal market, by 31 December 1992, that is, more than twenty years after the initial date set in the 1957 Treaty.[23]

Social Integration Next?

Delors achieved what he had set out to do. Somewhat ironically, perhaps, his success in the economic domain triggered public criticism about the narrow focus of the SEA as a vehicle for European integration. However, for a more focused agenda of social integration to receive a substantial boost, political consensus within an ever larger Community, comprising increasingly diverse member states, would prove a formidable obstacle. While still less than half its current size, the original membership of the Community had doubled by the mid-1980s.[24] Not even a gradual move away from decision-making by unanimity in favour of (qualified) majority voting could fully compensate for this, especially since sluggish economic growth continued to detract from any enthusiasm for the European cause at a national level. The SEA effectively confirmed the national sovereignty of the member states in matters of labour law as the removal of the requirement of unanimity was restricted to matters of occupational health and safety.[25] This latter change undoubtedly facilitated the adoption in 1989 of a framework Directive, outlining measures to encourage safety and health at the workplace.[26] But the mood of the times is perhaps best captured by the manner in which a formal charter on 'fundamental' worker rights came about in that same year.

Officially known as the Community Charter on Fundamental Social Rights of Workers,[27] the Charter did not create any groundbreaking new rights for employees in Europe.[28] Instead, it largely drew its inspiration from principles already contained in other international instruments, most notably the European Social Charter of 1961, various ILO Conventions, and the Treaty of Rome itself. The *raison d'être* of the Charter then was essentially political: to stress once again the importance of the social dimension that attaches to the establishment of the single European (economic) market. Technically, the Charter did not even constitute a legally enforceable document.[29] Even so, the member states failed to agree on a text acceptable to all. The United Kingdom declined to join the other eleven Community members in their Solemn Declaration on 9 December 1989. The immense symbolism that attached to the occasion becomes clear if one bears in mind that this date coincided with the 200th anniversary of the French Universal Declaration of Human rights in 1789.

The 1989 Charter lists the basic social rights of workers under the following twelve headings:[30]

1. Freedom of Movement
2. Employment and Remuneration
3. Improvement of Living and Working Conditions
4. Social Protection
5. Freedom of Association and Collective Bargaining
6. Vocational Training
7. Equal Treatment for Men and Women
8. Information, Consultation and Participation of Workers
9. Health Protection and Safety at the Workplace
10. Protection of Children and Adolescents
11. Elderly Persons
12. Disabled Persons.

The full text of the 1989 Charter is set out in Appendix 1. Without going into too much detail, it is clear that the above list displays a distinct emphasis on safeguarding the position of the individual. Any reference to collective rights is apparent as regards items 5 and 8 only. Intriguingly, these items concern the very aspects of the Charter that proved so problematic for the United Kingdom. Especially objectionable was the reference to a 'right' to resort to industrial action, including the right to strike, in the context of collective bargaining.[31] At the time, Britain under Thatcher had put its faith in reducing the role of the state domestically. The very perception of increasing power for Brussels through the back door of a social(ist) charter could only induce distrust if not outright contempt![32]

Primary responsibility for implementation of the Charter rested with the member states.[33] At a supranational level, the Charter laid the basis—albeit a most timid one—for more tangible (social) action in subsequent years. But for social policy to become a genuine part of the European integration effort, a more solid legal basis—and, in effect, a greater political will to act—was required. For the record, the Commission drew up an action program containing forty-seven specific proposals for Directives or other instruments in the wake of the Charter during the period 1990–92.[34] Apart from safety and health as well as equal opportunity, little if any progress was made with its implementation. A Directive requiring employers to inform their employees of the conditions applicable to their contract or employment relationship was adopted.[35] However, many other proposals were stalled, often because of opposition by the UK government. Hepple draws particular attention to draft Directives on the organisation of working time, the employment of atypical workers, and the posting of workers.[36] Most controversial by far was a proposal to establish a European works council in Community-scale companies. Clearly, its time had not yet come.

Maastricht: From European (Economic) Community to European Union

Following the SEA, a second major amendment to the Treaty of Rome was effected by the Treaty on European Union (TEU), also known as the Treaty of Maastricht (1992). The Maastricht treaty is an umbrella treaty with three distinct pillars. The core pillar is the EEC, henceforth known as the European Community (EC) in recognition of the broadened focus of the Community beyond things purely economic. Newly added—in official terms at least—spheres of interest include health, education, consumer protection and the environment. In one sense these can all be seen as 'soft' or 'social policy' areas. The two new 'outside' pillars are known as the Common Foreign and Security Policy (CFSP) and Cooperation in Justice and Home Affairs (CJHA), respectively. Any development in these outside pillars technically escapes the EC institutions and, in particular, the supervision normally exercised by the European Court of Justice. Instead, pursuant to the deal struck at Maastricht any initiatives for law-making in both areas would depend entirely on purely intergovernmental co-operation between the member states. Figure 6.2 shows the complexity of the Maastricht construct:

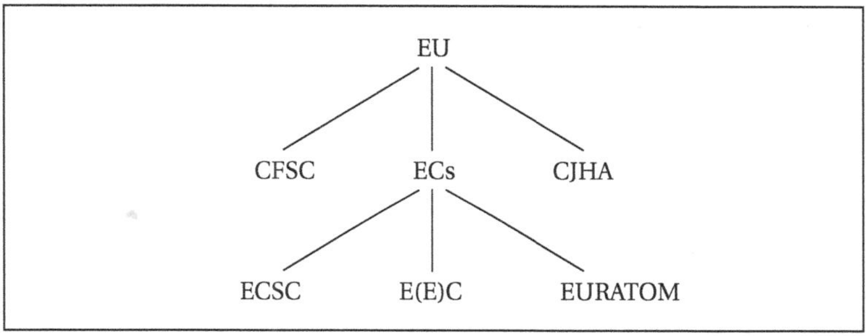

Figure 6.2: The European Union

As their titles suggest, the outside pillars have no connection with social policy (let alone labour law) whatsoever. Social policy under the Maastricht treaty was relegated to a separate Protocol—one of many—attached to the Treaty itself. The Protocol, signed by all twelve member states, allows eleven of these member states to enter into an Agreement on Social Policy. In unmistakable *déjà vu* fashion, the United Kingdom decided to opt out. The Agreement expands the scope for qualified majority voting. At the same time, however, a list of subject matters expressly requiring decision-making by unanimity is also included in the Agreement. The Agreement even comprises a list of so-called prohibited topics. These are topics that have specifically been precluded from regulation at Community level.

The effect of these three lists, in terms of facilitating progress towards creating a social Europe, is similar to driving a car with one foot firmly on the brake. Qualified majority voting henceforth applied to the suitably vague notion of working conditions, including employee information and consultation rights as well as (once again) equal treatment initiatives. Unanimity continued to be required when passing proposals for European laws on dismissal protection, collective representation of employees (including co-determination), and social security. Considered even more sensitive (from a national sovereignty perspective) and thus outside the jurisdiction of Europe entirely, were laws on the (prohibited) topics of strike or lock-out action, pay determination and, last but not least, freedom of association.

Maastricht: Subsidiarity

While the Agreement on Social Policy—unlike the Charter—had legal standing, its precise status was not free from controversy.[37] Some commentators wanted to treat the Agreement as an integral part of Community law. Others argued that it was simply an agreement at international law and thus outside the scope of the *acquis communautaire.*[38] But a much bigger problem for the future of an integrated policy on labour law was presented by a seemingly inconspicuous opening provision in the TEU. Article 3b enshrined the principle of subsidiarity in European parlance. The full text of this (in)famous provision reads as follows:

> The Community shall act within the limits of the powers conferred upon it by this Treaty and of the objectives assigned to it therein.
>
> In areas which do not fall within its exclusive competence, the Community shall take action, in accordance with the principle of subsidiarity, only if and in so far as the objectives of the proposed action cannot be sufficiently achieved by the Member States and can therefore, by reason of the scale or effects of the proposed action, be better achieved by the Community.
>
> Any action by the Community shall not be beyond what is necessary to achieve the objectives of this Treaty.

The meaning of Article 3b has been the subject of intense debate among scholars and policy-makers alike.[39] The second paragraph of the provision in the TEU is problematic. It seeks to combine the dual goals of efficiency and decentralisation in the decision-making process of the Community. Only, it does so in a manner that reflects a bias in favour of decentralisation. On one (benign) reading of Article 3b, the EU is considered to have reached a sufficient degree of sophistication for it to be no longer necessary, or indeed appropriate, that the advantages of Community-scale action over lower level (and, typically, national) regulation are taken as given. Hence the need for Community action to be openly justified on efficiency grounds in the future.

No great controversy need attach to such an interpretation of Article 3b. In effect, the case law of the European Court of Justice already reflects a more nuanced approach to the promotion of the integration ideal over time. This is illustrated by the evolution in judicial approach to the free movement of goods. The free movement of goods represents one of four core 'freedoms' upon which the common or internal market has been built in Europe. Specifically, the 1957 drafters of the Treaty of Rome considered it imperative that any unwarranted obstacles to internal Community trade be abolished. Under the Treaty, both tariff and non-tariff barriers to free trade are therefore prohibited. The former cover customs duties on imports and exports, including any charges having equivalent effect. The latter extend to quantitative restrictions on imports or exports, including, once again, any measures having an equivalent effect. Even in 1957, however, it was acknowledged that any ban on impediments to free trade could never be absolute. A range of exceptions, essentially on grounds of the broader public interest—protection of public morality, public security, public health, and the like—have been in place from the very beginning. Interestingly, especially during the formative period of the internal market, the Court of Justice chose to adopt an extremely narrow approach to the justifiability of any such national encroachments upon the integration effort.

Dassonville[40] and *Cassis de Dijon*[41] are two early cases in point. In *Dassonville* the Court ruled that a Belgian law prohibiting the import and sale of alcoholic spirits without an official document to certify the authenticity of the product in question and issued in the country of origin, was incompatible with Community law. The Belgian authorities unsuccessfully advanced protection of public health as the *ratio legis* for the national regulation. Similarly, in *Cassis de Dijon*, the European Court refused to accept that the import of French alcoholic beverages, lawfully produced in the originating country, could be stopped at the German border for failure to comply with more stringent standards applicable to the production of alcohol in the country of importation. The German argument that the promotion of free competition ought not be allowed to result in the condoning of 'unfair' competition was rejected.

Dassonville and *Cassis de Dijon*, it must be stressed, are early cases. By the time the Catalan advertising case came along,[42] a distinct shift in judicial policy had occurred. A regional, selective advertising ban for hard liquor on grounds of protecting public health in Spain was accepted by the European Court of Justice as not infringing the Community's free-movement-of-goods imperative. Trade-restricting measures introduced by member states then do not run foul of European law obligations where they can be shown to be temporary,[43] reasonable, necessary, proportionate and not arbitrary.

A more sinister interpretation of Article 3b is also possible. Proponents of the European cause fear that this provision amounts to the proverbial Trojan horse by handing eurosceptics a formidable platform to slow down, if not bring to an outright halt, European integration under the guise of addressing the so-called democratic deficit. Subsidiarity, so runs the argument, provides an opportunity to bring Europe closer to its people. It does so, not only by resisting the temptation to harmonise everything under the sun, but also because of the built-in presumption in favour of decentralised decision-making. The question put by eurosceptics then is seemingly straightforward. If the idea behind subsidiarity is to make decisions at a level that minimises alienation by the people they affect, why not avoid the risk of alienation altogether by allowing these citizens to make decisions for themselves? In other words, is it possible to interpret subsidiarity to mean total abstention of public regulation at any level in favour of self-regulation by private parties? Ironically, this was precisely the interpretation of subsidiarity favoured by the Catholic Church at one time,[44] albeit in a different context!

Deepening Versus Widening?

The basic problem with Article 3b is that it seeks to appease europhiles and eurosceptics alike. The issue is essentially political rather than legal in nature. It is quite feasible that, even without this provision on subsidiarity in the Treaty text, the desirability of new EU laws on labour law would have faced increasing disagreement among the various member states in any event. Differences in perception about the appropriate role of the state in matters of industrial relations are not new. Some countries—the United Kingdom, Scandinavia and the new member states from Eastern Europe, especially—typically favour a relatively hands-off approach to regulation in this area, whereas the Community's old guard (the Benelux countries, France, Germany and Italy) traditionally adopt a more hands-on stance. The latter see a continued, legitimate role for the state in regulating society in general and industrial relations in particular.

Perhaps in an attempt to diffuse the situation somewhat, the focus in Europe since Maastricht has shifted away from deepening towards widening the integration effort. In recent years the pace of accepting new member states has certainly picked up in remarkable fashion. While it took three decades for the initial EEC membership of six countries to double, by 1995 Sweden, Finland and Austria had brought membership of the EC to fifteen. A mere nine years later, the grand total had become twenty-five, with the 'bulk' admission of the Czech Republic, Cyprus, Estonia, Hungary, Latvia, Lithuania, Malta, Poland, Slovakia and Slovenia in 2004. Bulgaria and Romania were allowed to join in 2007. This has brought the current membership to an increasingly unwieldy twenty-seven countries. In fact, of all official applications for membership to date, only that of Turkey has repeatedly been held over—for now at least.

The tension between deepening and widening the EU can be seen against a broader backdrop. The entire history of the European integration movement is one of incremental change. At times this has necessitated adopting the classic 'two steps back for every step forward' approach. What may seriously handicap the deepening aspect into the foreseeable future, however, is not just the sheer number but also the type of new entrant post-1995. With respect, the countries from the 'new' Europe have so much catching up to do *vis-à-vis* those in the West that the pressure on slowing down integration throughout the enlarged EU risks controlling the European agenda for years to come. As discussed below, an official acknowledgment of the associated imperative to thoroughly overhaul the institutional decision-making structure of an enlarged EU has proved an additional factor of distraction (to further integration) in its own right.

Amsterdam

After the SEA and Maastricht, the Treaty of Amsterdam is the third major treaty to amend the 1957 Treaty of Rome. Signed in 1997 and in force since 1999, the Treaty of Amsterdam represents a missed opportunity to modernise the institutional structure of the EU in line with a broadening membership base. However, consensus did exist to incorporate the text of the Maastricht Agreement on Social Policy into the main body of the Treaty.[45] Amsterdam therefore discontinues the British opt-out situation that existed previously.[46] At the same time, Amsterdam also addresses concerns about the growing marginalisation of European social policy. A senior German labour law academic put it, with the benefit of hindsight perhaps rather too enthusiastically, as follows:

> For the first time the Treaty of Amsterdam contains at least a fragment of a social constitution of the Community ... [It] is to be seen as a confirmation of the welfare state model as established in the various Member States after World War II. And at the same time it is to be interpreted as an alternative to the simplistic neo-liberal approach of mere deregulation. Fundamental social rights as a point of orientation are an important benchmark for the future way of the Community: they might overcome the present wave of Euroscepticism and turn it into an identification with the underlying values [of the Community]. Lastly, they give a clear signal to the States which will join the European Union in the near future.[47]

In one sense the significance of the Amsterdam Treaty for social policy developments in Europe remains largely symbolic. The addition of a 'new' paragraph to the Preamble of the TEU is significant. In doing so, the member states merely reiterate their commitment, already articulated in the Preamble of the 1986 SEA, to fundamental social rights as defined in both the 1961 European Social Charter[48] and the 1989 Community Charter.[49] By the same token, though, Amsterdam has given the European Court of Justice a firmer basis for monitoring and steering social policy initiatives at the national and supranational levels. As for the other Community institutions, the Maastricht Agreement on Social Policy has triggered the adoption of several Directives on, most notably, European works councils (1994),[50] parental leave (1996)[51] and part-time work (1997).[52]

The Directive on European works councils is significant because it seeks to overcome the limits of national rules on works councils operating within companies that span multiple countries. Only large companies are envisaged. The Directive refers to them as Community-scale undertakings, that is, companies with an overall workforce of minimum 1000 employees[53] and employing at least 150 employees in each of two member states. The purpose of the Directive is to give employees in these businesses improved access to information and consultation rights with regard to transnational issues that may affect them.[54] However, the real importance of the 1994 Directive lies not so much in the substance of any new employee rights it creates but in the procedure chosen by its drafters to bring about these rights. Specifically, the Directive enhances the position of the so-called social partners on the European scene. It does so through the expectation that the establishment of these works councils, or an alternative mechanism for informing and consulting employees, largely becomes the product of negotiations between the representatives of employees and employers. The prescriptive provisions of the Directive only kick in when parties fail to agree among themselves.

Similarly the Directive on parental leave brings the position of the European social partners to the fore. Their emerging prominence in the development of European labour laws is further highlighted by the consideration that the text of the 1996 Directive is based on the first-ever European collective bargaining agreement negotiated pursuant to the Maastricht Agreement on Social Policy. On 14 December 2005 the organisations of UNICE and CEEP,[55] on the side of business, and ETUC,[56] on the side of the workers, reached a framework agreement on parental leave. In effect, the 2006 Directive elevates that agreement to the level of a European law.

The Directive on part-time work was adopted post-Amsterdam. Like its counterpart on parental leave, though, it gives binding effect to a prior agreement concluded between UNICE, CEEP and ETUC.[57] That a consensus could be reached at all is truly remarkable given the dual purpose of the agreement. Employee concerns about the scope for employer abuse of this form of atypical work somehow had to be reconciled with a genuine business need for flexibility in the organisation of working time. A similar tension between the need of employers for greater flexibility and the desire of employees to reconcile work and family life, without unduly compromising employment conditions including job security, can be found in the framework agreements on fixed-term employment contracts (1999) and 'telework' (2002).[58] Whereas the former was subsequently given legal effect by way of a Directive,[59] the latter remains voluntary in nature at the instigation of UNICE.[60] Negotiations towards an agreement on the working conditions of temporary agency workers failed altogether. Instead the Commission formulated its own proposal for a Directive in March 2002.[61]

Involvement by the social partners in the social policy decision-making process of the Community is nothing new. Only, what started as a purely consultative voice has been turned into a quasi-right to initiate the legislative process under the Maastricht Agreement on Social Policy. This shift in emphasis undoubtedly has brought new life to the Community's social integration agenda. But it has also raised questions about who the social partners are and how representative they can really be.[62] The main player on the side of business, UNICE, is the largest confederation of employer organisations in Europe. It was formally created in 1958 by the national employers' federations of the then six member states of the EEC.[63] In 2007 the organisation changed its name to BusinessEurope. Its current membership comprises forty national confederations from thirty-four countries in the EU and beyond.[64] All major national employer organisations in the Community are members of this confederation of European business. They include, for Great Britain: the Confederation of British Industry (CBI); for Germany: the *Bundesverband der Deutschen Industrie* (BDI) as well as the *Bundesvereinigung der Deutschen Arbeitgeberverbände* (BDA); and for France: the *Mouvement des Entreprises de France* (MEDEF).

Since the 1980s UNICE's partner in the social dialogue that takes place within the Community is ETUC.[65] Created in 1973, ETUC has arguably become the most important confederation of trade unions in Europe.[66] It maintains close ties with the International Confederation of Free Trade Unions (ICFTU), in particular. Like its counterpart on the employers' side, ETUC's reach goes beyond the EU in that it represents some 60 million employees belonging to seventy-six national trade union organisations in thirty-four countries.[67]

Important members include, for the United Kingdom: the Trade Union Congress (TUC); for Germany: the *Deutscher Gewerkschaftsbund* (DGB); and for France: each of the four main employee organisations divided along ideological lines.

Nice

The inability of the member states at Amsterdam to address the increasingly pressing issue of institutional reform, required to facilitate decision-making in an enlarged Community, meant that another attempt at amending the founding Treaty and the TEU had to be made sooner rather than later. The primary purpose of the Treaty of Nice, signed in 2001 and in force since 2003, was to revise the rules governing the composition and functioning of the core law-making bodies of the Commission, the Parliament, the Council, and the Court. While by no means considered a resounding success,[68] a rationalisation of sorts, together with an expansion of the scope for majority voting, was achieved at Nice. As regards labour law or, more generally, the social policy domain, the lack of progress was particularly pertinent, though.[69] Certainly, initial hopes for the inclusion of fundamental rights in the main body of the Treaty (and directly enforceable by the European citizens) once again faded 'like the morning haze before a rising sun'.[70] Instead a separate 'Charter' listing 'Fundamental Rights' of the European Union was adopted in late 2000.

The 2000 Charter is reminiscent of the 1989 Community Charter on Fundamental Social Rights of Workers. However, the range of rights contained in the 2000 document is wider than those that appear in the 1989 Charter. They clearly go beyond the employment setting. Not all the rights listed, while no doubt important, are genuinely fundamental in nature. Blanpain refers to 'an inflation' of rights that have been included in the 2000 Charter,[71] for example, a right of access to (job) placement services,[72] access to 'services of general economic interest' in order to promote 'the social and territorial cohesion of the Union',[73] and even a citizen's right to 'good administration' by the various EU institutions.[74] To add insult to injury, the legal effect of the 2000 Charter was an issue consciously avoided by its drafters. The official statement released at the conclusion of the Nice deliberations leaves no room for doubt in this regard:[75]

> The European Council welcomes the joint proclamation, by the Council, the European Parliament and the Commission, of the Charter of Fundamental Rights, combining in a single text the civil, political, economic, social and societal rights hitherto laid down in a variety of international, European or national sources. The European Council would like to see the Charter disseminated as widely as possible amongst the Union's citizens. In accordance with the Cologne conclusions, *the question of the Charter's force will be considered later.*

In the circumstances, the legal status of the 2000 Charter could only be addressed after the 2004 enlargement round of the Union had taken its course. The Lisbon Treaty of 2007, negotiated in the aftermath of the ill-fated Constitutional Convention, once ratified by all twenty-seven member states,[76] will elevate the contents of the Charter to a legally enforceable document. The full text of the Charter is reproduced in Appendix 2.

It would be misleading to confine a discussion of the Community's contemporary social dimension to the above Charter. Two European labour laws of note that were adopted at the start of the twenty-first century are Council Directives 2001/86/EC[77] and 2002/14/EC.[78] Both deal with employee rights to information and consultation. The 2001 Directive does so against the backdrop of legislation on the so-called European Company Statute. Best known under its Latin name of *Societas Europaea* (SE), the European Company is a legal construct for the establishment of businesses within the territory of the Community in the form of a public limited-liability company. The Statute for a European Company provides a uniform legal framework within which companies can (re-)organise their activities at Community level. In effect, the SE permits companies to function on the basis of a single (European) legislative and management system instead of being subject to multiple legal regimes nationally.[79] By contrast, no single European model procedure for the information and consultation of employees in the SE proved politically acceptable. The 2001 Directive merely ensures that no loss or reduction of any pre-existing employee rights under national law occurs in the SE. Of course, where no national rules exist on the matter, as in the case of the United Kingdom and Ireland, employees inevitably miss out.

The 2002 Directive goes one step further in that it establishes a uniform framework for informing and consulting employees throughout the Community. The employee information and consultation rights extend to the employer's development of business activities and economic situation, the structure and development of employment, and any decisions with the potential to substantially affect the organisation of work.[80] The requirements under the Directive are minima only and the practical implications for national law can therefore be expected to be limited. More affected, of course, are the United Kingdom and Ireland (together with the new member states from Central and Eastern Europe). Ironically, one of the founding member states with otherwise impeccable credentials as regards its social welfare model recently found itself in a legal wrangle for non-compliance with the 2002 Directive.[81]Under Belgian law, the main vehicle for informing and consulting employees is the works council. On the face of it, the 1948 Act on the Organisation of Business Activities requires the establishment of works councils in businesses employing fifty employees or more. In reality, the statutory requirement is only enforced in companies with a minimum workforce of 100 employees. Under the 2002 Directive a business needs to employ fewer than twenty employees in any one member state in order to qualify for an unconditional exemption.[82]

Constitutional Convention

The reforms introduced by the Treaty of Nice allowed for a reunification of sorts between East and West in Europe, typified by the addition (in the first instance) of ten member states.[83] This in turn added urgency to the need for a qualitative reappraisal of the Community. What should an enlarged EU look like? In particular, which ought to be the core principles upon which that Union is (being) built? How best to delineate the respective powers and responsibilities of the Union and its constituent member states in light of the subsidiarity concept? Further, how best to simplify the text of the various Treaties for the sake of providing greater clarity in contents? To address these questions a formal Convention on the Future of the European Union was convened in December 2001.[84]

The *modus operandi* of the Convention reflected a desire to involve the European citizen in an attempt to remedy a growing feeling of alienation from the European project. In a first phase, referred to as the listening phase, the various members of the Convention would inform themselves as to the various options open to the EU. Apart from hearings and written submissions, a special website was created to maximise the opportunity for input by the general public. The number of monthly visits to the site reportedly averaged 47 000, with a peak of some 100 000 hits towards the end of the Convention in June 2004.[85] Attempts at getting young people involved proved a mixed success, though. In particular, the organisation of a special 'Youth Convention' produced proposals deemed singularly unimaginative by the chair of the Convention proper, the former French president Giscard d'Estaing.[86]

The listening phase ran from February until July 2002. This was followed by an analysis phase and culminated in an outline for a constitutional treaty in October of that same year. The actual drafting of the treaty itself only started in early 2003. During this third phase various texts were prepared and circulated to members of the Convention.[87] All along there was an opportunity for the submission of amendments. The part of the treaty on the institutions of the Union alone triggered more than 650 suggestions for change![88]

Writing finished in June 2003 at which stage the Convention was officially brought to a close. Surprisingly, perhaps, the text of the proposed Constitution for Europe was generally well received by the various national governments.[89] Milton and Keller-Noëllet comment how much of the success of the Convention concerned the part that focused on the fundamentals.[90] They observe that:

> Fundamentals are principally about clarifying the relationship between the Union and the Member States, and the structure of the Union itself. They include the decision to reorganise completely the existing treaties, to institute a single 'Union' in place of, rather than alongside, the existing European Community, to define in simple terms the powers of the Union, to simplify its instruments and procedures, to improve the efficiency and legitimacy of its

> decision-making, and last but not least, to give the end product the title of 'Constitution'.[91]

Of course, the not-so-happy end to the story is all too familiar. Ratification of the treaty containing the text of the draft Constitution ran into trouble as soon as some member states decided to make ratification dependent on popular approval through a national referendum. Once French and Dutch voters registered a negative vote, the European Council considered that a 'period of reflection' was called for.[92] In July 2005 it was decided to suspend the ratification procedure. The draft constitutional treaty has since been replaced by the Treaty of Lisbon.

Lisbon

The Treaty of Lisbon was adopted on 18 October 2007. It is some 300 pages in length. Unlike the draft constitutional treaty, the Lisbon Treaty amends the EU (Maastricht) and EC (Rome) treaties without replacing them with a single text. As a result, Lisbon adds to the creeping—and, by now, bewildering—legal complexity of the post-SEA era. The EC treaty itself has been renamed the Treaty on the Functioning of the European Union. In common with earlier amendments to the original Treaty of Rome, several Protocols and Declarations have been attached to the Lisbon Treaty.

The official website of the EU presents the Treaty of Lisbon as a vehicle for 'taking Europe into the 21st century'.[93] Specifically, Lisbon is said to allow for a Europe that is more democratic and transparent. To this end, the role of the European Parliament in the law-making process has been strengthened by increasing the number of policy areas where the directly elected Parliament has to approve EU legislation together with the Council of (national) Ministers.[94] Further, the involvement by the various national parliaments in adopting EU laws is acknowledged for the first time. However, their role has been fashioned in purely negative terms: to monitor the legislative activities of the Union so as to ensure that it only acts where results can be better attained at EU level.[95] More dubious even, in terms of its effectiveness, is the provision for a new 'European citizens' initiative': it is meant to allow one million citizens from the member states to call on the Commission to come up with new proposals for legislation without, however, expanding the reach of Europe in the process.[96] Intriguingly, a further innovative feature of Lisbon is its express confirmation of the possibility that some member states may wish to withdraw from the Union at some stage in the future.

In addition to promoting internal democracy and transparency, Lisbon aims at making Europe more efficient. To this effect, qualified majority voting in the Council has been extended. From 2014 (!) onwards, the calculation of this qualified majority will be based on a double majority of member states and people.[97] Also from 2014 onwards, the size of the Commission will be reduced. To hold onto one Commissioner per country was considered unwieldy in an enlarged Union. Instead, the number of Commissioners is now being limited to two-thirds of the member states on a rotating basis. The maximum size of the European Parliament has similarly been contained at 751 members![98]

The direct impact of the Lisbon Treaty for social policy in general and labour law in particular, remains limited. However, at long last the Charter of Fundamental Rights has been incorporated into the main body of the EC Treaty, thus removing any doubts as to its legal status once and for all. It will be recalled that the Charter sets out in a single text the whole range of civil, political, economic and social rights enjoyed by European citizens. The Charter, once Lisbon has been ratified, formally binds the various EU institutions and the Member States when implementing Union law, while judicial supervision is entrusted to the European Court of Justice. However, the practical significance of the Charter must not be overstated. It largely articulates the EU's common (inherent) values. As such, it does not create any new powers for the Union. Even so, a Protocol annexed to the Lisbon Treaty once again introduces specific measures for the United Kingdom (and, on this occasion, Poland). The Protocol establishes exceptions with regard to the jurisdiction of the European Court of Justice and the protection of the rights recognised by the Charter in both countries.

The Treaty of Lisbon is scheduled to enter into force once it has been ratified by all (twenty-seven) member states. The self-imposed deadline for ratification is 31 December 2008. The ratification procedure itself is a matter for the national legislature. A referendum is only required under Irish law. That referendum was lost on 12 June 2008 by 53 to 47 per cent. At a European Council meeting, held in Brussels on 15 and 16 October 2008, Irish Prime Minister Brian Cowen confirmed his government's commitment to an 'acceptable' resolution of the issue[99] and the Council agreed to review the matter in December of that year.[100]

Social Europe: Quo Vadis?

By the mid-1990s it had become clear that to attach equal importance to social and economic policy developments in the EU can no longer be taken for granted.[101] The focus has shifted, with an increased emphasis placed on the cost of 'a social Europe' for business and the need for European industry to be competitive in a global market. Effectively, what happened is that the initial national debate about labour-market flexibility and deregulation in the various member states has since reached the supranational level as well. In the result, there has been a gradual, but persistent, move away from job security towards job creation, and from employment regulation towards employment promotion.

It is hard to regulate for deregulation. While the image of a growing social inertia at the turn of the century may be difficult to dispel, fundamental rights seem to have become the buzz word of the new millennium in the EU. Arguably, the Charter of Fundamental Rights serves as a stop-gap measure only and, in the long run, symbolic action of this nature may not suffice. Social Europe, if it is to be worthy of this label, needs to stand for more than merely the proclamation, no matter how solemn, of a minimum floor of 'inalienable' rights. Significant in this respect is the release, in late 2006, of a Green Paper entitled *Modernising Labour Law to Meet the Challenges of the 21st Century* by the European Commission.[102] The Green Paper asks some basic questions about the rebalancing of social equity and economic efficiency concerns. In some respects, the document allows us to draw parallels with the 'Forward with Fairness' approach of the Rudd government,[103] including its call for public input into the legislative encapsulation of ten minimum national employment standards for Australian workers. Chapter 7 looks in more detail at this issue.

Notes

1 Valticos and von Potobsky, *International Labour Law*, p. 17.
2 The 'question' of agricultural work was one of the first challenges to the competence of the ILO during the early years of its existence: ibid., p. 45. Interestingly, the country to raise the objection was France.
3 Betten, *International Labour Law*, p. 2.
4 Treaty of Versailles, Part XIII.
5 Emphasis added. The text of the Preamble is reproduced in Blanpain, *Codex (International Labour Law)*, 2007 update, p. 20. See also Landau, *The Influence of ILO Standards on Australian Labour Law & Practices*, p. 3.
6 Betten, *International Labour Law*, p. 7.
7 Legal developments at the level of the EU are discussed more fully later in this chapter.
8 For an overview of the main sources of international labour law, including various ILO publications, see Vranken, Chapter 2, 'Documentation', pp. 25–8.
9 Swepston, Chapter 7, 'International Labour Law', p. 143.
10 For a discussion of Australia's contemporary (common and labour) laws against the backdrop of international labour law standards as regards the right to strike, see Creighton and Stewart, *Labour Law*, p. 533ff.
11 ibid., p. 83. A fairly recent exception is the Industrial Relations Reform Act 1993 (Cth) adopted during the Keating years in an attempt to promote enterprise bargaining.
12 Australian Conciliation and Arbitration Commission (Full Bench) (1984) 294 CAR 175; 8 IR 35.
13 Workplace Relations Amendment (Work Choices) Act 2006 (Cth).
14 The French *Code civil* was adopted in 1804; the German *BGB* dates from 1896.
15 George, *Politics and Policy in the European Community*, p. 38.
16 Its main institutions are a Human Rights Commission and the Human Rights Court. The latter, unlike its EU counterpart (the European Court of Justice), is based in Strasbourg rather than Luxembourg.
17 Title III of Part Three (Policy of the Community).
18 Chapter 2 of Title III (Article 123 EEC).
19 The other pillar is the competition policy of the Community.
20 All took the form of Directives instead of Regulations. While both types of instruments are legally binding, Directives leave to the national authorities a certain choice as to the method of their implementation: Article 249 EC (189 EEC).
21 Blanquet, *L'Europe: vers l'harmonisation des législations sociales*, p. 234.
22 The Commission is the EC's executive body. In addition, it formulates proposals for new legislation and investigates complaints about compliance with existing laws.
23 Article 13 SEA. The 1957 Treaty had envisaged the progressive establishment of the common market over a period of twelve years, divided into three stages of four years each: Article 8 EEC.

24 Membership grew from six to nine following the admission of the United Kingdom, Ireland and Denmark in 1973. By 1986 the size of the Community had grown to twelve countries (Greece joined in 1981; Spain and Portugal followed suit in 1986). Sweden, Finland and Austria became members in 1995. However, the accession of an additional ten (ex-communist) countries on 1 May 2004, followed by Bulgaria and Romania in 2007, has taken the notion of diversity and the challenges this poses to an entirely new level.

25 Article 21 SEA.

26 Directive 89/391/EEC of 12 June 1989 on the Introduction of Measures to Encourage Improvements in the Health and Safety of Workers at Work, *Official Journal* L 183/1, 29 June 1989.

27 Commission of the European Communities, *Charter of the Fundamental Social Rights of Workers*. For a detailed analysis, see Bercusson, 'The European Community's Charter of Fundamental Social Rights', p. 624.

28 Strictly speaking, the Charter applies to employed and self-employed persons alike. Use of the term 'workers' in the title of the Charter is therefore deliberate.

29 Hepple, 'The Implementation of the Community Charter of Fundamental Social Rights', p. 644.

30 Blanpain, tongue in cheek perhaps, refers to these headings as 'the twelve commandments': *European Labour Law*, p. 238.

31 Clause 13 of the Community Charter 1989.

32 Particularly revealing about the relationship between Britain and the Community is Thatcher's so-called Bruges speech, delivered at the prestigious College of Europe in September 1988. See the discussion in Campbell, *Margaret Thatcher. Volume Two: The Iron Lady*, p. 603ff.

33 Clause 27 of the Charter.

34 COM (89) 568 (final).

35 Directive 91/553/EEC, *Official Journal* L 288/32, 18 October 1991.

36 Hepple, 'European Labour Law: The European Community', pp. 154–5.

37 ibid., p. 155; compare and contrast the assessment by Barnard, 'A Social Policy for Europe: Politicians 1:0 Lawyers', p. 15, and Weiss, 'The Significance of Maastricht for European Community Social Policy', p. 3. See also Fitzpatrick, 'Community Social Law after Maastricht', p. 199.

38 In free translation: 'the Community patrimony'. While suitably vague, the concept goes beyond the body (*corpus*) of Community law in a strict sense: Toth, *The Oxford Encyclopaedia of European Community Law. Volume I: Institutional Law*, pp. 9–10.

39 An official Protocol on the application of the subsidiarity principle, attached to the 1997 Treaty of Amsterdam, did not really add clarity.

40 *Procureur du Roi v Benoît and Gustave Dassonville*, Case 8/74, (1974) ECR 837; (1974) 2 CMLR 436.

41 *Rewe-Zentral AG v Bundesmonopolverwaltung für Branntwein*, Case 120/78, (1979) ECR 649; (1979) 3 CMLR 494.

42 Joint cases C-1/90 and C-176/90, (1994) 1 CMLR 887.

43 'Temporary' is any national measure adopted in the absence of a Community law on the matter.

44 Cass, 'The Word that Saves Maastricht? The Principle of Subsidiarity and the Division of Powers within the European Community', p. 1107.

45 The Amsterdam Treaty does so by adding a new Chapter 4 on Social Policy in Section II of the Treaty.

46 The Treaty of Amsterdam was signed on 2 October 1997. A few months earlier, on 1 May, Tony Blair had secured an election victory. It brought to an end the long reign of a Conservative government in the United Kingdom.

47 Weiss, 'The Future Role of the European Union in Social Policy', p. 493.

48 In its original version, the European Social Charter contained nineteen fundamental social rights. A 1996 revision extends the list to thirty-one. Of particular note is that this Council of Europe document henceforth comprises a 'right to dignity at work'.

49 For a particularly critical assessment, see Hepple, 'Towards a European Social Constitution', p. 291.

50 Directive 94/45/EC of 22 September 1994, *Official Journal* L 254/64, 30 September 1994.

51 Directive 96/34/EC of 3 June 1996, *Official Journal* L 145/4, 19 June 1996.

52 Directive 97/81/EC of 15 December 1997, *Official Journal* L 14/9, 20 January 1998.

53 Technically, the territorial scope of the Directive includes the so-called European Economic Area (EEA). Iceland, Liechtenstein and Norway thus come within the scope of the Directive.

54 For a more detailed analysis, see Engels and Salas, 'Transnational Information and Consultation: The European Works Council Directive', p. 525. See also Blanpain, *European Labour Law*, pp. 721–60. For a discussion in a broader context of worker participation, see Blanpain and Windey, *European Works Councils. Information and Consultation of Employees in Multinational Enterprises in Europe.* For a critical review of the Directive, see Rood, 'Some Thoughts on European Works Councils', p. 399.

55 UNICE stands for Union of Industrial and Employers Confederation of Europe. CEEP is French; in full, it reads *Centre Européen des Entreprises Publiques.* As its name suggests, the latter operates in the public sector. Agriculture also continues to be organised separately in the Community.

56 European Trade Union Confederation.

57 The agreement was formally concluded on 6 June 1997.

58 The agreement defines 'telework' as work that involves the use of information technology and that is carried out away from the employer's premises.

59 Directive 99/70/EC of 28 June 1999, *Official Journal*, L 175/43, 10 July 1999.

60 Blanpain, *European Labour Law*, p. 428.

61 COM/2002/0149 final, as amended by COM (2002) 701 final; ibid., p. 418.

62 Betten, 'The Role of Social Partners in the Community's Social Policy

Law-Making: Participatory Democracy or Furthering the Interests of Small Elites', pp. 252–60.

63 France, 'International Employers' Organisations', p. 70.
64 See the organisation's new website at www.businesseurope.eu
65 France, 'International Employers' Organisations', p. 71.
66 Windmuller and Pursey, 'The International Trade Union Movement', p. 86.
67 Blanpain, *European Labour Law,*, p. 138.
68 Mathijsen, *A Guide to European Union Law*, p. 22.
69 Blanpain labels the Treaty of Nice as 'socially, not so nice': *European Labour Law*, p. 257.
70 ibid.
71 ibid., p. 260. See also Betten, 'The EU Charter on Fundamental Rights: A Trojan Horse or a Mouse?' p. 151.
72 Charter of Fundamental Rights of the European Union, Article 29.
73 Charter of Fundamental Rights of the European Union, Article 36.
74 Charter of Fundamental Rights of the European Union, Article 41.
75 Emphasis added. See Conclusions of the Presidency, European Council, Nice, 7–10 December 2000, [2] at www.europarl.europa.eu/summits/nice1-en.htm
76 This is by no means a foregone conclusion. A national referendum in Ireland was lost in June 2008.
77 *Official Journal* L 294/22, 10 November 2001.
78 *Official Journal* L 80/29, 23 March 2002.
79 The legal basis of the Statute on the European Company is Regulation 2157/2001, *Official Journal* L 294/1, as modified in 2004: *Official Journal* L 168/1.
80 Blanpain, *European Labour Law*, pp. 763–4.
81 *Commission of the European Communities v Kingdom of Belgium*, Case C-320/06, *Official Journal* C 96/18, 28 April 2007.
82 Some flexibility exists. The member states can elect to apply the requirements of the Directive either to 'undertakings' employing a minimum of fifty employees or to 'establishments' with a minimum workforce of twenty.
83 Abolition of internal border controls on the free movement of people had to wait until the end of 2007. Access to the so-called Schengen area only became a reality for nine out of ten new member states from Central and Eastern Europe, including Malta but not Cyprus, on 21 December 2007. Border controls at airports were scheduled to be removed from 30 March 2008 onwards. Note that Britain and Ireland are not members of the 1985 Schengen agreement.
84 A detailed discussion from an insider's perspective can be found in Dehaene, *De Europese uitdaging: van uitbreiding tot integratie* (The European Challenge: from Expansion to Integration).
85 ibid., p. 72.
86 'Eurocrats in short trousers' is the expression used by Milton and Keller-Noëllet, with Bartol-Saurel, *The European Constitution: Its Origins, Negotiation and Meaning*, p. 43.

87 Unlike a purely intergovernmental conference, the Convention did not solely comprise representatives of the various national governments. There were also representatives of the national parliaments, the European Parliament and the Commission. The participation of the latter two groups especially gave the proceedings a distinctly European flavour: Dehaene, *De Europese uitdaging*, p. 46. The ten acceding countries and the three candidate countries (Bulgaria, Romania and even Turkey) were also represented. Finally, as every Convention member was entitled to a substitute, and there were a number of observers, the total number of participants exceeded 200: Milton and Keller-Noëllet, *The European Constitution*, p. 32.

88 Milton and Keller-Noëllet, *The European Constitution*, p. 41.

89 The text of the draft Treaty can be found at *Official Journal*, 16 December 2004 C 310/1.

90 Unfortunately, the same could not be said of the detailed provisions concerning the Union's substantive policies.

91 Milton and Keller-Noëllet, *The European Constitution*, pp. 47–8.

92 Declaration by the Heads of State or Government of the Member States of the Union on the Ratification of the Treaty establishing a Constitution for Europe (European Council, 16–17 June 2005): Mathijsen, *A Guide to European Law*, p. 25.

93 http://europa.eu/lisbon (accessed 14 December 2007).

94 This is known as the co-decision procedure.

95 In other words, the task of the national parliaments is to scrutinise the activities of the EU from a subsidiarity angle.

96 The scope for a citizens' initiative has been limited to Union action required to implement the Treaty of Lisbon.

97 Decisions must be taken by 55 per cent of the member states representing at least 65 per cent of the Union's population.

98 The number of members from each member state varies from six to ninety-six, depending on, in essence, population size.

99 'Government <committed> to finding treaty resolution—Cowen', *Irishtimes.com*, 17 October 2008.

100 European Council Conclusions, Brussels, 16 October 2008, text available at http://europa.eu

101 Neal, 'Do We Need a Social Policy for Europe?', p. 295.

102 Commission of the European Communities, *Modernising Labour Law to Meet the Challenges of the 21st Century*.

103 *Forward with Fairness* was the title of Labour's pre-election platform for workplace reform (April 2007). It is also the title of its subsequent policy implementation plan released in August 2007.

Chapter 7
From Collectivism to Individualism (and Back?)

Preliminary Observations

In the various national legal systems on the European Continent, the individual and collective dimensions of labour law have always co-existed without much internal tension. Individual labour law, typically in the form of statutory employment rights, is available to act as a social buffer whenever economic fluctuations put pressure on the 'output' of collective bargaining. Even after calls for economic flexibility became more persistent, particularly from the 1980s onwards, largely against a backdrop of globalisation and the associated need—perceived or otherwise—for business to be(come) internationally competitive, the sheer expanse of legislative individual employment rights has continued to form a formidable barrier to wholesale change. At no stage has the social welfare model been seriously questioned in contemporary Europe. The current focus on 'flexicurity' at the level of the EU does not represent a fundamental challenge either in this regard. On the contrary, flexicurity may be seen as an attempt at preserving the core aspects of the (continental) European system in place. Chapter 8 will be devoted to a fuller discussion.

At the supranational level of the EU, no real balance between individual and collective labour law ever existed. The 'golden era' of social regulation that typified the 1970s, through its focus on acquired employee rights, displayed a distinct individualistic flavour. Similarly, the various charters of fundamental rights that have since been promulgated adopt an individual (employee) focus. Acceptance of a jurisdiction for the Union to regulate in matters of collective labour law has proved problematic from the outset. It is a perception that is reinforced further by the continued (and, for now, successful) resistance by some member states to the elevation of certain core aspects of collective labour law—pay determination and industrial action, in particular—to the European social policy domain proper.

The story in Australia and New Zealand is once again strikingly different. Collectivist at heart, drastic swings of the labour law pendulum have occurred, in the last two decades or so, on both sides of the Tasman. New Zealand undoubtedly stands out as the most prominent case in point. In the Commonwealth of Australia, things have tended to be a bit more muddled due to, in no small part, Australia's federal make-up, together with inherent (constitutional) limitations to the federal labour power. Even so, both nations have unequivocally moved away from the core pillar upon which their systems of labour law were once built, that is, the compulsory conciliation and arbitration of industrial—collective—disputes in the 'public interest'. In their place has come a system of labour law that seeks to strike a better balance between the individual and collective components of labour law.

From Decentralisation to Deregulation in Europe

The economic recession of the 1970s had social repercussions that initially remained confined to the domain of collective bargaining. In continental Europe these effects were felt both as regards the outcome and the level of the bargaining. The practice of multi-level bargaining, in particular, whereby negotiation for selective minimum conditions of employment applicable throughout the entire private sector of the economy was topped up by negotiations at the level of individual sectors of industry and/or regions, often expanded upon in further bargaining at the actual place of work, came under severe pressure. Business increasingly objected to the cost and complexity associated with multiple layers of social regulation. In principle, a reduction in the number of bargaining levels could have been achieved through the removal of either the lower or higher levels at which these periodic negotiations for terms and conditions of employment were to occur in the future. Attempts by organised labour to maintain maximum solidarity through its preference for a centralised approach to collective bargaining proved futile, though. Over time the inevitable side-effect of a decentralised approach to bargaining was that employees with identical qualifications and working side by side in the same sector of industry risked being employed under different conditions, depending on which company happened to employ them.[1]

Under a 'layered' approach to collective bargaining, the bottom layer provides a minimum platform of employment conditions for the higher layers to build upon. Decentralised bargaining, especially when combined with a reduction in the number of bargaining levels, therefore opens up opportunities for increased business flexibility. In Europe, however, this flexibility is not without its limits, as any statutory minima in place typically cannot be contracted out. From the mid-1980s onwards, the trend towards decentralised bargaining was strengthened by calls for legislative deregulation. Deemed particularly problematic were inflexible legal rules regarding available types of work organisation other than permanent full-time employment, working time (whether averaged out over a weekly, trimester or annual period), and job security of 'permanent' employees.

The concept of deregulation is itself not without intrigue. Its origin can be traced to the United States, where deregulation formed a core principle underlying the economic policy of the Reagan administration. Conceptually, social deregulation stands for various public initiatives to reform substantially, or even abolish, major parts of basic labour legislation that mould the employment relationship. It can be considered 'negative' regulation, in that it reflects a tendency either not to regulate, to regulate less, or to reshape existing social laws. The ultimate goal is to promote economic flexibility by removing social 'rigidities' so as to encourage investment and, ultimately, employment. As such, deregulation on the Continent is not fundamentally different from the seemingly more 'positive', that is, proactive approach to labour regulation adopted in the United Kingdom under Margaret Thatcher.[2]

The current state of play regarding labour law reform on the Continent remains very much a work in progress. A recent listing of eighteen EU member states, ranked according to the 'stringency' of their employment protection legislation, confirms the ongoing discrepancy in flexibility between the legal regimes of the United Kingdom and Ireland, on the one hand, and their continental European counterparts.[3] As regards the latter countries, the main inroads to date concern a more flexible approach by the legislature to the calculation of working time, together with easier access for employers to temporary work arrangements. Reform of the statutory dismissal protection for employees in an open-ended employment relationship, that is, those employed under so-called indefinite contracts of employment, has proven significantly more difficult. The associated risk of developing a two-tier labour market in the process is both real and growing. This risk is openly acknowledged in the European Commission's 2006 discussion paper[4] on 'modernising' labour law for purposes of the twenty-first century. Chapter 8 examines that document in more detail. The focus in this chapter is upon developments in Australia and New Zealand.

Laboratories of Social Change in Australia and New Zealand

Australia and New Zealand form particularly rewarding objects of comparative study because of their demonstrated willingness to repeatedly engage in social experimentation. In the late nineteenth century, both countries did so by rejecting the British hands-off approach to the regulation of industrial relations in preference for a truly unique system of compulsory conciliation and arbitration. Some hundred years later, both countries have once again embarked upon a program of reform that is radical by international standards. The nature and philosophy of each wave of reform is fundamentally different, though. At first the focus was squarely on building a regulatory model for industrial dispute resolution, typified by active state involvement, not just in the establishment of the regulatory framework itself but also in the operation thereof. This amounted to a form of (undoubtedly benign) state paternalism. By comparison, the tone of the contemporary reform agenda is much more deconstructionist, with an emphasis on (individual and not just collective) freedom of choice against the backdrop of a minimum floor of rights. It reflects a controlled *laissez-faire* approach of sorts to industrial regulation.

The Traditional Model: Compulsory Conciliation and Arbitration

Compulsory conciliation and arbitration stood in direct contrast to the UK model of 'free' collective bargaining. The immediate trigger for its introduction in Australia and New Zealand was the large-scale industrial unrest on both sides of the Tasman that occurred during the 1890s. But, as indicated earlier,[5] a wider explanation for the extensive intervention by the state in the working lives of people may have to be found in the more general reliance on government assistance throughout the new colonies, especially in relation to basic infrastructure requirements (roads, telecommunications, hospitals, schools, and so on).

Unlike the situation in the United States, where the National Labor Relations Act effectively does away with the common law for those employees who come within the scope of the Wagner Act, Australia and New Zealand opted for a dual system of legal regulation from the outset. While the conciliation and arbitration system was also designed to operate at the collective level of labour law, the main participants were not an individual employer and the collective representative of his or her workforce, but rather the collective representatives of both business and labour. Further, this legislative model functioned against the backdrop of the—originally, exclusively English—common law at the individual employment level. The collectivist, statutory scheme sought to build upon the individualist features of the common law without meaning to replace it. The practical ramifications of such an approach have come to the fore in recent times, in that occasionally it has pitched a socially conservative legislature or government against a socially proactive judiciary. In New Zealand, for example, access to redundancy compensation has been linked to the judicial recognition of a common law implied duty for employers to treat their employees fairly.[6] In Australia as well, it was suggested at one stage that the common law similarly might have to come to the rescue of many employees whose employment relationship was terminated following the removal of statutory unfair dismissal protection for employees in small and medium-sized companies pursuant to 2005 amendments—the so-called Work Choices legislation—of the Workplace Relations Act 1996.[7]

The traditional conciliation and arbitration model is best described as centralist, compulsory and adversarial, as well as corporatist in nature. The model was centralist because of its administration by a single (independent) government body, the Arbitration Court. While no equivalent to the Arbitration Court exists in New Zealand today, its contemporary successor in Australia is the Australian Industrial Relations Commission. During the final years of the Howard administration responsibility for setting federal minimum wages was transferred from the Commission to a newly established Australian Fair Pay Commission pursuant to the Workplace Relations Amendment (Work Choices) Act 2005. The Rudd government has foreshadowed that the functions of both Commissions are to be returned to a single body—Fair Work Australia[8]—by 2010.

Less clear at this early stage are the flow-on effects, if any, of the changes proposed by the new Labor government as regards other traditional features of the conciliation and arbitration model. Briefly, the traditional model was compulsory as regards both the submission of industrial disputes and their resolution. It was adversarial in that its application required the existence of a dispute as a trigger. While the creation of a formal dispute might have sufficed in practice, the model nonetheless expected each party to argue its position in a quasi–court room setting. This in turn encouraged the parties to adopt extreme positions in order to maximise their chances of a favourable outcome. Because of the litigious nature of the conciliation and arbitration proceedings, it seemed inappropriate to refer to the union and management parties as social partners, as they continue to be known in continental Europe. Finally, the model was corporatist in that, again unlike the situation that generally prevails in Europe, the organisational structure of Australian and New Zealand unions displayed features of a pronounced craft or occupational tradition. As both countries lacked a tradition of industrial unionism, employers were regularly confronted with a multitude of unions, and this in turn necessitated the negotiation of multiple industrial documents in order to cover the employment conditions for all members of their workforce. Typically, the Keating reforms of the early 1990s notwithstanding, these awards and collective agreements tended to be entered into at an above-company, that is, regional or national, level.

By the late twentieth century the compulsory conciliation and arbitration model had resulted in a system that was top-heavy, with literally thousands of awards and agreements regulating employment conditions, often in minute detail. From an employer perspective, the system had become too rigid to be able to accommodate the specific needs of individual businesses. From an employee perspective, the model was rather condescending if not outright patronising in that access to legal remedies, in instances of unfair dismissal for example, tended to be union-controlled. And, from the perspective of the general public, the model had become distinctly out of tune with the broader government pursuit of deregulating the financial and economic markets in the wake of a brave new world of globalisation.

The Shape of Change

New Zealand

In New Zealand the shape of the industrial relations reforms can be traced via three major pieces of legislation adopted over a relatively short period of not quite fifteen years. Interestingly, each statute was adopted in the aftermath of a change in the government of the day. Until fairly recently, New Zealand effectively had a two-party first-past-the-post type of political system.[9] This allowed for radical swings of the pendulum in terms of government philosophy. Even so, a common theme in all labour legislation adopted since the mid-1980s can be detected. It is a theme New Zealand also shares with Australia and one best described in terms of a 'do-it-yourself' approach to industrial disputation and labour matters in general. Specifically, all of the legislation discussed below not only places great emphasis on decentralisation, it does so together with an increased focus on self-regulation and, hence, self-reliance by the various labour law parties including, most notably, the individual employee. Only the 2005 Work Choices legislation in Australia would go further since that particular statute reflected a legislative bias that was openly, and unashamedly, pro-business and pro–individual employer.

From Labour Relations Act 1987 (NZ) ...

In 1984 a Labour government under the leadership of David Lange gained office. The Lange government released a broad-based discussion paper, a green paper, on reforming the regulatory framework of industrial relations in New Zealand.[10] Public comment was sought on a range of questions that probed the strengths and weaknesses of the conciliation and arbitration system as it had evolved over the years. Some of these questions specifically addressed the role of trade unions, including their relationship with employers as well as employees. Other questions focused on the role of the state in industrial relations more generally, including the function of specialist bodies such as the Arbitration Court, when dealing with industrial disputation. This back-to-basics approach is particularly evident in the following extract from the green paper:[11]

> 6. The original objectives of the system were to minimise the incidence of strike action and to develop a system for the negotiation of wages and working conditions which impacts widely and in effect provides minimum standards for the majority of the workforce. In connection with these objectives Government regulation has focussed on the following strategies:
>   (a) to avoid disputes arising from competition between unions for members (inter-union disputes);
>   (b) to avoid disputes arising from an employer's refusal to recognise a union's right to negotiate;
>   (c) to provide employers and unions with assistance in the resolution of disputes by prescribing appropriate procedures;
>   (d) to have questions of compliance with awards dealt with by way of a legal process rather than through direct action;
>   (e) to promote the formation of independent trade unions, and the organising of workers into these unions;
>   (f) to provide for the negotiation of awards, which extend common wages and conditions of employment across an industry, for workers doing a particular job.
>
> 7. The approach taken in the remainder of the paper is to pose a series of questions about the appropriate form of Government regulation. To a large extent, the

> answers to the specific questions will reflect a wider view on wage fixing and related matters. The following two questions are intended to elicit these views.
>
> Question 1. Are the policy objectives enunciated in paragraph 6 the right ones, and have they been realised in practice?
>
> Question 2. What effect have these objectives and strategies had on the outcome of union/employer negotiations, i.e. does the balance of advantage favour unions, employers, or is it about equal?

The green paper triggered some 200 submissions, a very respectable number in view of the small size of New Zealand's overall population, and emanating from interest groups and individuals alike.[12] These provided the basis for the release of a policy document or white paper, in which the government's labour law philosophy was revealed more openly.[13] Specifically, the government concluded from the various submissions it had received that much of what went wrong with the incumbent system could be attributed to excessive government intervention in industrial relations. In light of this diagnosis, the remedy had an air of inevitability to it: reduce government interference; give the (employer and employee) parties greater opportunity to sort things out for themselves.

Key terms in the white paper were 'self-regulation' and 'self-reliance'. Two qualifications are called for, though. First, the role of unions themselves was not (as yet) questioned. In other words, the focus of the white paper was on collective self-regulation and on collective self-reliance. Second, the focus (again, for the time being) was on a reduced role for the state, not a total withdrawal. It explains why the compulsory nature of conciliation and arbitration was removed but not the conciliation and arbitration model itself. In fact, the new legislation adopted to implement the industrial relations reforms replaced the single Arbitration Court with an Arbitration Commission and a Labour Court. The former had jurisdiction to conciliate and, with both parties' consent, to arbitrate interest disputes. The latter was given jurisdiction to determine rights disputes and personal grievances. Intriguingly, as discussed in Chapter 5, under the Labour Relations Act 1987 individual employee access to the new Labour Court was made available to union members only.[14]

Via Employment Contracts Act 1991 (NZ) ...

The Labour Party lost the national general elections held in 1990. The incoming, conservative (National) government proclaimed to continue the 'good work' of the previous administration. It decided to do this by shifting the focus in industrial relations away from collective self-regulation towards individual self-reliance. Henceforth, the individual employment contract would constitute the core component of the new labour law regime. The Employment Contracts Act 1991 deliberately avoids any open use of the term 'union'. Collective bargaining, while not strictly prohibited, becomes deliberately geared towards individual companies and multi-employer bargaining requires the consent of each employer.[15] The Act abolishes the Arbitration Commission and replaces the Labour Court with an Employment Court. As indicated by this deliberate change in name, the Act directs the focus of the new Court to the enforcement of individual employment rights. Significantly, and this feature survived the 1991 legislation, access to the Employment Court is opened up to all employees regardless of union membership. Further, individual terms and conditions of employment are not allowed to be 'inconsistent' with the terms and conditions in any applicable collective employment contract.[16]

Unlike its predecessor, the 1991 legislation was not the product of extensive public consultation prior to its introduction, although the government's intentions had been made clear during the election campaign. In a knee-jerk reaction, no doubt, a re-elected Labour (coalition) government in 2000 repealed the Employment Contracts Act and replaced it with the Employment Relations Act in force today.

To Employment Relations Act 2000 (NZ)

A major objective of the Employment Relations Act 2000 is the promotion of collective bargaining which, according to observers, had 'collapsed dramatically' under the previous legislation.[17] However, the Employment Relations Act 2000 also seeks to steer a middle course between the 1991 legislation and the old award system. Specifically, the Act is said to strive for a proper balance between economic and social policy considerations.[18] Similarly the Act can be seen as an attempt at adjusting the balance between the individual and collective dimensions of labour law. The essence of the shift in policy perspective then is perhaps best captured by the following extract from the Explanatory Note that accompanied the Employment Relations Bill:[19]

> This Bill implements Government policy to repeal the Employment Contracts Act 1991 and introduces a better framework for the conduct of employment relations. That framework is based on the understanding that *employment is a human relationship* involving issues of mutual trust, confidence and fair dealing, and is *not simply a contractual, economic exchange.* This basis requires *specific recognition* in any regulation of the relationship—something *not satisfactorily achieved by general contract law.*

The rights of unions to bargain collectively have been restored. In a rather sad reflection on the industrial climate under the previous administration, the 2000 legislature felt compelled to state expressly that a union is entitled to represent its members in relation to any matter involving their collective interests as employees.[20] Less obvious, perhaps, especially in light of the much-reduced unionisation degree of the contemporary New Zealand workforce, is a legislative provision to the effect that, while collective bargaining can be initiated by a single employer, on the employees' side it once again becomes a union monopoly.[21] Multi-employer bargaining is permissible under the Act, but it comes with requirements attached[22] and, generally, continues to prove difficult in practice.[23] The 2000 Act preserves the specialist institutions of the Employment Tribunal, renamed the Employment Relations Authority, and the Employment Court. Not surprisingly, the role of the former Arbitration Commission in resolving disputes of interest has not been restored. However, aspects of the old compulsory arbitration system nonetheless appear to have been reintroduced in the wake of amending legislation, enacted in 2004, ostensibly for the purpose of giving teeth to a statutory duty of good faith bargaining discussed immediately below.

In an intriguingly innovative swoop, the 2000 legislature makes the right to bargain subject to an obligation for all parties to act in good faith. The obligation is reminiscent of, and inspired by, the statutory duty to bargain in good faith under the National Labor Relations Act in the United States. Specifically, it amounts to a proactive, constructive obligation for the parties to meet and confer with a view to reaching agreement. While the legislature left the actual detail to be worked out in a separate Code,[24] the statutory duty to bargain in good faith encompasses an obligation for the parties to recognise the representative authority of one another.[25] It also entails an obligation for the parties to supply each other with information 'reasonably necessary' to substantiate claims made for the purpose of the bargaining.[26]

A first Code of Good Faith for Bargaining for Collective Agreement was approved by the Minister for Labour on 1 May 2001. It has since been replaced with a new Code which came into force on 11 August 2005. The text of the Code was prepared by a government consultative committee, the so-called Good Faith Code Committee.[27] Pursuant to Section 1.3 of the Code good faith requires the parties:

> to be active and constructive in establishing and maintaining a productive employment relationship. This includes a requirement that the parties are responsive and communicative and do not do anything likely to mislead or deceive each other. Therefore, when bargaining for a collective agreement the parties need to consider whether their actions will establish and maintain the type of relationship required.

Breach of the good faith obligation allows either party to approach the court for a penalty.[28]

A Bridge Too Far? The Employment Relations Amendment Act 2004 (NZ)
Section 39 of the Employment Relations Act 2000 permits the Employment Court to have regard to the Code in determining whether unions and employers have dealt with each other in good faith when bargaining for a collective agreement. Logically, the good faith obligation does not force parties to reach an agreement. However, in an attempt to boost the success rate of collective bargaining, the

legislature amended the 2000 Act in 2004. Henceforth, the statute enshrines a general expectation that good faith bargaining will produce a collective agreement unless there is a 'genuine reason' not to, based on 'reasonable grounds'.[29] Expressly disallowed as genuine reasons for employers refusing to enter into a collective agreement are principled objections to collective bargaining itself and reluctance to negotiate a clause for the payment of a 'bargaining fee' by non-union employees.[30]

The concept of bargaining fee does not feature in the original legislation of 2000. Even so, under the 2000 Act only union members can be covered by a collective agreement.[31] In practice, employers prefer to treat all members of the workforce the same, regardless whether they are organised or not.[32] To avoid the impression of condoning freeloading and, indirectly at least, of facilitating employer attempts at undermining collective bargaining, in 2004 the government inserted a new Part 6B on 'bargaining fees' in the Employment Relations Act. This Part 6B allows employer and union to agree that non-unionised employees, who perform work that comes within the coverage clause of a particular collective agreement, pay a fee equivalent to (but not more than) the relevant union dues.[33]

The compulsory payment of a bargaining fee might be dismissed as just another illustration of the pervasive nature of the user-pay system that has come to typify general society in New Zealand from the late 1980s onwards. But it also constitutes a rather blunt tool for making union membership a more attractive proposition for individual employees in the twenty-first century. Even more fundamental is the potential for change triggered by the provisions in the 2004 Amendment Act on ensuring compliance with the good faith obligation. On one level the Employment Relations Amendment Act 2004 simply introduces a process that enables either party to seek the 'assistance' of the Employment Relations Authority in 'resolving' difficulties in concluding a collective agreement that may arise from time to time.[34] Here any powers of the Authority are purely facilitative[35] and result in the formulation of non-binding recommendations only.[36] On another level, however, if the difficulties in collective bargaining concern breaches of the good faith obligation that are considered 'deliberate, serious, and sustained', penalties apply.[37] Stronger, this type of breach further allows the Authority to make 'a determination fixing the provisions of the collective agreement being bargained for'.[38] Even though such remedy clearly is meant to be used as a last resort only,[39] it would seem that the ghost of compulsory arbitration is once again rearing its head!

The good faith obligation is not restricted to collective bargaining. It applies to all parties to an employment relationship, whether individual or collective. A separate Part 6 of the Employment Relations Act 2000 deals with terms and conditions of employment for individual employees. In principle, the individual parties are free to agree—in writing—upon such terms and conditions of employment as they think fit.[40] Where a collective agreement is applicable, additional terms and conditions may be negotiated provided the individual terms are not inconsistent with those in the collective instrument.[41] The 2000 Act prohibits unfair advantage taking[42] and provides for remedies, both by way of financial compensation and in the nature of a variation or cancellation of the individual employment agreement.[43] In an apparent signal to the judiciary,[44] the legislature in 2004 clarified that the statutory obligation of good faith goes beyond any implied duties of mutual trust and confidence that may exist at common law.[45] The duty even applies to dealings between the union and its own members.[46]

Australia

Labour law reform in Australia commenced during the same time period as in New Zealand. However, the initial approach to change in Australia was much more timid than in New Zealand. Various reasons may account for this state of affairs. Because of the federal make-up of the country, multiple levels of decision-making exist and these need to be in tune with one another in order for change, especially of a radical nature, to be possible. The restrictive manner in which the Commonwealth Constitution articulates the so-called industrial power adds an element of complexity in this regard, in particular where labour law reform emanates from the national legislature.[47] The position of relatively greater strength occupied by the ACTU, the central union movement in Australia, as compared to its New Zealand counterpart may also act as a buffer to wholesale change. Furthermore, differences in perception as to the need for change itself can be detected. To some extent these differences in perception are based on differences in the economic conditions that prevail in each country. While the economies of both Australia and New Zealand traditionally may have a solid core in farming, the additional availability of plentiful natural resources makes Australia somewhat less vulnerable in the international marketplace. In any event, when change in the regulatory framework for industrial relations did occur in Australia, it came more gradually and, arguably, with less emphasis on prior public consultation and debate.

The Pre-1996 (Hawke/Keating) Era: If It Ain't Broke ...

Upon taking office in 1983, the Labor government of Bob Hawke established an official committee charged with a comprehensive review of the existing industrial relations system. The committee produced a report in 1985, known as the Hancock Report after its chair—and professor of economics—Keith Hancock.[48] While the report contained numerous recommendations for amending the system then in place, its overwhelming conclusion was that conciliation and arbitration had served the community well for the best part of a century and therefore a complete overhaul was not warranted.[49] That conclusion was in line with the public submissions, roughly 150 in total, largely from stakeholders, received by the committee.[50] In implementing the Hancock Report, the Hawke government replaced the Conciliation and Arbitration Act 1904 with the Industrial Relations Act 1988. The 1988 Act has been described as 'little more than a consolidation measure', entailing 'no substantial change to the system as it had operated for eighty-five years'.[51]

Under the 1988 legislation the centralised system of compulsory conciliation and arbitration was kept intact. Even so, the Act contained some provisions that could facilitate decentralised (enterprise) collective bargaining, albeit under the (central) supervision of the Australian Industrial Relations Commission, by means of so-called certified agreements. A concerted effort at promoting enterprise bargaining had to wait until the Industrial Relations Reform Act 1993, though. Adopted under a Labor government led by Paul Keating, decentralised bargaining pursuant to the 1993 Act effectively came in two guises, that is, certified agreements and enterprise flexibility agreements. While these industrial instruments differed in their technical detail, particularly innovative was that the former required union involvement whereas the latter did not. The contents of each type of collective agreement could be freely negotiated on the proviso that an official seal of approval ('certification') would only be obtained where the terms and conditions of employment contained in the decentralised document did not seek to undercut those available under the relevant award. This approach to enterprise bargaining was legally founded on the corporations power of the Australian Constitution rather than the more traditional industrial power.[52]

The Workplace Relations Act 1996 (Cth)

When first elected in 1996, the conservative coalition under John Howard failed to obtain a majority in the Senate. While this limited the scope for radical change, the Workplace Relations Act 1996 expressed, for the first time in the history of Australian labour law, an unambiguous legislative preference for workplace bargaining. When compared to the legislation adopted under Keating, the object clause of the 1996 Act specifically listed among its principal objectives:[53]

> (b) ensuring that the primary responsibility for determining matters affecting the relationship between employers and employees rests with the employer and employees *at the workplace or enterprise level*; and ...
>
> (d) providing the means:
>
> (i) for wages and conditions of employment to be determined *as far as possible* by the agreement of employers and employees at the workplace or enterprise level ...

This promotion of decentralised bargaining came with a twist, though. The 1996 Act introduced a new type of agreement, referred to as an Australian Workplace Agreement or AWA. These agreements not only symbolised decentralisation. In addition, AWAs sought to bring about the individualisation of Australian labour law.

As defined under the statute, an AWA is a written agreement that deals with matters pertaining to the relationship between an employer and employee.[54] While each party may appoint a bargaining agent,[55] the employer and employee constitute the only persons that can enter into an AWA.[56] Unlike certified agreements or enterprise flexibility agreements under the 1993 (Keating) legislation, an AWA is to all extents and purposes an individual agreement—even though it allows an employer to enter into identical AWAs with some, most or indeed all members of the workforce!

In principle, the contents of an AWA could be negotiated freely between employer and employee from the outset. However, prior to the 2005 amendments, AWAs—not unlike certified agreements—had to be filed with and approved by the newly created office of the Employment Advocate. Approval depended on the Employment Advocate being satisfied that the contents of the AWA complied with the 'no disadvantage test'.[57] This meant that the terms and conditions of employment as stated in an AWA could not result, 'on balance', in a reduction in the 'overall' terms and conditions of employment applicable under the relevant award, federal or state law.[58] While the precise boundaries of contractual freedom thus remained suitably vague, AWAs at first did not replace the award system. Rather, AWAs and awards had to somehow co-exist. Stronger even, the first generation of AWAs was not allowed to undercut employment conditions contained in the relevant applicable collective document. It is a feature that certainly helps explain their limited appeal to employers under the original Workplace Relations Act 1996.

The Work Choices Act 2005 (Cth)

In one sense the changes introduced by the 1996 Act were incremental rather than revolutionary in nature. However, once the Coalition government gained control over both Houses of Parliament, from July 2005 onwards, more radical labour law reform became possible. Technically, the 2005 legislation on 'work choices' is a mere amendment of the Workplace Relations Act 1996. In terms of its contents, though, the Workplace Relations (Work Choices) Act 2005 'substantially rewrites'[59] the 1996 Act. It removes the no disadvantage test, previously applicable to AWAs, from the statute book. A new hierarchy of norms henceforth places these individual agreements at the top, outranking collective agreements and awards as the official source for regulating employment conditions. The elevation of AWAs to the main employment regulatory device is such that the contents of this type of individual employment contract prevail over collective industrial instruments, not just to the extent of any inconsistency with awards or collective agreements, but by replacing the award and collective agreement in their entirety. As regards the latter, the Act effectively places the Industrial Relations Commission on death row. Unlike the approach adopted by the New Zealand legislature in 1991, the Australian legislature has done so by stealth rather than through the outright abolition of that institution. By reducing the role of awards to regulating an ever-decreasing number of minimum employment conditions, referred to in the 2005 Act as 'allowable matters', the very reason for the existence of the Commission has come under direct threat.

The net effect of the 2005 Act is clear. Where an AWA exists between employer and employee, it becomes the sole source of 'negotiated' employment conditions. The Howard administration maintained that this is what self-regulation and self-determination is all about. Unfortunately, the 2005 Act is not really just about self-determination for either employees or, somewhat surprisingly, employers. Rather, it also shows a government determined to impose its will about what it deems good for business. The open one-sidedness of the Australian legislature in 2005 allows parallels to be drawn with a similar determination to promote the cause of labour as reflected in the 2004 amendments to the Employment Relations Act 2000 in New Zealand. The new statutory construct of prohibited matters provides an (Australian) case in point.

'Prohibited matters' is a familiar concept to labour lawyers in the United States. In enforcing the statutory duty of good faith bargaining under the 1935 Wagner Act, the National Labor Relations Board traditionally distinguishes between mandatory and non-mandatory bargaining topics. The latter comes in two varieties. Most non-mandatory topics are deemed permissive, in that parties may agree to negotiate upon issues that do not fit comfortably the (narrowly construed) notion of 'wages, hours, and other terms and conditions of employment' in the legislation.[60] The difference with mandatory bargaining topics is that only the pursuit of the latter can involve a lawful resort to industrial action. Occasionally, a non-mandatory topic may even be deemed illegal and hence prohibited. A classic example is a closed-shop provision compelling an employer to hire unionised labour exclusively. That type of provision would be deemed unlawful in Australia as well. However, the Work Choices Act 2005 goes considerably further than its American counterpart in limiting the scope for legitimate bargaining. A non-exhaustive list, to be expanded upon by means of separate government regulation, expressly prohibits parties from negotiating upon, *inter alia*, dismissal protection. The repercussions of this type of prohibition are potentially significant. Under the 2005 Act employees in companies with a total workforce of 100 or less are prevented from questioning the fairness of their dismissal. No Australian employee is allowed to question dismissals that occur for so-called operational reasons either, regardless of the size of the firm. As a result, because the matter is deemed a prohibited bargaining topic, employers risk fines for merely agreeing to discuss the introduction of extra-statutory job security measures with their own workforce!

A partial about-face occurred towards the end of Howard's reign. In 2007 amending legislation reintroduced aspects of the 'old' no disadvantage test in the shape of a 'new' fairness test applicable to employees with a maximum annual salary of $75 000. The application and enforcement of the fairness test was entrusted to two new government agencies established under the Workplace Relations Amendment (A Stronger Safety Net) Act 2007. The Office of the Workplace Ombudsman and the Workplace Authority replaced the former office of the Employment Advocate. The result of federal elections held in November of that same year has meant that the impact of the 2007 legislative changes remains untested, however.

Towards a National System of Australian Labour Law?

The Howard government may be criticised for getting the balance between economic efficiency and social equity wrong. However, on reflection, one good thing to come out of the Howard era has been a renewed interest in the pursuit of a single, national system of labour law for Australia. In the twenty-first century the disparate nature of multiple industrial relations systems operating at Commonwealth and state levels holds little appeal.[61] Unity, or at least national uniformity, and federalism need not be mutually exclusive. The use of the corporations power as a primary jurisdictional basis for the adoption of the Work Choices legislation may not have been the most elegant manner for seeking to bring about a unified approach to

Australian labour law, but it is not without precedent and, in any event, it has successfully withstood a constitutional challenge in the High Court.[62] The very principle of a national labour law regime warrants commendation, if only because it enhances transparency, economic efficiency and even social fairness, through the associated solidarity it imposes on workers regardless of the geographical area of their employment. The subsequent use and, in 2008, extension of National Employment Standards applicable to all Australian workers within the federal sphere also reflects a harmonising spirit on the part of the Rudd administration.

The Transition to Forward with Fairness Act 2008 (Cth)

While firmly committed to striking a different balance between economic flexibility and social stability, upon taking office the Rudd government nonetheless decided to proceed cautiously. In an apparent attempt to avoid abrupt change to the detriment of Australian business and the economy as a whole, the Rudd Labor government has enacted legislation that provides for a lengthy transition period before its new system of industrial relations, tellingly referred to as a new 'workplace' relations system on the government's official website,[63] is put into effect from 2010 onwards. As its Long Title suggests, the Workplace Relations Amendment (Transition to Forward with Fairness) Act 2008 does not repeal the Workplace Relations Act 1996. The core premise underlying the 2008 Act is that most institutions and legislative instruments in place pursuant to the 1996 legislation will continue to exist for now and, in some instances, well into the foreseeable future.

Even AWAs, easily the most controversial aspect of the Workplace Relations Act 1996, are being phased out over a period of several years only. Existing agreements are allowed to run their course until they expire or until the parties themselves decide to renegotiate them. Although new AWAs can no longer be entered into, individual employment contracts between an employer and an employee continue to be catered for. Referred to as Individual Transitional Employment Agreements or ITEAs by the 2008 legislature, this new type of industrial instrument represents the functional equivalent of the former AWAs. Their contents can be freely negotiated by the individual parties, subject to a revamped no disadvantage test in substitution for the 2007 fairness test and monitored by the Director of the Workplace Authority, an office introduced under Howard. In a by now familiar-sounding fashion, ITEAs are not allowed to reduce, 'on balance', the 'overall' terms and conditions of individual employees.[64] These restrictions mirror those applicable to the contents of AWAs under the 2007 amendments of the Workplace Relations Act 1996. Similarly, any individual agreements that pass the test still replace any pre-existing collective agreement or award otherwise applicable.

Post-2009 no guarantees attach to the continued availability of a special statutory instrument for the negotiation of individual employment contracts. Indications are that common law contracts only will be allowed, on a further proviso that they improve rather than detract from the employee position under the relevant collective agreement or award. Certainly, it would seem that Australia will not go down the path of New Zealand in dismantling the award system and the associated role of the central umpire in its entirety. On the contrary, it may be anticipated that there will continue to be a role for both awards and the Australian Industrial Relations Commission, albeit in a revamped format and quite probably under the new name of Fair Work Australia from 2010 onwards. In the interim, the 2008 legislature has put in train a process of award 'modernisation' to be carried out by the Commission for completion by the end of 2009. Intriguingly, any existing provisions on award rationalisation and simplification already in place under the Workplace Relations Act 1996[65] are repealed and replaced by a new part 10A entitled Award Modernisation. As stated in the 2008 Act, the ultimate goal is to have awards that are simple to understand and socially fair, yet economically sustainable and flexible. The declared objectives of award modernisation further suggest that the Rudd government sees a long-term future for awards in underpinning enterprise bargaining that is collective in nature and 'does not provide for statutory individual employment agreements'.[66]

While the actual process of rewriting awards is primarily a task entrusted to the Australian Industrial Relations Commission, the legislature preserves the (Howard) notion of so-called allowable matters as for the contents of these 'modern' (or, better perhaps, 'modernised') awards. The list of any such allowable award matters has been expanded from five to ten items. The extent to which the corollary of prohibited matters will disappear from the new labour law regime in its entirety remains unclear. While the government appears prepared to allow parties to bargain over a wider range of issues than they can at present under Work Choices, it wishes to exclude 'matters that are properly the prerogative of management'.[67] Managerial prerogative has a notoriously fluid contents. The 2008 Act specifically allows for the contents of restructured awards to include provisions relating to, but not inconsistent with, the newly proposed National Employment Standards (NES). The latter also number ten in total and were completed in draft form in June 2008.[68]

The National Employment Standards

The newly proposed National Employment Standards are contained in a document that is fifty pages in length.[69] Although released in mid-2008, the Rudd government plans that they will come into operation from 2010 onwards only. In this way it is being stressed that the statutory minima are to operate alongside the (yet-to-be-completed) modernised award system. The National Employment Standards mainly focus on working time, various forms of leave entitlement for employees (including flexibility to accommodate working parents) and the social as well as financial impact of economic restructuring decisions by business. By and large, the list represents an attempt at consolidating diverse measures already in place through awards and/or state legislation. Specifically, the minimum standards relate to the following matters:

1. Maximum weekly working hours
2. Employee requests for flexible working arrangements
3. Parental leave and related entitlements
4. Annual leave
5. Personal, carer's and compassionate leave
6. Community service leave
7. Long service leave
8. Public holidays
9. Notice of termination and redundancy pay
10. A Fair Work Information Statement.[70]

Upon closer examination it appears that not all of the statutory minimum employee rights will be granted unconditionally. Certainly, various qualifications attach to each entitlement. As a result, the picture that emerges can be rather complex at times.[71] A brief discussion of each of the ten employment standards follows.

The provision that the working hours for a full-time employee must not exceed thirty-eight hours remains subject to the employer's right to require that employees work 'reasonable' additional hours. Reasonableness in this context may differ from industry to industry[72] and from company to company,[73] which is not particularly conducive to promoting uniformity. Employee protection, such as any health and safety risks associated with working additional hours, as well as the employee's personal circumstances (including family responsibilities) clearly matter.[74] By the same token, though, the reasonableness of an employer request to work extra hours is also to be judged by reference to the employee's 'entitlement' to extra pay[75] and even by an employer giving advance notice about the requirement for the employee to work beyond the statutory maximum working week.[76]

Employees with school-age children may ask the employer for a change in their working arrangements in order to facilitate the care of these children. While any employee request for a flexible working arrangement may concern changes in working hours, it need not be so confined. Changes in patterns of work and even changes in the place of work are listed as further examples of employee requests for flexibility.[77] Requests must be in writing, state reasons, and the employer must respond within twenty-one days. The employer's response must be in writing and, if negative, motivated.[78]

Employees are entitled to twelve months of parental leave, extendable to twenty-four months subject to employer agreement.[79] The entitlement is unpaid, although parental leave can be combined with some (for example, annual) but not all (in particular, personal, compassionate and community service) forms of paid leave.[80] Parental leave must be taken over a single continuous period, no doubt to minimise disruption to the employer's business. While the actual commencement date of the leave period generally is for the employee to decide, the employer must be given timely (at least ten weeks in advance) notice in writing.[81] In any event, the leave must start not later than the birth of the child, but may begin up to six weeks prior to the expected date of delivery.[82]

In certain circumstances, the employer may require a pregnant employee to commence the parental leave within a period of six weeks before the expected date of birth. The employer may do so whenever concerns exist about the employee's fitness for work or health, subject to a compulsory (from the employee's perspective) medical examination.[83] Conversely, if that employee remains fit to perform some other work, she may ask to be transferred to another suitable job on the same terms and conditions of employment. Where no appropriate work is available, the pregnant employee is entitled to paid 'no safe job leave'.[84]

Employees who suffer a pregnancy-related illness are entitled to 'special' (unpaid) maternity leave regardless of the six-weeks period referred to above. Employer notice and, upon request, justification is required. Upon taking special maternity leave the entitlement to parental leave is reduced accordingly.[85]

Where the pregnant employee's partner wishes to take parental leave as well, this leave needs to be taken consecutively, immediately following the end of the first party's leave.[86] Even so, limited provision is made for concurrent leave by both partners of maximum three weeks around the delivery date.[87]

No job security, but rather employment security, attaches to parental leave. While employees are in principle entitled to return to their pre-leave position in the workplace, the employer is under no obligation to keep that position open. However, if the employer makes a decision during the period of parental leave that has a 'significant effect' on the employee's pre-leave position, the employee has a right to be informed and consulted about the effect of the decision.[88] In the circumstances an available position 'nearest in status and pay' and for which the employee is 'qualified and suited' must be offered.[89]

As a rule, the provisions regarding parental leave also apply in instances of child adoption.

Paid annual leave remains at four weeks, while shiftworkers—a concept to be defined in the modernised awards—will continue to receive five weeks. As before, the actual timing of taking annual leave is to be agreed between both parties, with employers being prohibited from 'unreasonably' refusing an employee request to take leave.[90] Interestingly, because it risks undermining the rationale behind the introduction of such leave and may even compromise the employee's health or safety, a 'modern' award will also be able to continue to contain provisions for the cashing out of paid annual leave.[91]

Equally unchanged is the provision that employees are entitled to ten days of—paid—personal or carer's leave. This form of leave allows an employee to be absent from work because of a personal illness or injury, including the illness or injury of a member of the employee's immediate family or household. Once again, the very spirit of this particular entitlement risks being compromised by award provisions that permit the cashing out of personal/carer's leave in the future.[92] If the ten-day period of carer's leave proves insufficient, the employee is entitled to two additional days of (unpaid) leave.[93] Unpaid carer's leave co-exists with paid compassionate leave, also of two days in length.[94]

Community service leave, for participation in jury service or the carrying out of another type of eligible (voluntary) community service activity, must be paid for by the employer—provided the employee's absence from work does not exceed ten days. Even then, the amount of payment is reduced by the jury service compensation paid or payable to the employee.[95]

While an employee's entitlement to long service leave is not new either, its inclusion in the National Employment Standards gives it a federal statutory basis.[96] The same goes for the listing of eight public holidays. Note, though, that a modern award or, for that matter, relevant state or territory laws, may substitute one or more of these days and may do so either wholly or in part.[97] As before, employers may reasonably request, but employees are allowed to reasonably refuse, work to be performed on a public holiday.[98]

As proposed, the National Employment Standards make no mention of employee protection against unfair dismissal. Instead an employee's entitlement to receive notice of employment termination is confirmed, as is the employer's entitlement to replace the notice period with the payment of any wages that otherwise would have been earned by that employee. The statutory provisions as regards the minimum length of the notice period mirror those originally contained in the Termination, Change and Redundancy case of 1984.[99] This federal award additionally created an employee entitlement to redundancy pay. The National Employment Standards not only confirm this entitlement, they also provide for the amount of payment to increase beyond the initial five years of employee service.[100] Redundancy is not confined to situations of employer insolvency or bankruptcy.[101] It also encompasses situations of employment termination at the initiative of the employer 'because the employer no longer requires the job done by the employee to be done by anyone, except where this is due to the ordinary and customary turnover of labour'.[102] Situations of business transmission do not normally qualify for redundancy pay.[103] Small businesses, that is, those employing fewer than fifteen employees, are exempt altogether.[104]

While they are meant to create a universally applicable safety net for all employees, the proposed National Employment Standards do not apply to a whole range of particularly vulnerable employees.[105] Not covered are employees employed on a fixed-term contract, neither are those employed for the performance of a specific task. Also excluded are casual and seasonal employees. Trainees or regular employees serving a probationary period are not covered either. Strangely, employees whose employment is terminated because of serious misconduct are excluded as well.[106]

Finally, the yet-to-be established office of Fair Work Australia is instructed to publish a so-called Fair Work Information Statement.[107] This Statement must contain, *inter alia*, information about the National Employment Standards themselves. A copy must be given by the employer to each employee and updated regularly.[108]

Where to from Here?

The 2008 Act is the first step in the Rudd reform agenda. Even so, the Transition to Forward with Fairness legislation sends some clear signals. There is a shift in focus away from individual bargaining as a primary vehicle for the negotiation of terms and conditions of employment. Instead, collective bargaining at the actual place of work becomes the focal point of the new labour law regime. The threshold for any such collective bargaining will be higher than under the previous Howard administration in two respects. Under the Transition to Forward with Fairness legislation the no disadvantage test applies to ITEAs and collective agreements alike. While the former are designed as temporary industrial instruments only, the latter are not. A less restrictive approach to the notion of allowable matters assists in giving renewed relevance to awards, any streamlining of their contents through the modernisation procedure notwithstanding. An expansion in the number of uniform ('national') statutory conditions of employment adds further meaning to the concept of a minimum floor of employee rights in Australia.

It is too early to tell whether the new balance between economic and social concerns will be acceptable to the community at large. In the short term, there appear to be lingering concerns in business circles about increased rigidity.[109] Conversely, organised labour displays notable anxiety about the perceived timidity of the government response to Work Choices some six months into the term of the Rudd administration.[110] The wait is on for the release of more detail as regards the second phase of the labour law reforms in Australia.

Notes

1 For an application to the Belgian context, see Vranken, *De collectieve arbeidsovereenkomsten in België van 1974 tot 1980. Evolutie en juridische evaluatie* (Collective Bargaining in Belgium During the Period 1974–1980. Evolution and Legal Evaluation).

2 For a comparative discussion of the continental European and English approaches to deregulation during the 1980s, see Vranken, 'Deregulating the Employment Relationship: Current Trends in Europe', p. 143.

3 In terms of stringency, the labour law systems of Portugal, Spain and Greece occupy first, second and third places, respectively. France is ranked fourth, Sweden fifth, Belgium sixth, Germany seventh, Italy eighth. The Netherlands and Denmark come in at numbers nine and fifteen, Ireland and the United Kingdom at seventeen and eighteen: Industrial Relations Services, 'Flexicurity in the Spotlight', p. 28.

4 Commission of the European Communities, *Modernising Labour Law to Meet the Challenges of the 21st Century*, p. 5.

5 See Chapter 2.

6 *Brighouse v Bilderbeck* [1995] 1 NZLR 158 at 165 (CA) (per Cooke P).

7 Stewart, with the assistance of Priest, 'The Work Choices Legislation: An Overview'.

8 Note that a Minimum Wage Panel, responsible for determining national minimum wages, will be set up within the otherwise unitary structure of Fair Work Australia. See Gillard, *Introducing Australia's New Workplace Relations System*, p. 9.

9 The first election using a mixed-member-proportional system of voting was held in 1996.

10 Department of Labour, *Industrial Relations. A Framework for Review*.

11 ibid., vol. 1, pp. 7–8.

12 The New Zealand Department of Labour published a summary of the various submissions received: *Industrial Relations. A Framework for Review—Summary of Submissions*.

13 Department of Labour, *Government Policy Statement on Labour Relations.*
14 Admittedly, the 1987 Act dropped a previously applicable additional requirement of award coverage for employees to gain access to the former Arbitration Court.
15 Section 18(2) of the Employment Contracts Act 1991 (NZ).
16 Note the use of the expression 'inconsistent' rather than conditions 'less favourable (to the employee)': Section 19(2) of the Employment Contracts Act 1991 (NZ).
17 Anderson, 'Transplanting and Growing Good Faith in New Zealand Labour Law', p. 8.
18 Hon. Margaret Wilson, Minister of Labour (and former law professor), 'The Employment Relations Act: A Statutory Framework for Balance in the Workplace', p. 5.
19 Explanatory Note, 1 (emphasis added).
20 Section 18(1) of the Employment Relations Act 2000 (NZ).
21 Section 40 of the Employment Relations Act 2000 (NZ).
22 These requirements include secret ballots of union members employed by each employer: Section 45 of the Employment Relations Act 2000 (NZ).
23 Anderson, 'Transplanting and Growing Good Faith in New Zealand Labour Law', p. 9.
24 Sections 35–39 of the Employment Relations Act 2000 (NZ). See Hughes, 'The Collective Bargaining Code of Good Faith' (2001), p. 59.
25 Section 32(1)(d)(i) of the Employment Relations Act 2000 (NZ).
26 Section 32(1)(e) of the Employment Relations Act 2000 (NZ).
27 The text of the Code is reproduced on the website of New Zealand's Department of Labour: www.ers.dol.govt.nz/goodfaith/code
28 Section 6.2 of the 2005 Code.
29 Section 33(1) of the Employment Relations Act 2000 (NZ) as amended.
30 Section 33(2) of the Employment Relations Act 2000 (NZ) as amended.
31 Section 56 of the Employment Relations Act 2000 (NZ).
32 Anderson, 'Transplanting and Growing Good Faith in New Zealand Labour Law', p. 9.
33 Section 69U of the Employment Relations Act 2000 (NZ) as amended.
34 Section 50A of the Employment Relations Act 2000 (NZ) as amended.
35 Section 50B of the Employment Relations Act 2000 (NZ) as amended.
36 Section 50H of the Employment Relations Act 2000 (NZ) as amended.
37 Section 4A of the Employment Relations Act 2000 (NZ) as amended.
38 Section 50J of the Employment Relations Act 2000 (NZ) as amended.
39 Determination of the agreement must be 'the only effective remedy': Section 50J(3)(c) of the Employment Relations Act 2000 (NZ) as amended.
40 Section 65 of the Employment Relations Act 2000 (NZ).
41 Section 61 of the Employment Relations Act 2000 (NZ).
42 Section 68 of the Employment Relations Act 2000 (NZ).
43 Section 69 of the Employment Relations Act 2000 (NZ).

44 Anderson, 'Transplanting and Growing Good Faith in New Zealand Labour Law', p. 6.
45 Section 3(a)(i) of the Employment Relations Act 2000 as amended.
46 Department of Labour, *Fact Sheet on Good Faith in Employment Relationships.*
47 Section 51 (xxxv) of the Constitution empowers the Commonwealth legislature to make laws with respect to 'conciliation and arbitration for the prevention and settlement of industrial disputes extending beyond the limits of any one State'. The traditional interpretation of these words effectively holds that the enactment of labour laws is a matter for the states in the first instance.
48 The report's full title is *Report of the Committee of Enquiry into Australian Industrial Relations Law and Systems.*
49 Creighton and Stewart, *Labour Law,* p. 56.
50 Gutman, Chapter 12, 'The Hancock Report: Last Hurrah for the System'.
51 Creighton and Stewart, *Labour Law,* p. 56.
52 Section 51 (xx) of the Constitution. Other aspects of the Industrial Relations Reform Act 1993 were based on the external relations power in Section 51 (xxix).
53 Section 3 of the Workplace Relations Act 1996 (Cth) (emphasis added).
54 Section 170VF(1) of the Workplace Relations Act 1996 (Cth).
55 Section 170VK(1) of the Workplace Relations Act 1996 (Cth). On the employee side, the term 'bargaining agent' is not restricted to a union.
56 Section 170VF(1) of the Workplace Relations Act 1996 (Cth).
57 Section 170VPB(1) and (4) of the Workplace Relations Act 1996 (Cth).
58 Section 170XA of the Workplace Relations Act 1996 (Cth).
59 Stewart, 'The Work Choices Legislation: An Overview', p. 1.
60 Section 8(d) of the National Labour Relations Act 1935.
61 By contrast, Belgium is a country that appears determined to move away from a unitary system of labour law. See Vanachter, 'Labour Law and the Division of Power between the Federal Level, the Communities and the Regions in Belgium', pp. 21–49.
62 The challenge to the constitutional validity of the 2005 Act was dismissed by a 5–2 majority in the High Court of Australia: *New South Wales v Commonwealth* [2006] HCA 52; 231 ALR 1 (14 November 2006).
63 See http://www.workplace.gov
64 Section 346D(1) of the Workplace Relations Act 1996 as amended by the Transition to Forward with Fairness Act 2008.
65 Part 10, Division 4 of the Workplace Relations Act 1996 (Cth).
66 Section 576A of the Workplace Relations Act 1996 as amended by the Transition to Forward with Fairness Act 2008 (Object Clause).
67 Gillard, *Introducing Australia's New Workplace Relations System,* p. 6.
68 Australian Government, *The National Employment Standards.* The text of this document is available in electronic format at www.workplace.gov.au
69 ibid.
70 ibid., Section 2(2).

71 A hands-on analysis of the proposed National Employment Standards as they emerged from the 'exposure draft' released in February 2008, including a useful comparison with pre-existing law, can be found in Punch and Sheils, 'NES & Award Modernisation—More Ingredients and a New Mixture?', pp. 1–8.
72 Section 12(4)(g) stipulates that 'the usual patterns of work in the industry' are a relevant consideration: The National Employment Standards.
73 Section 12 (4) (c) stipulates that 'the needs of the workplace' in which the employee is employed are a relevant consideration: ibid.
74 Sections 12 (4) (a) and (b): ibid.
75 Section 12 (4) (d): ibid.
76 Section 12 (4) (e): ibid.
77 Section 13 (1): ibid.
78 Section 13 (3) – (6): ibid.
79 The employer may only refuse an employee request for extension on 'reasonable business grounds': Section 22 (3): ibid.
80 Section 25: ibid.
81 Section 20: ibid.
82 Section 17: ibid.
83 Section 19: ibid.
84 Section 26: ibid.
85 Section 26 (7): ibid.
86 Section 18 (3) (b): ibid.
87 Section 18 (5) and (6): ibid.
88 Section 28: ibid.
89 Section 29: ibid.
90 Section 33 (2): ibid. Conversely, awards can stipulate that employees may be required to actually take up their annual leave entitlement in particular circumstances: Section 36 (1) (b): ibid.
91 Section 36 (1) (a): ibid.
92 Section 42: ibid.
93 Section 43: ibid.
94 Section 45: ibid.
95 Section 52 (4) and (5): ibid.
96 Section 53: ibid.
97 Listed are New Year's Day, Australia Day, Good Friday, Easter Monday, Anzac Day, Queen's Birthday, Christmas Day and Boxing Day. See Section 54: ibid.
98 Section 55 (2) and (3): ibid.
99 Compare Section 57 (ibid.) and Australian Conciliation and Arbitration Commission (Full Bench) (1984) 294 CAR 175, 18 IR 35.
100 See Section 60 of the National Employment Standards.
101 Note, though, that employers unable to pay can apply to the new office of Fair Work Australia for a reduction in the amount of redundancy pay owed to the employees. See Section 61: ibid.
102 Section 60 (1) (a): ibid.

103 Section 63: ibid.
104 Section 62 (1) (b): ibid.
105 Section 64: ibid.
106 Presumably, the general scope of the exclusion—beyond redundancy pay—is an error that will be corrected by the time the legislation takes its final form.
107 Section 65 of the National Employment Standards.
108 Section 66: ibid.
109 Scott, 'Minimum Standards Upset Employers', p. 9.
110 Norington, 'Ads Remind Labor of Vows', p. 2.

CHAPTER 8

Labour Law and Flexicurity

Introduction

In 2000, in a speech delivered at the Bathurst Panthers Leagues Club, Noel Pearson reflected on the woeful social problems experienced by Aboriginal people in Cape York Peninsula.[1] In his search for answers as to why social life for his people had declined notwithstanding a notable improvement in material circumstances over the past thirty years or so, Pearson drew a parallel with the changing role of labour law and the organised labour movement in Australian society generally. Pearson aptly pointed out the links that exist between a globalised economy, the decline of collectivism, and the very survival of the welfare state. Pearson observed as follows:

> The lower classes in developed countries have lost much of their political influence because of the shrinking and disorganisation of the only powerful group among them, the working class proper. The shift in the economy away from manufacturing, and economic globalisation which makes it possible to allocate production to the enormous unregulated labour markets outside the classical welfare states, have deprived the industrial workers in the developed

countries of their powerful position as sole suppliers of labour force to the most important part of the world economy. The lower classes are therefore now unable to defend the Welfare State. Nor is there any longer any political or economic reason for the influential strata of society to support the preservation of the Welfare State.

In his view, the welfare state 'will continue to face pressure to retreat' as, increasingly, it is being 'presented as an impediment to economic growth'. Pearson acknowledges that reform may be justified and, indeed, 'imperative' if the welfare state is to survive in the twenty-first century. But he argues strongly that to reform the welfare state is not to deny its continued role and existence:

> This country needs to develop a new consensus around our commitment to welfare ... our motivation to reform welfare must be based on the principle that dependency and passivity are a scourge and must be avoided at all costs ... Australians do not have an inalienable right to dependency, they have an inalienable right to a fair place in the real economy.

His plea effectively amounts to a rejection of the approach adopted by the World Bank in its *Doing Business* initiative—a project that seeks to provide a guide for evaluating business regulations that directly impact on economic growth.[2] But it also fits in, rather comfortably, with the philosophy that underpins the prevailing notion of flexicurity in the EU and constitutes the core focus of this final chapter of *Death of Labour Law?*

Labour law has reached a tipping point. For the greater part of the twentieth century its central preoccupation was with the quantity and quality of employee protection. This state of affairs started to change from the 1980s onwards. It would seem that the challenge for the future lies in a rebalancing of social protection in favour of economic flexibility in such a way as to avoid the former being usurped by the latter. In Europe a newly coined term in this regard is 'flexicurity'. It is a notion that takes pride of place in a 2006 discussion document (Green Paper) by the European Commission on modernising labour law to meet the challenges of the twenty-first century.[3] Parallels can be drawn with the legislative reform agenda of the newly installed Rudd government in Australia where a revamped system of collective (workplace) bargaining is foreshadowed to operate against the backdrop of a reinforced floor of statutory employee entitlements. These statutory entitlements are intended to act as a stable, protective social buffer against economic uncertainty now and into the future.

The jury remains out as regards the degree of social protection Western industrialised nations consider they can 'afford' to keep in this brave new world of globalisation and associated international competition. While the EU has a co-ordinating role at the supranational level only, the precise trade-off between the needs of business and labour is likely to differ somewhat between individual countries. Similarly, it is likely that Europe and Australia will strike the balance between economic flexibility and social security differently. History teaches that this need not cause alarm *per se*. Provided that a modernised labour law is not reduced to a mere listing of certain 'fundamental'—and therefore, almost inevitably, rather basic—social rights, the subject can have a future as an academic discipline in its own right.

On present indications, the focus of any such modernised labour law is the individual employee. Here Australian labour law, like its New Zealand counterpart, has shifted closer towards the continental European position. Again, this is not a cause for alarm. It certainly need not mean that the collective representative of workers has been outmanoeuvred. Rather, it must be acknowledged that unions ultimately signify a means towards an end. More important is that any void left because of the reduced prominence of unions is filled. By stepping in, the legislature is able to ensure that the position of the employee is not unduly compromised. The construct of flexicurity goes hand in hand with a renewed focus on the proactive (positive) role of the state in the regulation of industrial (or, in modern parlance, workplace) relations in Europe and Australasia alike.

Modernising the European Social Model

The Lisbon Agenda

In 2000 the European Council, comprising the heads of state or government of the member states together with the president of the EC Commission, met in Lisbon (Portugal). The general backdrop, and a first agenda item for the meeting, concerned ongoing preparations for a substantial enlargement of the EU's membership base with, in essence, former socialist countries from Central and Eastern Europe. On a more specific level, the Presidency Conclusions at the close of proceedings confirmed the purpose of the Lisbon meeting in terms of addressing the social—in the broadest sense of the word—ramifications of 'a quantum shift resulting from globalisation and the challenges of a new knowledge-driven economy'.[4] Both considerations, when combined, were said to add a sense of urgency to Europe's attempts at developing a strategy for change into the new century.

At Lisbon the European leaders formulated a strategic, and certainly ambitious, goal for 2010: for the EU to become 'the most dynamic and competitive knowledge-based economy in the world', capable of 'sustainable economic growth' and typified by 'more and better jobs' as well as 'greater social cohesion'.[5] To this effect an action plan was said to be needed. This plan needed to emphasise the right mixture of economic and social policy measures. The task ahead was expressed in the following terms:[6]

- Preparing the transition to a knowledge-based economy and society by better policies for the information society and R&D, as well as stepping up the process of structural reform for competitiveness and innovation and by completing the internal market;
- Modernising the European social model, investing in people and combating social exclusion;
- Sustaining the healthy economic outlook and favourable growth prospects by applying an appropriate macro-economic policy mix.

Of greatest interest, from a labour law perspective, was the focus on modernising the European social model. The Council considered that advances in the building of a knowledge economy must go hand in hand with the pursuit of an active and dynamic welfare state. The European social model, while acknowledged to be in need of adaptation, nevertheless must continue to 'underpin'[7] the transformation to the knowledge economy. Here special attention went to the need for Europe's education and professional training systems to accommodate those living and working in the 'knowledge society'.[8] Learning and training opportunities needed to be better tailored to people at different stages of their lives. The European Council distinguished three distinct categories of people: young persons, unemployed adults, and those in employment but at risk of seeing their skills overtaken by rapid change. Three main components of a new approach to education and training were identified: development of local learning centres, the promotion of new basic skills—in the information technologies, in particular—and increased transparency of qualifications.[9]

Increased transparency of qualifications forms an integral component of the so-called Bologna model for the establishment of a 'European area' of higher education by 2010. In Australia, the University of Melbourne has since developed its own 'Melbourne model' in partial response to these developments in Europe and elsewhere.[10] More generally, the EU emphasis on computer literacy allows further parallels to be drawn with a political commitment by the Rudd government to an education 'revolution' through, *inter alia*, increased access to computers and the internet for school-age children throughout Australia.[11]

For jurisdictional reasons, modernising the European social model by investing in people and rebuilding an active welfare state cannot be achieved by the EU acting alone. The member states were therefore called upon, in addition to the core EU institutions of the Council of Ministers and the European Commission, to take 'the necessary steps' to meet a series of reasonably specific targets. These were listed in the Presidency Conclusions of the Lisbon European Council meeting in the following terms:

> A substantial annual increase in per capita *investment in human resources*;
>
> The number of 18 to 24 year olds with only lower-secondary level education who are not in further education and training should be halved by 2010;
>
> Schools and training centres, all linked to the Internet, should be developed into multi-purpose local training centres accessible to all, using the most appropriate methods to address a wide range of target groups; *learning partnerships*

> *should be established between schools, training centres, firms and research facilities for their mutual benefit;*
>
> A European framework should define the new basic skills to be provided through *lifelong learning*: IT skills, foreign languages, technological culture, entrepreneurship and social skills; a European diploma for basic IT skills, with decentralised certification procedures, should be established in order to promote digital literacy throughout the Union;
>
> Define, by the end of 2000, the means for fostering the *mobility of students*, teachers and training and research staff both through making the best use of existing Community programmes (Socrates, Leonardo, Youth), by removing obstacles and through greater transparency in the recognition of qualifications and periods of study and training; to take steps to remove obstacles to teachers' mobility by 2002 and to attract high-quality teachers;
>
> A *common European format* should be developed for *curriculum vitae*, to be used on a voluntary basis in order to facilitate mobility by helping the assessment of knowledge acquired, both by education and training establishments and by employers.[12]

At its Lisbon meeting the European Council acknowledged that the pursuit of an active employment policy was both desirable and appropriate. The ultimate aim, though, was not just an increase in the overall number of jobs but, significantly, the creation of quality, value-added employment opportunities.[13] Four key areas were identified as requiring special attention. First, in the context of improving employability and reducing skills gaps across Europe, employment services ought to have access to a Europe-wide database on jobs and learning opportunities. Second, higher priority ought to be given to lifelong learning as a 'basic component' of the European 'social model'.[14] Further, the focus ought to be on increasing employment in services, including personal services. And, finally, furthering equal opportunities meant reducing occupational segregation, and better reconciling working life and family life, with particular emphasis on improvements in the provision of childcare.

Facing the Social—and Environmental—Challenge

A mid-term review of the Lisbon agenda for growth and employment was carried out in 2004. The Kok Report,[15] named after its chair and a former prime minister of the Netherlands, laments the lack of progress in implementing the Lisbon strategy. The overall criticism as regards an overloaded agenda, poor co-ordination and conflicting priorities is unequivocally directed towards both EU institutions and member states. But the latter are additionally singled out for having displayed a distinct lack of political will to act. The Report stresses the need to see the inter-relationship as well as interdependence of the component parts of the Lisbon strategy. The Report holds that:

> Improved economic growth and increased employment provide the means to sustain social cohesion and environmental sustainability. In their turn, social cohesion and environmental sustainability can contribute to a higher growth and employment.[16]

The link between social and environmental protection is no coincidence. In Europe neither is seen as contributing to a negative business climate *per se*. On the contrary, environmental policies are being promoted as opportunities for European businesses to gain a competitive edge in global markets. Specifically, by focusing on resource-efficient technologies that, so it is believed, 'other countries will eventually need to adopt', Europe may gain 'a first mover advantage'.[17]

To create the right climate for entrepreneurs, Europe must tackle three obstacles in particular. First, the overall burden of rules and regulations imposed on businesses, is arguably the most traditional and predictable. Here the Kok Report urges the Commission and the member states to pay particular attention to regulations that impact on the start-up of businesses. A second, related obstacle concerns the limited availability of finance. Company financing in Europe is said to be overly lending based and insufficiently risk capital based. Start-ups and small and medium-sized enterprises (SMEs) alike experience difficulties in attracting finance; they cannot meet the demands for guarantees by the traditional financial institutions. A third obstacle is that entrepreneurs are too often stigmatised when they fail, even though entrepreneurial activity carries an implied risk of failure.

Bankruptcy is said to trigger overly severe legal and social consequences in Europe as compared to, in particular, the United States. No doubt, the recent upheaval in the financial markets in the aftermath of the sub-prime lending debacle in that country warrants placing a cautionary gloss on the reading of that part of the Report!

As for the labour market reform agenda, the Kok Report urges member states to implement the recommendations of a 2003 European Employment Task Force, discussed more fully below, in order to increase the employment participation rate within the EU. Apart from the creation of new businesses, the Report identifies the need for greater 'adaptability' of both workers and companies.[18] The challenge for the European labour market is to find the right balance between (economic) flexibility and (social) security. Finding this balance is a shared responsibility for employees and employers, as well as for social partners and governments. Logically, adaptability of the workforce and education go hand in hand. As the Report puts it, rather laconically perhaps, 'lifelong learning is not a luxury'.[19] Further, in light of a greying European population, older workers are crucial. Special legal and financial incentives are required for workers to stay in the workforce longer, and for employers to hire and hold on to older workers. Much work remains to be done. Certainly, the European employment rate target for workers aged fifty and over—50 per cent by 2010—may seem unduly modest.

The Green Paper on Modernising Labour Law

In response to the above criticism in the Kok Report, the Lisbon strategy for growth and employment was officially relaunched in 2005.[20] One year later the EU sought to initiate public debate on how labour law in the EU could be adapted to support the Lisbon objective of achieving sustainable economic growth in light of the Community's overall commitment to full employment and social cohesion. The starting point for this debate was its 2006 Green Paper on modernising labour law.[21] The Green Paper in turn drew upon a 2003 report prepared by a group of experts, the so-called European Employment Task Force referred to above and with Wim Kok—the same person responsible for the 2004 interim report on the implementation of the original Lisbon agenda—as its chair.[22]

The 2003 report by the European Employment Task Force

expressed concern about the development of a two-tier labour market in Europe, with 'insiders' as winners and 'outsiders' as losers. The latter group was said to include anyone who is unemployed or has otherwise become detached from the labour market. Significantly, its coverage extends to employees working under precarious employment conditions and those employed informally, that is, in the unregulated (black market) economy. The challenge that presented itself was how to boost flexibility for business while simultaneously improving the social position of these 'outsiders'. The often-limited labour and social rights enjoyed by those in atypical employment relationships were acknowledged as having wider implications for the ability of these people to participate fully in society. The Task Force identified uncertainty about long-term employment prospects as affecting 'crucial' choices in people's private lives such as, for example, securing accommodation or planning a family.[23] If only the regulatory framework applicable to standard employment contracts could be adapted to facilitate greater flexibility for employees and employers alike, the need for recourse to precarious forms of employment in the first place would be reduced.[24] Accordingly, the Task Force urged the EU member states to review their own national laws as for the level of flexibility present in regular employment contracts in instances of, in particular, employment termination. Singled out for special attention were notice periods, the definition of unfair dismissal and, more generally, the costs and procedural requirements (that is, hurdles) surrounding individual as well as collective dismissal scenarios. The list may seem strikingly similar to the subject matter of the statutory dismissal reforms carried out towards the end of the Howard period in Australia.

The promotion of flexibility, when combined with a desire to boost employment security and reduce labour market segmentation, risks creating certain tensions that may end up pulling policy-makers in different directions. However, the realisation, and acknowledgment, that economic flexibility should not be viewed as an objective for its own sake but comes at a social cost that requires mitigation in a mature European society was clear enough. Rather than adopting a purely top-down approach by European or national legislatures, the drafters of the Green Paper believe that effective labour law reform crucially depends on involvement by the social partners and on a 'social dialogue' when 'framing collective and firm-level solutions'.[25] While the primary focus of the Commission document is on exploring the role of labour law in advancing a flexicurity agenda, other policy components of the flexicurity approach are listed as including lifelong learning, an active labour market policy, and more flexible social security rules.[26] Lifelong learning enables workers and business to keep pace with constantly changing skill requirements. Active labour market policies can and must encourage unemployed or inactive people to (re-)enter the labour market. Flexible social security rules in turn cater for the transitional needs of anyone in between jobs or temporarily leaving the labour market.

In scrutinising the role of labour law against the broader backdrop of a labour market that is fairer, more economically responsive and socially inclusive, the Green Paper articulates its own objectives in the following terms:

- To identify key challenges which have not yet yielded an adequate response and which reflect a clear deficit between the existing legal and contractual framework, on the one hand, and the realities of the world of work, on the other. The focus is mainly on *the personal scope of labour law rather than on issues of collective labour law.*
- To engage member state governments, the social partners and other relevant stakeholders in an open debate about how labour law can assist in promoting flexibility combined with employment security, *independently of the form of contract,* thereby ultimately contributing to increase employment and to reduce unemployment.
- To stimulate discussion on how different types of contractual relations, *together with employment rights applicable to all workers,* could facilitate job creation and assist both workers and enterprises by easing labour market transitions, assisting lifelong learning and fostering the creativity of the whole workforce.
- To contribute to the Better Regulation agenda[27] by promoting the modernisation of labour law, taking into account the overall *benefits and costs* involved, so as to enable *individual workers as well as businesses* to grasp more clearly what are their *rights and obligations.* Consideration needs to be given to the *problems*

faced especially by SMEs in dealing with the administrative costs imposed by both the Community and national legislation.[28]

The Concept of Flexicurity

The precise origins of the term 'flexicurity' are a matter of some debate. In the literature references to both the Netherlands and Denmark can be found.[29] Dutch Professor Hans Adriaansens, a sociologist, reportedly used the term in speeches and interviews in the mid-1990s. But flexicurity is also a notion that can be traced to a government policy pursued by the Danish government under the leadership of prime minister Rasmussen during the 1990s. At its core, the Danish/Dutch 'model' is perhaps best described in terms of a pyramid or triangle with three interrelated components as follows:[30]

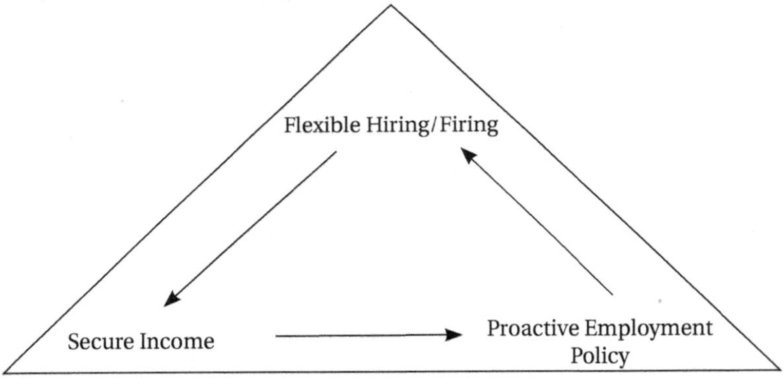

Figure 8.1: Flexicurity

The above model operates in an anti-clockwise fashion. The starting point, and a central feature at the top of the pyramid, is a relaxed approach to the regulation of hiring and firing, typified by limited conditions attached to the use of non-standard employment contracts and, in particular, a largely unrestricted approach to employee dismissal. In exchange, generous unemployment benefits are available through the state social security system to anyone who finds themselves 'in between' jobs. While the provision for financial assistance from the public purse is by no means restricted to short-term help only, it in turn forms an integral part of a proactive labour market policy directed at creating rights to, as well as obligations of, lifelong, continuing education and training in order to maximise employability of the employable.

The general idea behind flexicurity has now spread throughout Europe.[31] Ultimately each EU member state will have to make its own assessment how best to translate the concept into its individual national system of labour law. Even so, the Green Paper identifies six common matters in need of review in this regard. In dire need of some considerable creative thinking thus are employment 'transitions', but also the boundaries between labour law and commercial law, the problem of so-called three-way relationships triggered by temporary agency work arrangements, the organisation of working time, employee mobility, and labour law enforcement (including undeclared work). A brief explanation regarding the meaning and relevance of each of these items is set out below.

Employment Transitions

The focus of the Green Paper under this heading is on the promotion of employee mobility. Questions asked concern the traditional emphasis in national labour and social security laws on protecting the particular job held by dependent employees. The Commission document draws attention to a particular side-effect of this approach in that it potentially hampers, discourages even, voluntary and involuntary employee mobility alike. Instances of employment transition referred to in the Green Paper include not only dismissal and unemployment scenarios as prime cases of so-called involuntary employee mobility. Also targeted, expressly, are situations of carer's leave, education and training leave, and even voluntary career breaks. The Green Paper asks whether it might be useful to consider the introduction of more flexible employment protection legislation in conjunction with well-designed assistance to the unemployed, both in the form of passive (income compensation) and active (career training) labour market policies. It further asks whether collective bargaining between the social partners could play a role in promoting—and, presumably, guiding—any 'transitions between different contractual forms for upward mobility over the course of a fully active working life'.[32] Recent labour law reforms in the Netherlands,[33] Austria[34] and Spain[35] are all cited as meaningful examples of national legislation aimed at facilitating such employment transitions.

Uncertainty with Regard to the Law

This aspect of the Green Paper goes to the very core of the personal scope of application of labour law. The traditional binary distinction between employed and self-employed is said to no longer adequately depict the economic and social reality of work. Specifically, the emergence of various forms of 'non-standard' work has obscured the boundaries between labour law and commercial (corporate) law. Here the Green Paper posits the obvious question whether greater clarity may be needed in the legal definition of employees and contractors by the national authorities. However, the Green Paper raises this question for the specific purpose of exploring ways to facilitate 'bona fide'[36] transitions from employment to self-employment and *vice versa*. In the same vein, it asks whether a 'floor of rights'[37] needs to deal with the working conditions of all, regardless of the form of the contractual framework under which work is being performed. This in turn invites consideration of the impact of any such minimum legal requirements on job creation and worker protection. The regulation of the working conditions for self-employed commercial agents is cited as indicative action at the supranational level of the EU in this regard. In order to provide basic protection to independent commercial agents in their dealings with the principals who engage their services, Directive 86/653/EEC lays down uniform rules as regards, in particular, payment of remuneration, conditions for the conversion of fixed-term contracts into contracts of indefinite length, and compensation at the time of termination of any contracts.[38]

Three-Way Relationships

The growing incidence of temporary agency work as well as the practice of subcontracting has drawn attention to legal uncertainties that arise when people are hired by one company to perform work at the premises of another. The resulting 'dual employer' relationship necessitates a clear distribution of the responsibilities between the initial hiring firm and the end user of the employee. From a labour law perspective, the bottom line is that the employment rights of the employee are safeguarded in an appropriate fashion. In Europe special problems arise when both employers operate under different national laws. How to ensure adequate employee protection without unduly tampering with the operation of the internal market?

The Green Paper acknowledges that temporary agency work is regulated in most EU countries. Typically, the member states use a mixture of legislation, collective bargaining agreements and industry self-regulation. A proposed EC Directive seeks to avoid discriminatory treatment of agency workers *vis-à-vis* 'regular' employees in user companies.[39] Adoption of the proposal has been blocked by some member states for over five years. The Green Paper asks whether there may be a need to clarify the employment status of temporary agency workers.[40] Specifically, it asks whether the legal responsibilities of the various parties within a multiple employment relationship ought to be clarified in order to determine who is accountable for compliance with employment rights.[41]

Subcontracting also establishes a three-way relationship between the parties. In some member states the principal contractor is made legally liable for the obligations of their sub-contractors. While this facilitates monitoring compliance with employment legislation, it presents a potential obstacle to the Community principle of free movement of services. The Green Paper points at case law by the European Court of Justice to suggest that such an approach can be compatible with Community law provided the national measure satisfies the requirements of necessity and proportionality.[42] It asks whether the subsidiary liability of the contractor for the actions of subcontractors is both 'effective and feasible' or whether, alternatively, adequate employee protection can be ensured in other ways.[43]

Working Time

The only issue raised in connection with working time in the Green Paper concerns the link between flexibility in the organisation of working time and the occupational health and safety of employees. While the issue directly relates to a stalemate reached in the EU Council in the immediate lead-up to the release of the Green Paper, the underlying concern about the negative implications of flexible working time for employee wellbeing is a longstanding one in European law-making. In November 2006 a special meeting of the Employment, Social Policy, Health and Consumer Affairs Council failed to reach agreement on a revision of Directive 2003/88/EC[44] which in turn is built upon an original working time Directive dating from 1993.[45] The original (1993) Directive was itself the product of a political compromise and the sheer number of qualifications and exceptions it contained earned the Directive a rather dubious reputation as a 'tortuous and difficult instrument' to administer.[46]

Key issues in contention from the very beginning were provisions on so-called individual opt-out and on-call time. The former concerns the ability (or inability) of employees to opt out of the maximum 48-hour working week. The latter seeks to address the question how to calculate working time in scenarios of employees being on call, and thus available for work, even though they remain 'inactive' during some of that time. The United Kingdom, which consistently expressed its opposition to the regulation of working time ever since the 1993 Directive, strongly supports the concept of maintaining the individual opt-out. As for on-call time, the European Court of Justice has ruled on three occasions during the past decade that the full period of time during which an employee is at the disposal of the employer counts as working time.[47]

The Green Paper asks how best to modify the existing (minimum) requirements as regards the organisation of working time in order to provide greater flexibility for both employers and employees while at the same time ensuring 'a high standard' of protection for the health and safety of employees. A related question invites suggestions as to which aspects of the organisation of working time ought to be tackled 'as a matter of priority' by the Community.[48] The answers to these questions undoubtedly will be influenced by a subsequent political agreement, reached on 10 June 2008, in which the member states paved the way for new Directives on working time and on working conditions for temporary agency workers.[49]

Employee Mobility

In the past the EU has largely left the definition of 'employee' to the member states. The Green Paper questions the wisdom of this approach, especially given the transnational operation of many businesses in Europe. Continued reliance on national rather than EU law potentially hampers the Community's social policy goal of striking a balance between flexibility and security for employees. While the Green Paper indirectly acknowledges the futility of seeking agreement on a single definition of employee (for purposes of EU law) in the current political climate, it invites constructive suggestions for 'more convergent' definitions in the various EU Directives.[50]

Enforcement Issues

Labour markets depend on effective enforcement mechanisms for their efficient functioning. The Green Paper identifies 'undeclared' work as a 'particularly worrying and enduring feature of today's labour markets', especially when viewed in conjunction with cross-border movement of employees. Undeclared work is said to constitute 'the main contributing factor to social dumping'. Furthermore, it exploits workers and distorts competition.[51] The issue undoubtedly acquires extra significance in light of the massive expansion of the EU membership's base towards the East.

The Green Paper calls for more effective co-operation between the various enforcement agencies at the national level. In this regard, it suggests that strengthened administrative co-operation at the EU level may also assist member states in tackling abuse and evasion of employee protective labour rules. The paper asks whether greater administrative co-operation may be needed to boost effectiveness in the enforcement of Community labour law. The paper suggests that the social partners may be able to play a role in facilitating such co-operation.[52] Finally, it raises the question of whether further EU initiatives might be needed to combat undeclared work.[53]

Summary and Provisional Evaluation

When viewed individually, no single item on the above list of six presents itself as particularly revolutionary. As a package, however, the items can act as a formidable impetus and guide for labour law reform. Of course, the flexicurity 'model' does not entail a precise blueprint. Rather, it constitutes a general reference point for change only. Ultimately, each member state will have to come up with its own answer to the challenges posed by globalisation. At the level of the EU, one major limitation is jurisdictional in nature. Fifty years of European integration notwithstanding, the power to regulate labour law remains overwhelmingly national rather than supranational. This limits what the EU can do, unless an 'Australian' solution of sorts were to be found—in line with a creative (centralist) reinterpretation of that country's Commonwealth constitution as regards the relationship between the federal and state powers in matters of labour law. Willingness to change, on the other hand, is an entirely different matter. In principle, the EU has the ability to offer an approach to the regulation of labour law that differs from past practice. In this regard the concept of flexicurity presents an opportunity for the EU to lead from the top, with new ideas and a fresh outlook on labour law. Significantly, the Green Paper signals that the ultimate goal ought not to be just more jobs but better jobs. Extra jobs to be created should not come at a social cost of inferior employment conditions.

The Green Paper does not advocate a *tabula rasa* approach to labour law regulation. It does not seek to start from scratch, not even when dealing with the most problematic issue of employment transitions. Thus, for example, existing (national) dismissal laws need not be done away with in their entirety. In effect, while the proclaimed focus is on flexibility as well as security, the undertone overall remains heavily protectionist. As a result, the Green Paper raises more questions than it answers. How to restructure employment conditions for all without ending up with a mere lowest common denominator of employee protection? How much to improve the conditions of anyone employed other than on a full-time basis and/or in an open-ended employment relationship with the employer while still avoiding the risk that both objectives end up cancelling each other out, especially given the seemingly endless expansion of the group of workers once known as atypical employees? Will it be necessary to put a cap on that group of employees, if only to limit the size of those who, in terms of their employment conditions, are doomed to stay second-class citizens *vis-à-vis* the relative comfort and security full-time employees in open-ended employment relationships undoubtedly will continue to enjoy, even after any labour law revamp has been executed? The fact that the definition of 'employee' itself continues to stir controversy is a painful reminder of the sheer scale of the problem.

Common Principles on Flexicurity

The Green Paper provides a basis for consultation and reflection. In June 2007 the European Commission moved to a next stage by drafting eight 'common principles' on flexicurity.[54] These were formally accepted by the Council of the European Union in December 2007 and can be summarised as follows:

1 Flexicurity is about more and better jobs, adaptability and social inclusion.
2 Flexicurity requires an integrated approach to contractual employment arrangements, comprehensive lifelong learning strategies, effective (active) labour market policies, and adequate yet sustainable social security systems.
3 Flexicurity, by definition, is not about a single model or strategy to be super-imposed on all. For flexicurity to be effective, it needs to be tailored to the specific circumstances of individual countries. Even so, flexicurity always implies a balance to be struck between the rights and responsibilities of all parties (employers, employees, job seekers and public authorities).
4 Flexicurity is about overcoming labour market segmentation.
5 Flexicurity is to be pursued both at micro and at macro economic levels.
6 Flexicurity is about promoting equal opportunities for both genders.
7 Flexicurity requires a climate of trust among the social partners.
8 Any costs associated with flexicurity ought to be spread fairly between public authorities and private parties, with particular attention to the specific situation occupied by SMEs.[55]

As anticipated, these common principles stress the need to simultaneously work towards flexible contractual arrangements for the employment of workers, active labour market policies, comprehensive lifelong learning and training strategies, and modern social protection systems that provide adequate income support during periods of unemployment. To assist the member states in bringing about flexicurity, the Commission additionally set out a number of typical 'pathways', effectively four packages of suggestions, that cater for differences in the regulatory frameworks of individual member states.[56] These pathways have been developed on the basis of a report prepared by a Flexicurity Expert Group with Professor Wilthagen from the University of Tilburg as its *rapporteur*.[57] While the Report is careful not to identify individual countries, in the Commission's opinion these pathways, whether viewed individually or in combination with one another, address pertinent challenges in the various member states.

Flexicurity Pathway I: Tackling Contractual Segmentation

This pathway is meant to be of greatest interest to countries where the main problem is labour market segmentation, with decreasing numbers of haves and ever-rising numbers of have-nots in employment. These are countries where open-ended contracts of employment are traditionally seen as the primary vehicle for full labour law protection, including access to training opportunities and social security benefits. Belgium can be viewed as a representative case in point.

This first pathway seeks to improve the position of people, often but not always new job entrants, employed under precarious contractual arrangements (fixed-term work, agency work, on-call work) by providing adequate protection from the very beginning of their employment relationship while still facilitating the transition of these employees to better contractual arrangements over time. To this effect it is suggested that open-ended contracts be redesigned so that they are more readily available to newcomers on the job market. Rather than starting with a series of fixed-term or agency contracts, as is often the case currently, an open-ended contract could be made available immediately but any associated job security and other entitlements would be built up progressively over time. The Commission refers to this approach to employment relationships as the 'tenure track' approach. It quasi-guarantees automatic progress to better contractual conditions and reduces the risk of employees getting 'stuck' in less protective employment arrangements.

Conversely, employees employed under open-ended contracts may need to settle for 'redesigned' rules as regards, in particular, economic dismissals. The Commission's Communication to various EU institutions on this score is suitably vague, though. The document does not state outright that redundancies ought to become easier for employers to execute. Instead, the emphasis is on 'addressing bureaucracy', including length of procedures, transparency of outcomes, and generally 'making the process more reliable'.[58]

To further assist in making temporary employment a less marginal proposition into the future, the first pathway calls for improved training facilities. It is acknowledged that temporary employees are often unable to access on-the-job training opportunities because employers are reluctant to invest in transient workers. The installation of training funds and training institutions at above-company levels of the industry branch or the region would address the problem. To enhance participation in this form of lifelong learning, public authorities ought to consider meaningful incentives for employers and employees alike, including financial assistance and tax credits. Simultaneously, active labour market policies need to be (re-) designed to support not only the long-term unemployed but also those who experience frequent intervals of unemployment. Closer co-operation between public authorities and temporary work agencies is offered by way of a practical suggestion. Finally, the social security systems could be remodelled to allow temporary workers to accumulate rights and make entitlements portable across firms or industry. The Commission sees particular merit in offering higher benefits during shorter spells of unemployment.

Flexicurity Pathway II: Tackling a Lethargic Workforce

This pathway is said to be of greatest interest to countries with low job mobility, both within and between companies. Its focus is on increasing investment in the employability of workers in two principal ways. First, it would allow and expect employees within companies to continuously update their skills in order to be better prepared for future changes in production methods and organisation of work. Second, this pathway seeks to look beyond the employee's current job and current employer by putting in place a system that facilitates job transitions that are both safe (in terms of employment conditions) and successful (in terms of business needs) whenever company restructuring results in redundancies.

This second pathway is directed at countries where the primary source of employment security is created by and within large companies. Employees there tend to develop a strong attachment to their employer which results in low labour market mobility. When these countries additionally operate generous social security systems, it can prove particularly difficult to 'persuade' any employees who become unemployed to actively seek and accept alternative employment. The net result tends to be long-term unemployment for a relatively large part of a country's population at working age.

Apart from ensuring conditionality of social security benefits and effective monitoring of job search efforts, it is suggested under this pathway that companies step up their investment in lifelong learning and, therefore, the employability of their workforce. Specifically, skills development programs could be developed that offer personal training and career programs to each employee. The Commission suggests that such programs could even be made an integral component of the employment contract, including an obligation for employees to meet the agreed upgrade in skill requirements. As for the promotion of employee mobility across different companies, the Commission is less specific in its suggestions. 'Early intervention' is meant to avoid situations where the search for a new job is delayed until an actual redundancy occurs. Here the Commission calls for 'joint action by all concerned': employers, social partners, public employment services and even temporary work agencies are invited to co-ordinate their activities in order to prevent redundant employees becoming long-term unemployed.

Two proposals formulated by the European Expert Group on Flexicurity somehow did not make it into the Commission Communication on flexicurity pathways. Both address the position of older employees. As part of an approach to systematic lifelong learning, the Expert Group considered that job rotation schemes could not only allow for productivity levels to be maintained but might also strengthen employee motivation. Further, career trajectories, including training as required, for older employees might prevent their early exit from the labour market by allowing these workers to take on less demanding tasks over time.[59]

Flexicurity Pathway III: Tackling Social Exclusion and Upward Mobility Problems

In some countries the key challenge for the future may be the occurrence of substantial gaps in skills and opportunities among segments of the population. Employment participation rates may be high overall, but low skill levels can prevent certain specific groups (for example, single parents, migrants) from entering the labour market whereas others may lack opportunities to upscale in terms of job quality. The main emphasis of this third pathway therefore is on lifelong learning policies that start at the bottom, that is, at the initial schooling system.

Under this pathway early school leaving is to be 'fought' and the general qualification levels of all school leavers improved. Among the adult population illiteracy and innumeracy problems need to be addressed, but ought to extend to easy access of language and computer training both inside and outside the workplace. Public authorities may wish to improve upon any existing (financial or other) incentives for companies to invest in their workforce. Particularly innovative is the suggestion that individual training accounts be put in place that allow employees to spend a certain amount of working time on personal development in co-operation, of course, with their employers.

The financial implications of this third pathway could be considerable. In the Commission's view, improvements in basic education need to be implemented as a priority, but it acknowledges that results may take some time to eventuate. Improved workplace training requires private investment 'supported by public incentives'.[60] By the same token, though, to make the recruitment of lowly skilled employees an attractive proposition for business, adjustments are required on the fronts of both active labour market policies and social security systems. As for the former, the focus needs to be on providing adequate training in order to achieve upward mobility and sustainable—rather than merely quick—reintegration. As for the latter, the mixture between offering positive (for example, supplementary benefits) as well as negative (for example, conditional benefits) incentives needs to be geared towards minimising the chances of some people simply transferring their membership from the living poor to the working poor.

Flexicurity Pathway IV: Tackling Long-Term Unemployment and the Black Market

This pathway seeks to address problems faced by countries with relatively high numbers of people on long-term unemployment benefits, typically in the aftermath of substantial economic restructuring. The main problem to arise is that, even when new jobs become available, these tend to be in the service industry, often with precarious employment conditions. As a result, benefit recipients have difficulty 'seizing' any employment opportunities and when they do, they are tempted to work informally only.

In a way this final pathway is the least relevant from an Australian perspective. As indicated in the Report by the European Expert Group on flexicurity, the focus here is on countries that have only just begun their transition process towards a market-based economy. In these countries, past employment and income security were overwhelmingly provided by the state or state-run companies. Typically, social security systems in turn provided long-term benefits but no regular checks as to the availability of employees for work or even their continued ability to work. It represents an approach that facilitates and, arguably, stimulates labour market exit and informal work at the expense of transition into new employment.[61]

The main suggestion under this fourth flexicurity pathway is for adequate levels of protection, that is, decent employment conditions, to be offered to all employees—including those employed informally in emerging sectors of the economy. Improving the rights of informal workers and providing access to professional training may make the regularisation of informal work a less futile proposition. Any resulting increase in the size of the regular workforce should have a beneficial effect for the country's tax revenue. This in turn would allow for additional financial resources to be devoted to labour (and taxation) inspectorates in combating the black market economy.

Where to from Here?

Mission for Flexicurity

The ball is now firmly in the camp of the various member states. While each of the above pathways focuses on a different key challenge, all four have been prepared by the Commission for purposes of guidance and inspiration only. No total *carte blanche* exists. Implementation of the flexicurity agenda at the level of the individual member states is closely monitored by the Commission and regular national reports need to be submitted to it.

The EU member states are expected to report on the implementation of their own national pathways in the last quarter of 2008, with follow-up reports to be submitted in 2009 and 2010. To assist the member states in the preparation of their first national report, the Commission launched a public initiative in March 2008, referred to as Europe's Mission for Flexicurity.[62] The Mission for Flexicurity initiative allows the Commission to monitor the member states' progress with their national implementation of the common flexicurity principles. Further, the initiative seeks to ensure the full integration of these common principles in future activities of the Community.

The Mission for Flexicurity in essence stands for the establishment of a small working group, composed of European Community officials and representatives of the European social partners. The group's *modus operandi* is to visit a limited number of self-selecting (yet not totally random) member states for in-depth discussions about the state of play regarding the development and implementation of the Common Principles on Flexicurity at national and sub-national levels. Following these visits, the Mission is expected to prepare a report for presentation to the December 2008 meeting of the European (Employment and Social Affairs) Council.

National State of Play

Of course, the starting position for individual countries can vary significantly. Research carried out by the European Foundation for the Improvement of Living and Working Conditions, an autonomous body of the EU to assist in the formulation of policy on social and work-related matters,[63] examined the extent to which flexicurity is reflected in the regulatory framework of the various EU member states. Published in 2007,[64] national differences were recorded as regards each of the components that make up the flexicurity pyramid.

In terms of hiring and firing, the regulatory regimes of Latvia and Spain were found to be the most rigid overall. When looking at commencement and termination of employment separately, difficulties as regards hiring were most pronounced in France and Greece, whereas dismissal laws were most rigid in Latvia, the Netherlands, Portugal and Slovenia. By contrast, the most flexible labour markets, in terms of regulation of recruitment and employment termination, include, not surprisingly, the United Kingdom and Denmark but also, rather surprisingly, Belgium and Hungary.[65] In terms of hiring, the study examined the relative ease with which fixed-term contracts can be used for the performance of temporary tasks, the maximum cumulative duration of any such fixed-term contracts, and minimum pay levels. As regards firing, the particular focus was on rules governing redundancy. Factors taken into account all sought to determine whether and, if so, to what extent, redundancy was treated as a special form of dismissal. These included, for instance, the requirement to notify a third party (typically, a government agency) or the requirement to seek prior approval from a third party. Also included was the requirement to mitigate the social impact of economic restructuring decisions, by considering reassignment or retraining options as an alternative to termination. Finally, as regards business restructuring, the European Foundation checked whether priority rules might apply in carrying out terminations for redundancy and/or in terms of the re-employment of any employees made redundant.

In terms of income support, the Scandinavian countries (Sweden and Denmark, in particular) and the older member states (Luxembourg, Belgium, France, Germany, Austria and the Netherlands, especially) fared best. The lowest level of social security protection was found to exist in the three Baltic countries. But the figures were also quite low for Slovakia, Hungary, Poland, Ireland, Malta and the Czech Republic.[66] The Foundation Report notes a common trend across social security systems in the EU to switch from welfare orientation to more proactive employment policies, in particular as regards dealing with the social aftermath of economic restructuring.[67]

The Report adopts a broad approach to the pursuit of active labour market policies in the EU member states. Acknowledged as typical forms of active labour market programs are training and development, job rotation and job sharing, employment incentives, integration of disabled individuals, direct job creation and start-up initiatives. Denmark and the Netherlands are singled out for their relatively high expenditure on active labour market policies. Generally, the older member states of the EU-15 score considerably better than the EU-10 newcomers.[68]

Interestingly, the Report found no major differences between the member states in terms of total expenditure on education. However, there are noticeable national variations as regards the significance attached to lifelong learning by the social partners. From the late 1980s onwards, lifelong learning has grown in importance as a topic for collective bargaining in most member states. Centralised bargaining, at a national and industry level, has been the preferred option in Austria, Belgium, Denmark, France, the Netherlands and Spain. In Germany and Italy, in particular, centralised bargaining has been supplemented by negotiations on employee training and development at the level of individual companies. In the United Kingdom and Ireland, among others, collective bargaining has so far had only a limited impact on lifelong learning initiatives.[69]

Labour Law and Flexibility: Back to the Future?

The future of labour law is intrinsically linked to the future shape of labour law itself. While it would be presumptuous to assume too much in terms of what this future may hold, it is clear that the labour law of old is either gone, as in New Zealand, or under considerable strain, as in Europe and Australia. Increasingly, labour law is expected to somehow combine aspects of both social stability and economic flexibility. In the process, the *raison d'être* of labour law—employee protection—risks being compromised or, at the very least, obscured. On one interpretation, labour law in the future can only be 'allowed' to be protective provided it does so without upsetting the overriding need of business for flexibility. The purpose of labour law thus becomes subordinate to the imperatives of a globalised economy.

The effectiveness of a revamped labour law inevitably becomes more difficult to measure. Parallels can be drawn with taxation law. If seen largely as an exercise in revenue gathering, it is relatively straightforward to determine how well tax law meets this core objective. Once other, at times competing, goals are thrown into the equation, however, say tax law is additionally expected to perform a social (for example, income redistribution) function, the picture becomes more blurred. Another parallel is between labour law and environmental law. If the purpose of the latter is simply to protect the environment, its effectiveness is easy to assess. Of course, environmental laws never operate in a vacuum; they cannot be studied in the abstract. Similarly, for labour law, it is trite to observe that a social paradise cannot be built on top of an economic graveyard. Environmental protection does have repercussions for the economy or, at least, it impacts on how economic activities are being conducted. The point is, though, that, if cause and effect are too readily confused, an apparent focus on environmental protection may easily turn into a focus on protecting the economic interests of business whenever environmental concerns are being raised. The same goes for labour law. Labour law should never become downgraded to a study of legal rules for the protection of the economy whenever employee protection is at issue. Not only would this affect the face and shape of any such labour law, it would no longer be labour law worthy of that name.

Social protection and economic viability are values that are inevitably linked, as are environmental and economic concerns. The difficulty with contemporary labour law lies in the fact that social and economic issues have become more intrinsically intertwined than ever before.

To strive for ever more perfect economic prosperity, for its own sake, is meaningless. Policy-makers in Europe and Australia are united in their desire for the right mix of economic and social priorities, yet seem prepared to strike a different balance. The current approach to flexicurity at the level of the EU suggests that the European Commission prefers to err on the side of employee protection, if only to preserve the European social model. The provision for a statutory minimum floor of employee rights in Australia, notwithstanding, the Labor government by contrast is loath to appear unduly anti-business. In seeking to tackle the challenges for the future, both the EU and Australia are prepared to err on the side of caution—only they come to the issue from opposite ends of the spectrum.

Under the Australian version of flexicurity, economic flexibility is to be achieved primarily through workplace bargaining in order to be better able to take account of the specific needs of business at the actual place of work. It represents an approach to the determination of employment conditions for employees that stands in sharp contrast to the centralised system of wage-fixing of old. Under the Rudd administration any negative social implications are to be cushioned by means of an expanded social safety net of ten rather than five statutory minimum employment conditions. While commendable, by European (civil law) standards the legislative floor of employee rights remains distinctly modest. That perception alters little when a streamlined system of modern awards—yet to be put into effect—is additionally factored into the overall picture.

Clearly every system of labour law ultimately needs to strike its own balance between economic flexibility and social stability. In doing so, advanced Western societies ought to resist the temptation to reduce the contents of their labour laws to a mere listing of certain basic social rights for employees or even, more generally, workers.

Such rights, especially when presented as 'fundamental' and 'universal' in nature, risk having to be phrased in terms so rudimentary as to deprive them of genuine meaning. Further, once their solemn promulgation has occurred, it can provide an excuse for political inaction going forward. The risks are real, as illustrated by the multiple initiatives at cataloguing, from 1989 onwards, core employee rights at the supranational level of the EU. As political statements of intent, fundamental rights can serve a purpose. As enforceable legal entitlements, their relevance is decidedly questionable. Once labour law mutates into an applied course in human rights, it simply ceases to exist.

Notes

1 'The Light on the Hill', Ben Chifley Memorial Lecture, delivered by Noel Pearson, 12 August 2000. An electronic version of the text is available at www.capeyorkpartnerships.com/team/noelpearson/lightonhill-12-8-00.htm-55k

2 www.doingbusiness.org

3 Commission of the European Communities, *Modernising Labour Law to Meet the Challenges of the 21st Century.*

4 Lisbon European Council 23 and 24 March 2000, Presidency Conclusions, p. 1. The text is available electronically at http://www.europarl.europa.eu/summits/lis1-en.htm

5 ibid., p. 2.

6 ibid.

7 ibid., p. 9.

8 ibid., p. 7.

9 ibid.

10 Vranken, 'Legal Education Reform in Australia and the Impact of Globalisation: A Comparative Perspective'.

11 Australian Government, *First 100 Days: Achievements of the Rudd Government.*

12 Lisbon European Council, Presidency Conclusions, pp. 7–8 (emphasis added).

13 'More and better jobs': ibid., p. 8. It can be seen as a direct reaction to, and a rejection of, the creation of so-called McJobs in the United States. See also *Question and Answer: A New Start for the Lisbon Strategy,* MEMO 05/34, Brussels, 2 February 2005.

14 Lisbon European Council, Presidency Conclusions, p. 8.

15 *Facing the Challenge: The Lisbon Strategy for Growth and Employment.* Report from the High Level Group chaired by Wim Kok. An electronic version can be found at www.europa.eu.int/comm/Lisbon-strategy/index-en.html

16 ibid., p. 6 (Executive Summary).

17 ibid., p. 35.
18 ibid., p. 32.
19 ibid., p. 33.
20 Commission Communication to the Spring 2005 European Council, 'Working Together for Growth and Jobs. A New Start for the Lisbon Strategy', p. 24.
21 Commission of the European Communities, *Modernising Labour Law to Meet the Challenges of the 21st Century.*
22 Report of the Employment Task Force, *Jobs, Jobs, Jobs: Creating More Employment in Europe,* November 2003, cited in the Commission's Green Paper, p. 3.
23 ibid.
24 In Europe the share of non-standard employment, including self-employment, increased from 36 per cent in 2001 to nearly 40 per cent of the EU-25 workforce in 2005. Part-time employment accounted for some 60 per cent of employment creation since 2000. Single-person businesses constituted 10 per cent of all workers in 2005: ibid., pp. 7–8.
25 ibid., p. 3.
26 ibid., p. 4.
27 *Better Regulation for Growth and Jobs in the European Union* is the heading of a Communication from the Commission to the Council and the European Parliament.
28 ibid. (emphasis added).
29 European Foundation for the Improvement of Living and Working Conditions, *Approaches to Flexicurity: EU Models,* pp. 7–9.
30 Madsen describes the Danish flexicurity approach in terms of a 'golden triangle': See Madsen, 'How Can It Possibly Fly? The Paradox of Dynamic Labour Market in a Scandinavian Welfare State', p. 331.
31 European Foundation for the Improvement of Living and Working Conditions, *Approaches to Flexicurity: EU Models,* p. 8.
32 Commission of the European Communities, *Modernising Labour Law to Meet the Challenges of the 21st Century,* p. 10 (question 6).
33 Flexicurity and Security Act (*wet flexibiliteit en zekerheid*) 1998.
34 Severance (*Abfertigung*) Act 2002.
35 Specifically, a Spanish decree of June 2006 is cited as seeking to reduce the financial cost for employers when temporary employment arrangements are converted into open-ended contracts.
36 Commission of the European Communities, *Modernising Labour Law to Meet the Challenges of the 21st Century,* p. 12 (question 7).
37 ibid. (question 8).
38 *Official Journal* L 382, 31 December 1986. It must be noted, however, that as indicated by the Long Title of the Directive, technically this European law merely seeks to co-ordinate the laws of the member states in this matter.
39 Commission of the European Communities, Amended Proposal for a Directive of the European Parliament and the Council on Working

Conditions for Temporary Workers, Brussels 28 November 2002; COM (2002) 701 final.

40 Commission of the European Communities, *Modernising Labour Law to Meet the Challenges of the 21st Century*, p. 13 (question 10).

41 ibid. (question 9).

42 Case C-60/03 (*Wolff and Müller*) [2004] ECR I-9553.

43 Commission of the European Communities, *Modernising Labour Law to Meet the Challenges of the 21st Century*, p. 13 (question 9).

44 *Official Journal*, L 299/9, 18 November 2003.

45 Directive 93/104/EC concerning Certain Aspects of the Organisation of Working Time, *Official Journal*, L 307/18, 13 December 1993.

46 Blanpain, *European Labour Law*, p. 300.

47 See cases C-303/98 (*Simap*) [2000] ECR I-7963; C-151/02 (*Jaeger*) [2003] ECR I-8389; and C-14/04 (*Dellas*) [2006] 2 CMLR 39.

48 Commission of the European Communities, *Modernising Labour Law to Meet the Challenges of the 21st Century*, p. 14 (question 11).

49 'Commission strongly welcomes today's political agreement on Working Time and Working Conditions for Temporary Agency Workers'.

50 Commission of the European Communities, *Modernising Labour Law to Meet the Challenges of the 21st Century*, p. 14 (question 12).

51 ibid.

52 ibid., p. 15 (question 13).

53 ibid. (question 14).

54 Commission of the European Communities, *Towards Common Principles of Flexicurity*.

55 Council of the European Union, 16201/07, SOC 523, ECOFIN 503, Brussels, 6 December 2007. The text of the 'common principles' is contained in an annex to this document. For ease of reference, it is reproduced in full in Appendix 3 in this book.

56 Annex I (Flexicurity Pathways) of the Communication from the Commission to the Council, the European Parliament, the European Economic and Social Committee and the Committee of Regions: Commission of the European Communities, *Towards Common Principles of Flexicurity*, p. 14ff.

57 European Expert Group on Flexicurity, *Flexicurity Pathways: Turning Hurdles into Stepping Stones*. An electronic version of the Report is available at http://ec.europa.eu/employment-social/employment-strategy/pdf/flexi-pathways-en.pdf

58 Annex I of the Commission Communication, Commission of the European Communities, *Towards Common Principles of Flexicurity*, p. 14.

59 European Expert Group on Flexicurity, *Flexicurity Pathways: Turning Hurdles into Stepping Stones*, p. 27.

60 Annex I of the Commission Communication: Commission of the European Communities, *Towards Common Principles of Flexicurity*, p. 18.

61 European Expert Group on Flexicurity, *Flexicurity Pathways: Turning Hurdles into Stepping Stones*, p. 21.

62 European Commission, *Mission for Flexicurity: Terms of Reference.*
63 The Foundation has its own website at www.eurofound.europa.eu
64 European Foundation, *Approaches to Flexicurity: EU Models.* The study covers twenty-five of the twenty-seven EU member states. It predates the admission of Bulgaria and Romania to membership on 1 January 2007.
65 ibid., p. 11.
66 ibid., p. 20.
67 ibid., p. 17 quoting a 2005 study by the European Industrial Relations Observatory, *Redundancies and Redundancy Costs.*
68 ibid., p. 21.
69 ibid., pp. 22–3.

Epilogue

The Australian Government introduced the Fair Work Bill into the House of Representatives on 25 November 2008. Before the Bill can be adopted into law it will need to pass scrutiny of a full Senate Committee inquiry in 2009. It is anticipated that the new legislation will take effect on 1 January 2010. The Australian Government hopes that certain key aspects of the Bill—in particular the provisions on the bargaining framework and unfair dismissal—can become operative from 1 July 2009 onwards.

The proposed legislation seeks to replace the Workplace Relations Act 1996 (Cth) in its entirety. The text of the Bill, entitled A Bill for an Act relating to Workplace Relations and for Related Purposes, is 575 pages in length. It is accompanied by an equally formidable Explanatory Memorandum comprising 429 pages. The Fair Work Bill 2008 is divided into six chapters. The main substantive provisions can be found in chapters two and three.

Entitled Terms and Conditions of Employment, chapter two contains the much anticipated National Employment Standards as well as the provisions on Modern Awards and Enterprise Agreements. Award terms are divided into three categories: permissive, mandatory and prohibited terms. Permissive terms include provisions on outworkers and industry-specific redundancy schemes. A mandatory term of note is the provision for a so-called flexibility term. A flexibility term is defined in Section 144 of the Bill as a term enabling individual employees and their employer to agree on an arrangement by which the effect of the award is varied 'in order to meet the genuine needs of the employee and employer'. One crucial proviso is that the employee must be 'better off overall' as a result of the individual flexibility arrangement. Prohibited award contents include, *inter alia*, terms about the union's right of entry to employer premises. The 'better off overall' test also applies to enterprise agreements in relation to employees covered by an award, with the exception of employees employed under an individual flexibility arrangement.

Chapter three is headed Rights and Obligations of Employees, Employers, Organisations etc. The statutory provisions for the protection of employees against unfair dismissal can be found here. Chapter three also spells out the legal rules as regards protected industrial action.

Compliance and enforcement issues fall within the jurisdiction of the proposed Fair Work Divisions within the Federal Court of Australia and the Federal Magistrates Court.

While the Explanatory Memorandum states that the proposed legislation is simpler and substantially shorter than the current Workplace Relations Act 1996 (Cth), the Fair Work Bill 2008 by no means amounts to easy bedside reading. Even so, initial commentary in the general press suggests that both labour and industry are reasonably happy with the formal outcome of extensive, if not always open, consultations with the various stakeholders. In the same vein, Malcolm Turnbull for the Opposition has indicated the Coalition's acceptance of the Government's mandate for labour law reform. But politics is a fickle business. Only the future can tell.

Appendix 1

Community Charter of the Fundamental Social Rights of Workers (1989)*

TITLE I. FUNDAMENTAL SOCIAL RIGHTS OF WORKERS

Freedom of Movement

1. Every worker of the European Community shall have the right to freedom of movement throughout the territory of the Community, subject to restrictions justified on grounds of public order, public safety or public health.
2. The right to freedom of movement shall enable any worker to engage in any occupation or profession in the Community in accordance with the principles of equal treatment as regards access to employment, working conditions and social protection in the host country.
3. The right of freedom of movement shall also imply:
   - harmonisation of conditions of residence in all Member States, particularly those concerning family reunification;

---

* Commission of the European Communities, *Community Charter of the Fundamental Social Rights of Workers*, Office for Official Publications of the European Communities, Luxembourg, ISBN 92-826-0975-8, © European Communities, 1990

- elimination of obstacles arising from the non-recognition of diplomas or equivalent occupational qualifications;
- improvement of the living and working conditions of frontier workers.

Employment and Remuneration

4. Every individual shall be free to choose and engage in an occupation according to the regulations governing each occupation.
5. All employment shall be fairly remunerated. To this effect, in accordance with arrangements applying in each country:
    - workers shall be assured of an equitable wage, i.e. a wage sufficient to enable them to have a decent standard of living;
    - workers subject to terms of employment other than an open-ended full-time contract shall receive an equitable reference wage;
    - wages may be withheld, seized or transferred only in accordance with the provisions of national law; such provisions should entail measures enabling the worker concerned to continue to enjoy the necessary means of subsistence for himself and his family.
6. Every individual must be able to have access to public placement services free of charge.

Improvement of Living and Working Conditions

7. The completion of the internal market must lead to an improvement in the living and working conditions of workers in the European Community. This process must result from an approximation of these conditions while the improvement is being maintained, as regards in particular the duration and organisation of working time and forms of employment other than open-ended contracts, such as fixed-term contracts, part-time working, temporary work and seasonal work.

    The improvement must cover, where necessary, the development of certain aspects of employment regulations such as procedures for collective redundancies and those regarding bankruptcies.

8. Every worker of the European Community shall have a right to a weekly rest period and to annual paid leave, the duration of which must be harmonised in accordance with national practices while the improvement is being maintained.
9. The conditions of employment of every worker of the European Community shall be stipulated in laws, in a collective agreement or in a contract of employment, according to arrangements applying in each country.

Social Protection

According to the arrangements applying in each country:

10. Every worker of the European Community shall have a right to adequate social protection and shall, whatever his status and whatever the size of the undertaking in which he is employed, enjoy an adequate level of social security benefits.

    Persons who have been unable either to enter or re-enter the labour market and have no means of subsistence must be able to receive sufficient resources and social assistance in keeping with their particular situation.

Freedom of Association and Collective Bargaining

11. Employers and workers of the European Community shall have the right of association in order to constitute professional organisations or trade unions of their choice for the defence of their economic and social interests.

    Every employer and every worker shall have the freedom to join or not to join such organisations without any personal or occupational damage being thereby suffered by him.
12. Employers or employers' organisations, on the one hand, and workers' organisations, on the other, shall have the right to negotiate and conclude collective agreements under the conditions laid down by national legislation and practice.

    The dialogue between the two sides of industry at European level which must be developed, may, if the parties deem it desirable, result in contractual relations, in particular at inter-occupational and sectoral level.

13. The right to resort to collective action in the event of a conflict of interests shall include the right to strike, subject to the obligations arising under national regulations and collective agreements.

In order to facilitate the settlement of industrial disputes the establishment and utilisation at the appropriate levels of conciliation, mediation and arbitration procedures should be encouraged in accordance with national practice.

14. The internal legal order of the Member States shall determine under which conditions and to what extent the rights provided for in Articles 11 to 13 apply to the armed forces, the police and the civil service.

Vocational Training

15. Every worker of the European Community must be able to have access to vocational training and to receive such training throughout his working life. In the conditions governing access to such training there may be no discrimination on grounds of nationality.

The competent public authorities, undertakings or the two sides of industry, each within their own sphere of competence, should set up continuing and permanent training systems enabling every person to undergo retraining, more especially through leave for training purposes, to improve his skills or to acquire new skills, particularly in the light of technical developments.

Equal Treatment for Men and Women

16. Equal treatment for men and women must be assured. Equal opportunities for men and women must be developed.

To this end, action should be intensified wherever necessary to ensure the implementation of the principle of equality between men and women as regards in particular access to employment, remuneration, working conditions, social protection, education, vocational training and career development.

Measures should also be developed enabling men and women to reconcile their occupational and family obligations.

Information, Consultation and Participation for Workers

17. Information, consultation and participation for workers must be developed along appropriate lines, taking account of the practices in force in the various Member States.

    This shall apply especially in companies or groups of companies having establishments or companies in several Member States of the European Community.

18. Such information, consultation and participation must be implemented in due time, particularly in the following cases:
    - when technological changes which, from the point of view of working conditions and work organisation, have major implications for the work force are introduced into undertakings;
    - in connection with restructuring operations in undertakings or in cases of mergers having an impact on the employment of workers;
    - in cases of collective redundancy procedures;
    - when trans-frontier workers in particular are affected by employment policies pursued by the undertaking where they are employed.

Health Protection and Safety at the Workplace

19. Every worker must enjoy satisfactory health and safety conditions in his working environment. Appropriate measures must be taken in order to achieve further harmonization of conditions in this area while maintaining the improvements made.

    The measures shall take account, in particular, of the need for the training, information, consultation and balanced participation of workers as regards the risks incurred and the steps taken to eliminate or reduce them.

    The provisions regarding implementation of the internal market shall help to ensure such protection.

Protection of Children and Adolescents

20. Without prejudice to such rules as may be more favourable to young people, in particular those ensuring their preparation for work through vocational training, and subject to derogations

limited to certain light work, the minimum employment age must not be lower than the minimum school-leaving age and, in any case, not lower than 15 years.

21. Young people who are in gainful employment must receive equitable remuneration in accordance with national practice.

22. Appropriate measures must be taken to adjust labour regulations applicable to young workers so that their specific needs regarding development, vocational training and access to employment are met.

    The duration of work must, in particular, be limited—without it being possible to circumvent this limitation through recourse to overtime—and night work prohibited in the case of workers of under 18 years of age save in the case of certain jobs laid down in national legislation or regulations.

23. Following the end of compulsory education, young people must be entitled to receive initial vocational training of a sufficient duration to enable them to adapt to the requirements of their future working life; for young workers, such training should take place during working hours.

Elderly Persons

According to the arrangements applying in each country:

24. Every worker of the European Community must, at the time of retirement, be able to enjoy resources affording him or her a decent standard of living.

25. Every person who has reached retirement age but who is not entitled to a pension or who does not have other means of subsistence, must be entitled to sufficient resources and to medical and social assistance specifically suited to his needs.

Disabled Persons

26. All disabled persons, whatever the origin and nature of their disablement, must be entitled to additional concrete measures aimed at improving their social and professional integration.

    These measures must concern, in particular, according to the capacities of the beneficiaries, vocational training, ergonomics, accessibility, mobility, means of transport and housing.

TITLE II. IMPLEMENTATION OF THE CHARTER

27. It is more particularly the responsibility of the Member States, in accordance with the national practices, notably through legislative measures or collective agreements, to guarantee the fundamental social rights in this Charter and to implement the social measures indispensable to the smooth operation of the internal market as part of a strategy of economic and social cohesion.
28. The European Council invites the Commission to submit as soon as possible initiatives which fall within its powers, as provided for in the Treaties, with a view to the adoption of legal instruments for the effective implementation, as and when the internal market is completed, of those rights which come within the Community's area of competence.
29. The Commission shall establish each year, during the last three months, a report on the application of the Charter by the Member States and by the European Community.
30. The report of the Commission shall be forwarded to the European Council, the European Parliament and the Economic and Social Committee.

APPENDIX 2

Charter of Fundamental Rights of the European Union (2000)*

CHAPTER I. DIGNITY

Article 1. Human Dignity

Human dignity is inviolable. It must be respected and protected.

Article 2. Right to Life

1. Everyone has the right to life.
2. No one shall be condemned to the death penalty, or executed.

Article 3. Right to the Integrity of the Person

1. Everyone has the right to respect for his or her physical and mental integrity.
2. In the fields of medicine and biology, the following must be respected in particular:
    - the free and informed consent of the person concerned, according to the procedures laid down by law,

---

* http://eur-lex.europa.eu/ © European Communities

- the prohibition of eugenic practices, in particular those aiming at the selection of persons,
- the prohibition on making the human body and its parts as such a source of financial gain,
- the prohibition of the reproductive cloning of human beings.

Article 4. Prohibition of Torture and Inhuman or Degrading Treatment or Punishment

No one shall be subjected to torture or to inhuman or degrading treatment or punishment.

Article 5. Prohibition of Slavery and Forced Labour

1. No one shall be held in slavery or servitude.
2. No one shall be required to perform forced or compulsory labour.
3. Trafficking in human beings is prohibited.

CHAPTER II. FREEDOMS

Article 6. Right to Liberty and Security

Everyone has the right to liberty and security of person.

Article 7. Respect for Private and Family Life

Everyone has the right to respect for his or her private and family life, home and communications.

Article 8. Protection of Personal Data

1. Everyone has the right to the protection of personal data concerning him or her.
2. Such data must be processed fairly for specified purposes and on the basis of the consent of the person concerned or some other legitimate basis laid down by law. Everyone has the right of access to data which has been collected concerning him or her, and the right to have it rectified.
3. Compliance with these rules shall be subject to control by an independent authority.

Article 9. Right to Marry and Right to Found a Family

The right to marry and the right to found a family shall be guaranteed in accordance with the national laws governing the exercise of these rights.

Article 10. Freedom of Thought, Conscience and Religion

1. Everyone has the right to freedom of thought, conscience and religion. This right includes freedom to change religion or belief and freedom, either alone or in community with others and in public or in private, to manifest religion or belief, in worship, teaching, practice and observance.
2. The right to conscientious objection is recognised, in accordance with the national laws governing the exercise of this right.

Article 11. Freedom of Expression and Information

1. Everyone has the right to freedom of expression. This right shall include freedom to hold opinions and to receive and impart information and ideas without interference by public authority and regardless of frontiers.
2. The freedom and pluralism of the media shall be respected.

Article 12. Freedom of Assembly and of Association

1. Everyone has the right to freedom of peaceful assembly and to freedom of association at all levels, in particular in political, trade union and civic matters, which implies the right of everyone to form and to join trade unions for the protection of his or her interests.
2. Political parties at Union level contribute to expressing the political will of the citizens of the Union.

Article 13. Freedom of the Arts and Sciences

The arts and scientific research shall be free of constraint. Academic freedom shall be respected.

Article 14. Right to Education

1. Everyone has the right to education and to have access to vocational and continuing training.

2. This right includes the possibility to receive free compulsory education.
3. The freedom to found educational establishments with due respect for democratic principles and the right of parents to ensure the education and teaching of their children in conformity with their religious, philosophical and pedagogical convictions shall be respected, in accordance with the national laws governing the exercise of such freedom and right.

Article 15. Freedom to Choose an Occupation and Right to Engage in Work

1. Everyone has the right to engage in work and to pursue a freely chosen or accepted occupation.
2. Every citizen of the Union has the freedom to seek employment, to work, to exercise the right of establishment and to provide services in any Member State.
3. Nationals of third countries who are authorised to work in the territories of the Member States are entitled to working conditions equivalent to those of citizens of the Union.

Article 16. Freedom to Conduct a Business

The freedom to conduct a business in accordance with Community law and national laws and practices is recognised.

Article 17. Right to Property

1. Everyone has the right to own, use, dispose of and bequeath his or her lawfully acquired possessions. No one may be deprived of his or her possessions, except in the public interest and in the cases and under the conditions provided for by law, subject to fair compensation being paid in good time for their loss. The use of property may be regulated by law in so far as is necessary for the general interest.
2. Intellectual property shall be protected.

Article 18. Right to Asylum

The right to asylum shall be guaranteed with due respect for the rules of the Geneva Convention of 28 July 1951 and the Protocol of 31 January

1967 relating to the status of refugees and in accordance with the Treaty establishing the European Community.

Article 19. Protection in the Event of Removal, Expulsion or Extradition

1. Collective expulsions are prohibited.
2. No one may be removed, expelled or extradited to a State where there is a serious risk that he or she would be subjected to the death penalty, torture or other inhuman or degrading treatment or punishment.

CHAPTER III. EQUALITY

Article 20. Equality before the Law

Everyone is equal before the law.

Article 21. Non-Discrimination

1. Any discrimination based on any ground such as sex, race, colour, ethnic or social origin, genetic features, language, religion or belief, political or any other opinion, membership of a national minority, property, birth, disability, age or sexual orientation shall be prohibited.
2. Within the scope of application of the Treaty establishing the European Community and of the Treaty on European Union, and without prejudice to the special provisions of those Treaties, any discrimination on grounds of nationality shall be prohibited.

Article 22. Cultural, Religious and Linguistic Diversity

The Union shall respect cultural, religious and linguistic diversity.

Article 23. Equality between Men and Women

Equality between men and women must be ensured in all areas, including employment, work and pay. The principle of equality shall not prevent the maintenance or adoption of measures providing for specific advantages in favour of the under-represented sex.

Article 24. The Rights of the Child

1. Children shall have the right to such protection and care as is necessary for their well-being. They may express their views

freely. Such views shall be taken into consideration on matters which concern them in accordance with their age and maturity.

2. In all actions relating to children, whether taken by public authorities or private institutions, the child's best interests must be a primary consideration.
3. Every child shall have the right to maintain on a regular basis a personal relationship and direct contact with both his or her parents, unless that is contrary to his or her interests.

Article 25. The Rights of the Elderly

The Union recognises and respects the rights of the elderly to lead a life of dignity and independence and to participate in social and cultural life.

Article 26. Integration of Persons with Disabilities

The Union recognises and respects the right of persons with disabilities to benefit from measures designed to ensure their independence, social and occupational integration and participation in the life of the community.

CHAPTER IV. SOLIDARITY

Article 27. Workers' Right to Information and Consultation within the Undertaking

Workers or their representatives must, at the appropriate levels, be guaranteed information and consultation in good time in the cases and under the conditions provided for by Community law and national laws and practices.

Article 28. Right of Collective Bargaining and Action

Workers and employers, or their respective organisations, have, in accordance with Community law and national laws and practices, the right to negotiate and conclude collective agreements at the appropriate levels and, in cases of conflicts of interest, to take collective action to defend their interests, including strike action.

Article 29. Right of Access to Placement Services

Everyone has the right of access to a free placement service.

Article 30. Protection in the Event of Unjustified Dismissal
Every worker has the right to protection against unjustified dismissal, in accordance with Community law and national laws and practices.

Article 31. Fair and Just Working Conditions

1. Every worker has the right to working conditions which respect his or her health, safety and dignity.
2. Every worker has the right to limitation of maximum working hours, to daily and weekly rest periods and to an annual period of paid leave.

Article 32. Prohibition of Child Labour and Protection of Young People at Work
The employment of children is prohibited. The minimum age of admission to employment may not be lower than the minimum school-leaving age, without prejudice to such rules as may be more favourable to young people and except for limited derogations.

Young people admitted to work must have working conditions appropriate to their age and be protected against economic exploitation and any work likely to harm their safety, health or physical, mental, moral or social development or to interfere with their education.

Article 33. Family and Professional Life

1. The family shall enjoy legal, economic and social protection.
2. To reconcile family and professional life, everyone shall have the right to protection from dismissal for a reason connected with maternity and the right to paid maternity leave and to parental leave following the birth or adoption of a child.

Article 34. Social Security and Social Assistance

1. The Union recognises and respects the entitlement to social security benefits and social services providing protection in cases such as maternity, illness, industrial accidents, dependency or old age, and in the case of loss of employment, in accordance with the rules laid down by Community law and national laws and practices.
2. Everyone residing and moving legally within the European Union is entitled to social security benefits and social advantages

in accordance with Community law and national laws and practices.

3. In order to combat social exclusion and poverty, the Union recognises and respects the right to social and housing assistance so as to ensure a decent existence for all those who lack sufficient resources, in accordance with the rules laid down by Community law and national laws and practices.

Article 35. Health Care

Everyone has the right of access to preventive health care and the right to benefit from medical treatment under the conditions established by national laws and practices. A high level of human health protection shall be ensured in the definition and implementation of all Union policies and activities.

Article 36. Access to Services of General Economic Interest

The Union recognises and respects access to services of general economic interest as provided for in national laws and practices, in accordance with the Treaty establishing the European Community, in order to promote the social and territorial cohesion of the Union.

Article 37. Environmental Protection

A high level of environmental protection and the improvement of the quality of the environment must be integrated into the policies of the Union and ensured in accordance with the principle of sustainable development.

Article 38. Consumer Protection

Union policies shall ensure a high level of consumer protection.

CHAPTER V. CITIZENS' RIGHTS

Article 39. Right to Vote and to Stand as a Candidate at Elections to the European Parliament

1. Every citizen of the Union has the right to vote and to stand as a candidate at elections to the European Parliament in the Member State in which he or she resides, under the same conditions as nationals of that State.

2. Members of the European Parliament shall be elected by direct universal suffrage in a free and secret ballot.

Article 40. Right to Vote and to Stand as a Candidate at Municipal Elections

Every citizen of the Union has the right to vote and to stand as a candidate at municipal elections in the Member State in which he or she resides under the same conditions as nationals of that State.

Article 41. Right to Good Administration

1. Every person has the right to have his or her affairs handled impartially, fairly and within a reasonable time by the institutions and bodies of the Union.
2. This right includes:
   - the right of every person to be heard, before any individual measure which would affect him or her adversely is taken;
   - the right of every person to have access to his or her file, while respecting the legitimate interests of confidentiality and of professional and business secrecy;
   - the obligation of the administration to give reasons for its decisions.
3. Every person has the right to have the Community make good any damage caused by its institutions or by its servants in the performance of their duties, in accordance with the general principles common to the laws of the Member States.
4. Every person may write to the institutions of the Union in one of the languages of the Treaties and must have an answer in the same language.

Article 42. Right of Access to Documents

Any citizen of the Union, and any natural or legal person residing or having its registered office in a Member State, has a right of access to European Parliament, Council and Commission documents.

Article 43. Ombudsman

Any citizen of the Union and any natural or legal person residing or having its registered office in a Member State has the right to refer to the Ombudsman of the Union cases of maladministration in the activities of the Community institutions or bodies, with the exception of the Court of Justice and the Court of First Instance acting in their judicial role.

Article 44. Right to Petition

Any citizen of the Union and any natural or legal person residing or having its registered office in a Member State has the right to petition the European Parliament.

Article 45. Freedom of Movement and of Residence

1. Every citizen of the Union has the right to move and reside freely within the territory of the Member States.
2. Freedom of movement and residence may be granted, in accordance with the Treaty establishing the European Community, to nationals of third countries legally resident in the territory of a Member State.

Article 46. Diplomatic and Consular Protection

Every citizen of the Union shall, in the territory of a third country in which the Member State of which he or she is a national is not represented, be entitled to protection by the diplomatic or consular authorities of any Member State, on the same conditions as the nationals of that Member State.

CHAPTER VI. JUSTICE

Article 47. Right to an Effective Remedy and to a Fair Trial

Everyone whose rights and freedoms guaranteed by the law of the Union are violated has the right to an effective remedy before a tribunal in compliance with the conditions laid down in this Article.

Everyone is entitled to a fair and public hearing within a reasonable time by an independent and impartial tribunal previously established by law. Everyone shall have the possibility of being advised, defended and represented.

Legal aid shall be made available to those who lack sufficient resources in so far as such aid is necessary to ensure effective access to justice.

Article 48. Presumption of Innocence and Right of Defence

1. Everyone who has been charged shall be presumed innocent until proved guilty according to law.
2. Respect for the rights of the defence of anyone who has been charged shall be guaranteed.

Article 49. Principles of Legality and Proportionality of Criminal Offences and Penalties

1. No one shall be held guilty of any criminal offence on account of any act or omission which did not constitute a criminal offence under national law or international law at the time when it was committed. Nor shall a heavier penalty be imposed than that which was applicable at the time the criminal offence was committed. If, subsequent to the commission of a criminal offence, the law provides for a lighter penalty, that penalty shall be applicable.
2. This Article shall not prejudice the trial and punishment of any person for any act or omission which, at the time when it was committed, was criminal according to the general principles recognised by the community of nations.
3. The severity of penalties must not be disproportionate to the criminal offence.

Article 50. Right not to be Tried or Punished Twice in Criminal Proceedings for the Same Criminal Offence

No one shall be liable to be tried or punished again in criminal proceedings for an offence for which he or she has already been finally acquitted or convicted within the Union in accordance with the law.

CHAPTER VII. GENERAL PROVISIONS

Article 51. Scope

1. The provisions of this Charter are addressed to the institutions and bodies of the Union with due regard for the principle of subsidiarity and to the Member States only when they are implementing Union law. They shall therefore respect the rights, observe the principles and promote the application thereof in accordance with their respective powers.

2. This Charter does not establish any new power or task for the Community or the Union, or modify powers and tasks defined by the Treaties.

Article 52. Scope of Guaranteed Rights

1. Any limitation on the exercise of the rights and freedoms recognised by this Charter must be provided for by law and respect the essence of those rights and freedoms. Subject to the principle of proportionality, limitations may be made only if they are necessary and genuinely meet objectives of general interest recognised by the Union or the need to protect the rights and freedoms of others.
2. Rights recognised by this Charter which are based on the Community Treaties or the Treaty on European Union shall be exercised under the conditions and within the limits defined by those Treaties.
3. In so far as this Charter contains rights which correspond to rights guaranteed by the Convention for the Protection of Human Rights and Fundamental Freedoms, the meaning and scope of those rights shall be the same as those laid down by the said Convention. This provision shall not prevent Union law providing more extensive protection.

Article 53. Level of Protection

Nothing in this Charter shall be interpreted as restricting or adversely affecting human rights and fundamental freedoms as recognised, in their respective fields of application, by Union law and international law and by international agreements to which the Union, the Community or all the Member States are party, including the European Convention for the Protection of Human Rights and Fundamental Freedoms, and by the Member States' constitutions.

Article 54. Prohibition of Abuse of Rights

Nothing in this Charter shall be interpreted as implying any right to engage in any activity or to perform any act aimed at the destruction of any of the rights and freedoms recognised in this Charter or at their limitation to a greater extent than is provided for herein.

APPENDIX 3

The Common Principles of Flexicurity (2007)*

(1) Flexicurity is a means to reinforce the implementation of the Lisbon Strategy, create more and better jobs, modernise labour markets, and promote good work through new forms of flexibility and security to increase adaptability, employment and social cohesion.

(2) Flexicurity involves the deliberate combination of flexible and reliable contractual arrangements, comprehensive lifelong learning strategies, effective active labour market policies, and modern, adequate and sustainable social protection systems.

(3) Flexicurity approaches are not about one single labour market or working life model, nor about a single policy strategy: they should be tailored to the specific circumstances of each Member State. Flexicurity implies a balance between rights and responsibilities of all concerned. Based on the common principles, each Member State should develop its own flexicurity arrangements. Progress should be effectively monitored.

---

* http://register.consilium.europa.eu © European Communities, 2000–2008. Please note that any references contained in the register are not legally binding. Only legal acts published in the *Official Journal of the European Union* are binding.

(4) Flexicurity should promote more open, responsive and inclusive labour markets overcoming segmentation. It concerns both those in work and those out of work. The inactive, the unemployed, those in undeclared work, in unstable employment, or at the margins of the labour market need to be provided with better opportunities, economic incentives and supportive measures for easier access to work or stepping-stones to assist progress into stable and legally secure employment. Support should be available to all those in employment to remain employable, progress and manage transitions both in work and between jobs.

(5) Internal (within the enterprise) as well as external flexicurity are equally important and should be promoted. Sufficient contractual flexibility must be accompanied by secure transitions from job to job. Upward mobility needs to be facilitated, as well as between unemployment or inactivity and work. High-quality and productive workplaces, good organisation of work, and continuous upgrading of skills are also essential. Social protection should provide incentives and support for job transitions and for access to new employment.

(6) Flexicurity should support gender equality, by promoting equal access to quality employment for women and men and offering measures to reconcile work, family and private life.

(7) Flexicurity requires a climate of trust and broadly-based dialogue among all stakeholders, where all are prepared to take the responsibility for change with a view to socially balanced policies. While public authorities retain an overall responsibility, the involvement of social partners in the design and implementation of flexicurity policies through social dialogue and collective bargaining is of crucial importance.

(8) Flexicurity requires a cost effective allocation of resources and should remain fully compatible with sound and financially sustainable public budgets. It should also aim at a fair distribution of costs and benefits, especially between businesses, public authorities and individuals, with particular attention to the specific situation of SMEs.

Bibliography

Aaron, B, Chapter 16, 'Labour Courts and Organs of Arbitration', in BA Hepple (ed.), *Labour Law*, vol. XV, in *International Encyclopedia of Comparative Law*, JCB Mohr, Tübingen, 1985.

Anderson, G, 'Just a Jump to the Left? New Zealand's Employment Relations Act 2000' (2001) 14 *Australian Journal of Labour Law* 62.

——, 'Transplanting and Growing Good Faith in New Zealand Labour Law' (2006) 19 *Australian Journal of Labour Law* 1.

Arup, C, 'Labour Market Regulation as a Focus for a Labour Law Discipline' in R Mitchell (ed.), *Redefining Labour Law. New Perspectives on the Future of Teaching and Research*, Centre for Employment and Labour Relations Law, Occasional Monograph Series, No. 3, Melbourne, 1995, 29.

——, and Mitchell, R, (eds), *Labour Law and Labour Market Regulation: Essays on the Construction, Constitution and Regulation of Labour Markets and Work Relationships*, Federation Press, Annandale, NSW, 2006.

——, Gahan, P, Howe, J, Johnstone, R, Mitchell, R, and O'Donnell, A, (eds), *Labour Law and Labour Market Regulation: Essays on the Construction, Constitution and Regulation of Labour Markets and Work Relationships*, Federation Press, Sydney, 2006.

Australian Government, *The National Employment Standards*, available at www.workplace.gov.au

Australian Labor Party, *Forward with Fairness. Labor's Plan for Fairer and More Productive Australian Workplaces*, April 2007.

——, *Forward with Fairness. Policy Implementation Plan*, August 2007.

Bakels, HL, and Opheikens, L, *Schets van het Nederlands arbeidsrecht*, 6th edn, Kluwer, Deventer, 1982.

Barnard, C, 'A Social Policy for Europe: Politicians 1:0 Lawyers' (1992) 8 *International Journal of Comparative Labour Law and Industrial Relations* 15.
Bercusson, B, 'The European Community's Charter of Fundamental Social Rights' (1990) 53 *The Modern Law Review* 624.
Bergel, JL, 'Principal Features and Methods of Codification' (1988) 48 *Louisiana Law Review* 1073.
Betten, L, *International Labour Law*, Kluwer, Deventer, 1993.
——, 'The Role of Social Partners in the Community's Social Policy Law-Making: Participatory Democracy or Furthering the Interests of Small Elites', in C Engels and M Weiss (eds), *Labour Law and Industrial Relations at the Turn of the Century. Liber Amicorum in Honour of Prof Dr Roger Blanpain*, Kluwer Law International, The Hague, 1998, 239.
——, 'The EU Charter on Fundamental Rights: A Trojan Horse or a Mouse?' (2001) 17 *International Journal of Comparative Labour Law and Industrial Relations* 151.
Biagi, M, 'Forms of Employee Representational Participation', in R Blanpain, and C Engels (eds), *Comparative Labour Law and Industrial Relations in Industrialized Market Economies*, 7th edn, Kluwer Law International, The Hague, 2001, 483.
Blanpain, R, *De Wet op de arbeidsovereenkomst*, Kluwer, Antwerpen, 1978.
——, *Schets van het Belgisch arbeidsrecht*, 2nd edn, Die Keure, Brugge, 1984.
——, *Case Law (International Court of Justice)*, in R Blanpain (ed.), *International Encyclopaedia for Labour Law and Industrial Relations*, Kluwer Law International, The Hague, 2005 update.
——, 'Belgium', in R Blanpain (ed.), *International Encyclopaedia for Labour Law and Industrial Relations*, Kluwer Law International, The Hague, 2006 update.
——, *European Labour Law*, 10th edn, Kluwer Law International, The Hague, 2006.
——, *Codex (International Labour Law)*, in R Blanpain (ed.), *International Encyclopaedia for Labour Law and Industrial Relations* Kluwer Law International, The Hague, 2007 update.
Blanpain, R, and Weiss, M, (eds), *Changing Industrial Relations and Modernisation of Labour Law. Liber Amicorum in Honour of Professor Marco Biagi*, Kluwer Law International, The Hague, 2003.
Blanpain, R, and Windey, P, *European Works Councils. Information and Consultation of Employees in Multinational Enterprises in Europe*, Peeters, Leuven, 1994.
Blanquet, F, *L'Europe: vers l'harmonisation des législations socials*, cited in R Blanpain (ed), *European Labour Law*, 10th edn, Kluwer Law International, The Hague, 2006, 234.
Brooks, B, and Engels, C (eds), *Employed or Self-Employed*, in R Blanpain (gen. ed.), Bulletin of Comparative Labour Relations, Kluwer, Deventer, No. 24, 1992.

—— (eds), 'General Overview', in B Brooks and C Engels (eds), *Employed or Self-Employed*, in R Blanpain (gen. ed.), Bulletin of Comparative Labour Relations, Kluwer, Deventer, No. 24, 1992, 1.

Brudney, JJ, 'Employee Majority Bargaining Systems: Comparing Developments in the United States and Australia', seminar under the auspices of the Centre for Employment and Labour Relations Law, University of Melbourne, 16 June 2008.

Camerlynck, GH, and Lyon-Caen, G, *Droit du Travail*, Dalloz, Paris, 1975.

Campbell, J, *Margaret Thatcher. Volume Two: The Iron Lady*, Pimlico, London, 2004.

Cass, DZ, 'The Word that Saves Maastricht? The Principle of Subsidiarity and the Division of Powers within the European Community' (1992) 29 *Common Market Law Review* 1107.

Cella, GP, and Treu, T, 'National Trade Union Movements', in R Blanpain and C Engels (eds), *Comparative Labour Law and Industrial Relations in Industrialized Market Economies*, Kluwer Law International, The Hague, 2001, 445.

Collins, H, 'Methods and Aims of Comparative Contract Law' (1991) 11 *Oxford Journal of Legal Studies* 396.

Commission Communication to the spring 2005 European Council, 'Working Together for Growth and Jobs. A New Start for the Lisbon Strategy', *Official Journal*, 16 March 2005, C 64; COM (2005) 24.

Commission of the European Communities, *Charter of the Fundamental Social Rights of Workers*, Office for Official Publications of the European Communities, Luxembourg, 1990.

——, Green Paper: *Modernising Labour Law to Meet the Challenges of the 21st Century*, Brussels, 22 November 2006, COM (2006) 708 final.

——, *Towards Common Principles of Flexicurity*, COM (2007) 359 final.

Commission strongly welcomes today's political agreement on Working Time and Working Conditions for Temporary Agency Workers, press release, IP/08/912, Brussels, 10 June 2008.

Communication from the Commission to the Council and the European Parliament, *Better Regulation for Growth and Jobs in the European Union*, COM (2005) 0097 (final).

Craver, CB, 'The Relevance of the NLRA and Labor Organisations in the Post-Industrial Global Economy' (2006) 57 *Labor Law Journal* 133.

Creighton, B, and Stewart, A, *Labour Law*, 4th edn, Federation Press, Sydney, 2005.

Dannin, E, 'Why At-Will Employment is Bad for Employers and Just Cause is Good for Them' (2007) *Labor Law Journal* 5.

De Groot, C, *Netherlands Labour and Co-Determination Law in an EEC Perspective*, Kluwer, Deventer, 1990.

Dehaene, J-L, *De Europese uitdaging: van uitbreiding tot integratie*, Van Halewyck, Leuven, 2004.

Department of Employment and Industrial Relations Working Environment Branch, *Industrial Democracy and Employee Participation—Policy Discussion Paper*, Canberra, 1986.

Department of Foreign Affairs and Trade, *Workplace Relations in Australia*, About Australia Fact Sheet Series, September 2008.
Department of Labour, *Industrial Relations. A Framework for Review*, 2 vols, Government Printer, Wellington, 1985.
——, *Government Policy Statement on Labour Relations*, Government Printer, Wellington, September 1986.
——, *Industrial Relations. A Framework for Review—Summary of Submissions*, Government Printer, Wellington, 1986.
——, *Report of the Committee Enquiring into Dependent Contracting*, Government Printer, Wellington, 1988.
——, *Fact Sheet on Good Faith in Employment Relationships*, available at www.ers.dol.govt.nz/goodfaith/code (accessed 29 February 2008).
Despax, M, and Rojot, J, 'France', in R Blanpain (ed.), *International Encyclopaedia for Labour Law and Industrial Relations*, Kluwer, Deventer, 1987 update.
Dickens, L, Jones, M, Weekes, B, and Hart, M, *Dismissed: A Study of Unfair Dismissal and the Industrial Tribunal System*, Blackwell, Oxford, 1985.
Durand, P, 'Le particularisme du droit du travail' (1945) *Droit Social* 298.
Engels, C, 'Belgium', in B Brooks and C Engels (eds), *Employed or Self-Employed*, in R Blanpain (gen. ed.), *Bulletin of Comparative Labour Relations*, Kluwer, Deventer, No. 24, 1992, 29.
——, and Salas, L, 'Transnational Information and Consultation: The European Works Council Directive', in R Blanpain, and C Engels (eds), *Comparative Labour Law and Industrial Relations in Industrialized Market Economies*, 7th edn, Kluwer Law International, The Hague, 2001, 525.
——, and Weiss, M, (eds), *Labour Law and Industrial Relations at the Turn of the Century. Liber Amicorum in Honour of Prof Dr Roger Blanpain*, Kluwer Law International, The Hague, 1998.
European Commission, *Mission for Flexicurity: Terms of Reference*, Brussels, 8 February 2008.
European Council Conclusions, Brussels, 16 October 2008, available at http://europa.eu
European Expert Group on Flexicurity, *Flexicurity Pathways: Turning Hurdles into Stepping Stones*, June 2007, available at http://ec.europa.eu/employment-social/employment-strategy/pdf/flexi-pathways-en.pdf
European Foundation for the Improvement of Living and Working Conditions, *Approaches to Flexicurity: EU Models*, Office for Official Publications of the European Communities, Luxembourg, 2007.
European Industrial Relations Observatory, *Redundancies and Redundancy Costs*, European Foundation for the Improvement of Living and Working Conditions, Dublin, 2005, available at http://www.eurofound.eu.int/pubdocs/2005/75/en/1/ef0575en.pdf
Facing the Challenge: The Lisbon Strategy for Growth and Employment, Report from the High Level Group chaired by Wim Kok, Office for Official Publications of the European Communities, Luxembourg, 2004, available at www.europa.eu.int/comm/Lisbon-strategy/index-en.html

Finkin, MW, 'Law Reform American Style: Thoughts on a Restatement of the Law of Employment', in R Blanpain and M Weiss (eds), *Changing Industrial Relations and Modernisation of Labour Law. Liber Amicorum in Honour of Professor Marco Biagi*, Kluwer Law International, The Hague, 2003, 139.

First 100 Days: Achievements of the Rudd Government, February 2008, available at www.pm.gov.au/first-100-days.doc

Fitzpatrick, B, 'Community Social Law after Maastricht' (1992) 21 *Industrial Law Journal* 199.

Frame, A, *Salmond. Southern Jurist*, Victoria University Press, Wellington, 1995.

France, D, 'International Employers' Organisations', in R Blanpain and C Engels (eds), *Comparative Labour Law and Industrial Relations in Industrialized Market Economies*, 7th edn, Kluwer Law International, The Hague, 2001, 55.

Freedland, MR, *The Contract of Employment*, Clarendon Press, Oxford, 1976.

Fudge, J, 'Fragmenting Work and Fragmenting Organisations: The Contract of Employment and the Scope of Labour Regulation' (2006) 44 *Osgoode Hall Law Journal* 609.

Gahan, P, and Mitchell, R, 'The Limits of Labour Law and the Necessity of Interdisciplinary Analysis' in R Mitchell (ed.), *Redefining Labour Law: New Perspectives on the Future of Teaching and Research*, Centre for Employment and Labour Relations Law, Occasional Monograph Series No. 3, Melbourne, 1995, 62.

George, S, *Politics and Policy in the European Community*, Oxford University Press, Oxford, 1991.

Getman, JG, and Blackburn, JD, *Labor Relations. Law, Practice and Policy*, 2nd edn, Foundation Press, Mineola, 1983.

Gillard, J, (Minister for Employment and Workplace Relations), *Introducing Australia's New Workplace Relations System*, speech given at the National Press Club, Canberra, 17 September 2008.

Gladstone, A, 'Settlement of Disputes over Rights', in R Blanpain and C Engels (eds), *Comparative Labour Law and Industrial Relations in Industrialized Market Economies*, 7th edn, Kluwer Law International, The Hague, 2001, 629.

Goldman, AL, and White, RH, 'The United States of America', in R Blanpain (ed.), *International Encyclopaedia for Labour Law and Industrial Relations*, Kluwer Law International, The Hague, 2002 update.

'Government <committed> to finding treaty resolution—Cowen', *Irishtimes.com*, 17 October 2008.

Gutman, GO, 'The Hancock Report: Last Hurrah for the System', in *Arbitration in Contempt*, Proceedings of the Inaugural Seminar of the HR Nicholls Society, Melbourne, 28 February – 2 March 1986, Chapter 12, available at www.hrnicholls.com.au/nicholls/nichvol1 (accessed 11 March 2008).

Hanza, G, *Comparative Law and Antiquity*, Akadémiai Kiadó, Budapest, 1991.

Hardy, S, 'Great Britain', in R Blanpain (ed.), *International Encyclopaedia for Labour Law and Industrial Relations*, Kluwer Law International, The Hague, 2007 update.

Hepple, B, 'Individual Labour Law', in GS Bain (ed.), *Industrial Relations in Britain*, Blackwell, Oxford, 1983, 393.
——, 'Introduction', in B Hepple (ed.), *The Making of Labour Law in Europe. A Comparative Study of Nine Countries up to 1945*, Mansell Publishing, London and New York, 1986, 1.
——, 'The Implementation of the Community Charter of Fundamental Social Rights' (1990) 53 *The Modern Law Review* 643.
——, 'European Labour Law: The European Community', in R Blanpain and C Engels (eds), *Comparative Labour Law and Industrial Relations in Industrialized Market Economies*, 5th edn, Kluwer Law International, The Hague, 1993, 143.
——, 'Towards a European Social Constitution', in C Engels and M Weiss (eds), *Labour Law and Industrial Relations at the Turn of the Century. Liber Amicorum in Honour of Prof Dr Roger Blanpain*, Kluwer Law International, The Hague, 1998, 291.
House of Representatives, Standing Committee on Employment, Workplace Relations and Workforce Participation, *Making It Work: Inquiry into Independent Contracting and Labour Hire Arrangements*, Canberra, August 2005.
Hueck, A, and Nipperdey, HC, *Lehrbuch des Arbeitsrechts*, 7th edn, Verlag F Vahlen, Berlin/Frankfurt, 1963.
Hughes, J, 'The Collective Bargaining Code of Good Faith' (2001) 26 *New Zealand Journal of Industrial Relations* 59.
Husson, M (ed.), *Travail flexible, salariés jetables. Fausses questions et vrais enjeux de la lutte contre le chômage.* Editions La Découverte, Paris, 2006.
Industrial Relations Services, 'Flexicurity in the Spotlight', *European Industrial Relations Review*, December 2006, 27.
International Labour Organization, *Labour Courts, An International Survey of Judicial Systems for the Settlement of Disputes*, Studies and Reports Series A (Industrial Relations), No. 40, International Labour Office, Geneva, 1938.
Jacobs, A, 'The Netherlands', in R Blanpain (ed.), *International Encyclopaedia for Labour Law and Industrial Relations*, Kluwer Law International, The Hague, 2004 update.
Javillier, JC, *Droit du travail*, 2nd edn, LGDJ, Paris, 1988.
Kahn-Freund, O, 'Legal Framework', in A Flanders and HA Clegg (eds), *The System of Industrial Relations in Great Britain. Its History, Law and Institutions*, Basil Blackwell, Oxford, 1954, 42.
——, 'Comparative Law as an Academic Subject' (1966) 82 *Law Quarterly Review* 40.
——, 'On Uses and Misuses of Comparative Law' (1974) 37 *The Modern Law Review* 1.
Kamba, WJ, 'Comparative Law: A Theoretical Framework' (1974) 23 *International and Comparative Law Quarterly* 485.
Kassalow, EM, *Trade Unions and Industrial Relations: An International Comparison*, Random House, New York, 1969.

Landau, EC, *The Influence of ILO Standards on Australian Labour Law and Practices*, Monograph 30, Industrial Relations Research Centre, University of New South Wales, 1990.
Lewis, R, 'The Role of the Law in Employment Relations', in R Lewis (ed.), *Labour Law in Britain*, Basil Blackwell, Oxford, 1986, 1.
Lisbon – European Council 23 and 24 March 2000, Presidency Conclusions, 1, available at http://www.europarl.europa.eu/summits/lis1-en.htm
——, *Question and Answer: A New Start for the Lisbon Strategy*, MEMO 05/34, Brussels, 2 February 2005.
Macintyre, S, and Mitchell, R, 'Introduction', in S Macintyre and R Mitchell (eds), *Foundations of Arbitration. The Origins and Effects of State Compulsory Arbitration 1890–1914*, Oxford University Press, Melbourne, 1989, 1.
Madsen, PK, 'How Can It Possibly Fly? The Paradox of Dynamic Labour Market in a Scandinavian Welfare State', in JL Campbell, JA Hall and OK Pedersen (eds), *National Identity and the Varieties of Capitalism: The Case of Denmark*, DJOF Publishing/ McGill University Press, Kopenhagen/ Montreal, 2006, 321.
Mallard, T (Minister for Labour), 'Stronger Protection for Casual and Temp Workers', 22 June 2008, available at http://beehive.govt.nz
Mathijsen, PSRF, *A Guide to European Union Law*, 9th edn, Sweet & Maxwell, London, 2007.
May, R, Walsh, P, Harbridge, R, and Thickett, G, *Unions and Union Membership in New Zealand: Annual Review for 2002*, Industrial Relations Centre, Victoria University of Wellington, Working Paper 1/03, Wellington, 2003.
McCallum, RC, 'A Modern Renaissance: Industrial Law and Relations under Federal Wigs 1977–1992' (1992) 14 *Sydney Law Review* 401.
Merryman, JH, *The Civil Law Tradition. An Introduction to the Legal Systems of Western Europe and Latin America*, 2nd edn, Stanford University Press, Stanford, CA, 1985.
Milton, G, and Keller-Noëllet, J, with Bartol-Saurel, A, *The European Constitution: its Origins, Negotiation and Meaning*, John Harper Publishing, London, 2005.
Mitchell, R (ed.), *Redefining Labour Law. New Perspectives on the Future of Teaching and Research*, Centre for Employment and Labour Relations Law, Occasional Monograph Series, No. 3, Melbourne, 1995.
Neal, AC, 'Do We Need a Social Policy for Europe?', in R Blanpain and M Weiss (eds), *Changing Industrial Relations and Modernisation of Labour Law. Liber Amicorum in Honour of Professor Marco Biagi*, Kluwer Law International, The Hague, 2003, 287.
Norington, B, 'Ads Remind Labor of Vows' (2008) *The Australian*, 23 June, 2.
Orr, G, and Murugesan, S, 'Mandatory Secret Ballots Before Employee Industrial Action, (2007) 20 *Australian Journal of Labour Law* 272.
Pearson, N, *The Light on the Hill*, Ben Chifley Memorial Lecture, 12 August 2000, available at www.capeyorkpartnerships.com/team/noelpearson/lightonhill-12-8-00.htm-55k
Punch, P, and Sheils, M, 'NES & Award Modernisation—More Ingredients and a New Mixture?' (2008) 3 *Industrial Law News* 1.

Ramm, T, '*Laissez-faire* and State Protection of Workers', in B Hepple (ed.), *The Making of Labour Law in Europe. A Comparative Study of Nine Countries up to 1945*, Mansell Publishing, London and New York, 1986, 73.
——, 'Workers' Participation, the Representation of Labour and Special Labour Courts', in B Hepple (ed.), *The Making of Labour Law in Europe. A Comparative Study of Nine Countries up to 1945*, Mansell Publishing, London and New York, 1986, 242.
Rasking, J, and Tegenbos, G, '138 miljoen voor vakbonden', *De Standaard Online*, 10 April 2006.
Rawling, M, 'The Regulation of Outwork and the Federal Takeover of Labour Law' (2007) 20 *Australian Journal of Labour Law* 189.
Report of the Committee of Enquiry into Australian Industrial Relations Law and Systems, 2 vols, Australian Government Publishing Service, Canberra, 1985.
Report of the Committee of Inquiry into Industrial Democracy, Government Printer, Wellington, 1989.
Report of the Employment Task Force, *Jobs, Jobs, Jobs: Creating More Employment in Europe*, November 2003, cited in the Commission of the European Communities, *Modernising Labour Law to Meet the Challenges of the 21st Century*, COM (2006), 3.
Report on the Functioning of the Transitional Arrangements set out in the 2003 Accession Treaty, cited in the *Commission of the European Communities, Modernising Labour Law to Meet the Challenges of the 21st Century*, COM (2006), 48: 8 February 2006, 11 (n. 31).
Richardson, Ivor (Sir), 'The Role of the Courts in Industrial Relations' (1987) 12 *New Zealand Journal of Industrial Relations* 113.
Riley, J, 'A Fair Deal for the Entrepreneurial Worker? Self-Employment and Independent Contracting Post Work Choices' (2006) 19 *Australian Journal of Labour Law* 246.
Rood, MG, 'Some Thoughts on European Works Councils', in C Engels and M Weiss (eds), *Labour Law and Industrial Relations at the Turn of the Century. Liber Amicorum in Honour of Prof Dr Roger Blanpain*, Kluwer Law International, The Hague, 1998, 399.
Sappideen, C, Vines, P, Grant, H, and Watson, P, *Torts. Commentary and Materials*, 9th edn, Lawbook Co., Sydney, 2006.
Schregle, J, 'Comparative Industrial Relations: Pitfalls and Potential' (1981) 120 *International Labour Review* 15.
Scott, S, 'Minimum Standards Upset Employers' (2008) *The Australian Financial Review*, 15 February, 9.
Senate Commission Report 1977, in R Blanpain, *De Wet op de arbeidsovereenkomst*, Kluwer, Antwerpen, 1978.
Stallybrass, WTS, *Salmond's Law of Torts*, 9th edn, Sweet and Maxwell, London, 1936.
Stewart, A, with the assistance of Priest, E, 'The Work Choices Legislation: An Overview', available at www.federationpress.com.au/pdf/WorkChoicesLegislation 0206.pdf (accessed 14 February 2006).
Summers, CW, Wellington, HH, and Hyde, A, *Labor Law. Cases and Materials*, 2nd edn, University Casebook Series, Foundation Press, Mineola, 1982.

Swepston, L, Chapter 7, 'International Labour Law', in R Blanpain, and C Engels (eds), *Comparative Labour Law and Industrial Relations in Industrialized Market Economies*, 7th edn, Kluwer Law International, The Hague, 2001, 135.

Szakats, A, and Mulgan, MA, *Dismissal and Redundancy Procedures*, 2nd edn, Butterworths, Wellington, 1990.

'There's Money in Mopping', (2005), *The Economist*, 10 December, 38–40.

Toth, AG, *The Oxford Encyclopaedia of European Community Law. Volume I: Institutional Law*, Clarendon Press, Oxford, 1990.

Tunc, A, 'L'Enseignement du droit comparé: présentation' (1988) *Revue internationale de droit comparé* 703.

Underhill, E, 'Labour Hire and Independent Contracting in Australia: Two Inquiries, How Much Change?' (2006) 19 *Australian Journal of Labour Law* 306.

Valticos, N, and von Potobsky, G, *International Labour Law*, 2nd edn, Kluwer, Deventer, 1995.

Vanachter, O, 'Labour Law and the Division of Power Between the Federal Level, the Communities and the Regions in Belgium', in O Vanachter and M Vranken (eds), *Federalism and Labour Law: Comparative Perspectives*, Intersentia, Antwerpen/Oxford/New York, 2004, 21.

Vranken, M, *De collectieve arbeidsovereenkomsten in België van 1974 tot 1980. Evolutie en juridische evaluatie*, Acco, Leuven/Amersfoort, 1984.

——, 'Deregulating the Employment Relationship: Current Trends in Europe' (1986) 7 *Comparative Labor Law* 143.

——, 'Specialisation and Labour Courts: A Comparative Analysis' (1988) 9 *Comparative Labor Law Journal* 497.

——, 'Autonomy and Individual Labour Law: A Comparative Analysis' (1989) 5 *International Journal of Comparative Labour Law and Industrial Relations* 100.

——, 'An Australasian Approach to Industrial Democracy?' (1991) 4 *Australian Journal of Labour Law* 81.

——, 'Comparativism and Australian Labour Law', in R Mitchell (ed.), *Redefining Labour Law. New Perspectives on the Future of Teaching and Research*, Centre for Employment and Labour Relations Law, Occasional Monograph Series, Melbourne, 1995, 121.

——, *Fundamentals of European Civil Law and Impact of the European Community*, Federation Press, Sydney, 1997.

——, 'Common Law versus Specialist Jurisdiction in Labour Law' in DR Nolan (ed.), *The Australasian Labour Law Reforms. Australia and New Zealand at the End of the Twentieth Century*, Federation Press, Sydney, 1998, 21.

——, 'The Role of Specialist Labour Courts in an Environment of Substantive Labour Law Deregulation: A New Zealand Case Study' (1999) 15 *International Journal of Comparative Labour Law and Industrial Relations* 303.

——, 'Documentation', in R Blanpain, and C Engels (eds), *Comparative Labour Law and Industrial Relations in Industrialized Market Economies*, 7th edn, Kluwer Law International, The Hague, 2001, 25.

——, 'Legal Education Reform in Australia and the Impact of Globalisation: A Comparative Perspective' (2008) 14 *Revue Juridique Polynésienne* 21.
Wedderburn, Lord, *The Worker and the Law*, 3rd edn, Penguin, Harmondsworth, 1986.
——, 'Labour Law: Autonomy from the Common Law?' (1987) 9 *Comparative Labor Law Journal* 219.
——, 'Labour Law: From Here to Autonomy?' (1987) 16 *Industrial Law Journal* 1.
Weiss, M, 'The Significance of Maastricht for European Community Social Policy' (1992) 8 *International Journal of Comparative Labour Law and Industrial Relations* 3.
——, 'The Future Role of the European Union in Social Policy', in C Engels and M Weiss (eds), *Labour Law and Industrial Relations at the Turn of the Century. Liber Amicorum in Honour of Prof Dr Roger Blanpain*, Kluwer Law International, The Hague, 1998, 489.
——, 'Modernising the German Works Council System: A Recent Amendment' (2002) *International Journal of Comparative Labour Law and Industrial Relations* 251.
——, 'Labour Law', in J Zekoll and M Reimann (eds), *Introduction to German Law*, 2nd edn, Kluwer International, The Hague, 2005, 299.
——, and Schmidt, M, 'Germany', in R Blanpain (ed.), *International Encyclopaedia for Labour Law and Industrial Relations*, Kluwer Law International, The Hague, 2000 update.
——, Simitis, S, and Rydzy, W, 'The Settlement of Labour Disputes in the Federal Republic of Germany', in T Hanami and R Blanpain (eds), *Industrial Conflict Resolution in Market Economies. A Study of Australia, the Federal Republic of Germany, Italy, Japan and the USA*, 2nd edn, Kluwer, Deventer, 1989, 81.
Wheeler, HN, 'The Labor Movement in the 21st Century', in C Engels and M Weiss (eds), *Labour Law and Industrial Relations at the Turn of the Century. Liber Amicorum in Honour of Prof Dr Roger Blanpain*, Kluwer Law International, The Hague, 1998, 221.
Wilson, M, 'The Employment Relations Act: A Statutory Framework for Balance in the Workplace' (2001) 26 *New Zealand Journal of Industrial Relations* 5.
Windmuller, JP, and Pursey, SK, 'The International Trade Union Movement', in R Blanpain and C Engels (eds), *Comparative Labour Law and Industrial Relations in Industrialized Market Economies*, 7th edn, Kluwer Law International, The Hague, 2001, 73.
Woods, NS, *Industrial Conciliation and Arbitration in New Zealand*, Government Printer, Wellington, 1963.
Ziskind, D, 'Cultural Bias in Labor Law Comparison' (1984) 6 *Comparative Labor Law* 275.
Zweigert, K, and Kötz, H, *An Introduction to Comparative Law*, 3rd edn, Clarendon Press, Oxford, 1998.

Index

Kolibri 360 GmbH
Ferdinand-Jühlke-Straße 7
99095 Erfurt, Deutschland
produktsicherheit@kolibri360.de